APR 5 2005

THE EMANCIPATION OF MUSIC FROM LANGUAGE

THE EMANCIPATION
OF MUSIC
FROM LANGUAGE

*Departure from
Mimesis in
Eighteenth-Century
Aesthetics*

JOHN NEUBAUER

*Yale University Press
New Haven and London*

Copyright © 1986 by Yale University. All rights reserved.
This book may not be reproduced, in whole or in part, in
any form (beyond that copying permitted by Sections 107
and 108 of the U.S. Copyright Law and except by review-
ers for the public press), without written permission
from the publishers.

Designed by Nancy Ovedovitz and set in Galliard type by
Eastern Graphics. Printed in the United States of
America by Edwards Brothers, Inc., Ann Arbor,
Michigan.

Library of Congress Cataloging-in-Publication Data

Neubauer, John, 1933–
    The emancipation of music from language.
    Bibliography: p.
    Includes index.
    1. Music—18th century—Philosophy and aesthetics.
2. Music and literature. I. Title.
ML3849.N48 1986   781′.09′033   85–14355
ISBN 0–300–03577–2 (alk. paper)

The paper in this book meets the guidelines for perma-
nence and durability of the Committee on Production
Guidelines for Book Longevity of the Council on Library
Resources.

10   9   8   7   6   5   4   3   2   1

for Ursel

CONTENTS

PREFACE

The debts one accumulates in the course of a major project are too numerous and too weighty to be appropriately acknowledged. Nevertheless, I wish to express my deep appreciation for the help and stimulation I have received from several of my former Pittsburgh colleagues, foremost among them Clark Muenzer, Don Franklin, Wayne Slawson, and Phil Koch. Earlier versions of some chapters were read by Alex Gelley, Dorrit Cohn, and Ulrich Weisstein, and I received kind and helpful comments in the final stage from Frits Noske and Claude Palisca. For her interest and efficient help, I am grateful to Ellen Graham at Yale University Press. Jean van Altena's excellent editing helped me to eliminate many errors and inconsistencies.

The John Simon Guggenheim Foundation provided me with the luxury of a year's uninterrupted research, and I am grateful not only for its support, but for the opportunity of having been associated with this magnificent institution.

My thanks go to Texas Tech Press for allowing me to use a revised version of an article already published as the Goethe chapter.

Complete information for the abbreviated documentation in the text is given at the end under "Literature Cited." All the translations of foreign texts are my own unless indicated otherwise, or unless the reference is to a translation.

Amsterdam, April 12, 1985

THE EMANCIPATION OF MUSIC FROM LANGUAGE

INTRODUCTION

I

Two eighteenth-century authors describe music as a pleasant entertainment but a morally and aesthetically inferior art that must be made to serve better causes:

> Musick is certainly a very agreeable Entertainment, but if it would take the entire Possession of our Ears, if it would make us incapable of hearing Sense, if it would exclude Arts that have a much greater Tendency to the Refinement of humane Nature: I must confess I would allow it no better Quarter than Plato has done, who banishes it out of his Commonwealth. [Addison, *The Spectator*, March 21, 1711]

> After all, singing is nothing more than a pleasant and emphatic reading of verse. [Gottsched, *Critische Dichtkunst* 725]

One would search in vain for similar passages in the vast nineteenth-century literature on music; from the Romantic era onward, the relation between music and language reverses itself, and all the arts aspire, as Schopenhauer and Pater say, to the condition of music:

> The poems of the lyrist can express nothing that did not already lie hidden in that vast universality and absoluteness in the music that compelled him to figurative speech. Language can never adequately render the cosmic symbolism of music. [Nietzsche, *The Birth of Tragedy*, sect. 6]

> By means of arranging lines and colors, with the pretext of an arbitrary subject borrowed from life or nature, I obtain symphonies, harmonies that represent nothing absolutely real in the vulgar sense of the word since they do not express directly any idea; but they compel us to reflect, as music compels us to reflect, without the aid of ideas or images, simply by means of the mysterious affinities that exist between our brain and those arrangements of colors and lines. [Gauguin][1]

> Either by the musician's will or unknown to him, the modern one among the meteors, the symphony, approaches thought that no longer claims kinship with everyday expression only. [Mallarmé][2]

I believe that these passages accurately characterize an inversion in the hierarchy of the arts and a major shift in aesthetics that was induced by the emergence of classical instrumental music. Instrumental music had been written before, of course, and at times it had even enjoyed great popularity. But, for a number of divergent reasons, foremost among them the absence of a religious and philosophical rationale, such music was never considered to be the purest, most essential form of music. The absence of verbal content seemed to reduce it to entertainment, a facile pleasure for the senses or a puzzle for the mind. The gradual growth of instrumental music in the eighteenth century, culminating in the production of sonatas, symphonies, and chamber music, forced an aesthetic revaluation of major import, whose implications went well beyond the confines of music proper. Here, for the first time in the history of Western aesthetics, an art that subordinated didactic messages and representations of specific contents to pure forms was acclaimed as profound art. Though instrumental pieces often continued to be interpreted as representations (of moonlight or a pastoral scene, for example), a new understanding of the arts emerged, and the struggle to legitimize instrumental music became the first, decisive battle about nonrepresentational art. In interpreting the emergence of the new aesthetics as breaking the ground for abstract art, I hope to throw new light on a well-known subject.

II

Since I will trace the emergence of a new music aesthetics with sparse reference to music itself, I should explain why I consider this a subject in its own right, and not some arid no-man's-land from which uncharted roads lead to the more fertile fields of artistic practice or the philosophy, psychology, and sociology of the arts. Such a rationale seems particularly needed in light of both the recent attacks on the traditional presuppositions of intellectual history and the backlash against the growth of literary theory.

The analogy between music aesthetics and literary theory makes apt the introductory words of René Wellek's *History of Modern Criticism*, which note the existence of a "deep gulf between theory and practice throughout the history of literature" and plead that we recognize the history of criticism as "a topic which has its own inherent interest, even without relation to the history of the practice of writing; it is simply a branch of the history of ideas which is in only loose relationship with the actual literature produced at the time. No doubt one can show the influence of the theory on the practice and, to a minor degree, of the practice on the theory, but this . . . should not be confused with the internal history of criticism." Hence the relationship between Wordsworth's theory and poetry is irrelevant to Wellek's project, for "the historian of criticism need only ask what Wordsworth meant by his doctrine, whether what he said makes sense, and what were the context, the background, and the influence on other critics of his theory" (6–7). In a similar vein Dahlhaus asserts that music aesthetics is shaped more by the philosophical and literary traditions that provide its categories than by music itself, which is its subject matter (*Rom. Musikästh.* 171).

What, more precisely, does this semi-independence of music aesthetics imply? One old and popular empiricist prejudice holds that aesthetic theories are just speculations parasitic on practice. By this account, music aesthetics would always have to wait for the empirical data of composition. Yet history amply proves that theories of the arts often precede or at least co-determine practice. Late-Renaissance theories about Greek music inspired experiments with a rhetorical and monodic style that eventually contributed to the birth of opera; in the case of Gluck, Wagner, and Schoenberg, theory surely played a decisive role in developing a new kind of music. The primacy of practice is a fine weapon against normative aesthetics, but it assigns a derivative status to reflections on the arts, just as empiricist theories of science belittle the role of hypotheses and theories. As the central subject of my book—the theoretical justification and acceptance of instrumental music—demonstrates, theories may adjust to an existing practice, and in such cases they limp behind. But in the case I am going to discuss, the lag was due to the profundity of the changes required in the aesthetics of all the arts. Once the theory adjusted, it allowed and even encouraged the development of novel artistic modes. The history of music aesthetics suggests that theory and practice in the arts tend to leapfrog, so that the creative work occasionally shapes the theory, whereas at other times theoretical reflection inspires creativity. If theory were always to wait for practice, it would have little relevance to it.

Another, equally common prejudice admits the independence of theoretical reflection but assigns a negative role to it, by pointing out that most theories have subsequently turned out to be fallacious or at least incompatible with the artistic practice they were designed to explain. Yet neither correctness nor adequacy to a specific artistic practice is the right standard by which to judge a theory. Some theories are interesting in their own right, others because of their clash with practice, others again because they inspire a mode of creativity, no matter how "wrong" or inconsistent they may be qua ideas. The humanist Girolamo Mei may or may not have understood Greek music accurately; what matters is that his ideas powerfully inspired Vincenzo Galilei and the Camerata to write significant new music.

Above all, ideas on music serve as a lifeline between music and the larger artistic, social, and intellectual concerns of a community. In this sense they are not just reflections on practice but often its very foundation and its interpreter to the community at large. Even the sharpest critics of Pythagorean and Platonic theories of music will have to admit, for instance, that these theories bolstered the prestige of music during the Middle Ages. Looking outward, theories of music may have profound bearing on the other arts and on philosophy, religion, and even politics, as the eighteenth century well demonstrates. My own interest in the subject originated with the discovery that problems of music engaged the minds of all those who have come to epitomize the age. Leibniz, Addison, Batteux, Euler, Diderot, d'Alembert, Rousseau, Frederick the Great, Moses Mendelssohn, Herder, Sir William Jones, Adam Smith, Lessing, and Kant—to name only a few—contributed decisively to eighteenth-century music aesthetics, and their reflections on the subject generally shaped, in turn, their thinking.

I offer these thoughts not to advocate the primacy of theory or to belittle the impact of artistic and social forces on it but to suggest that theories of the arts, and of music in particular, should be viewed from complementary rather than mutually exclusive angles, and that none of the emergent views will give a full perspective on the subject. My own perspective will be primarily literary and philosophical. While I have conscientiously tried to satisfy professional musicologists, I hope they will be generous enough to look upon my work not as a musicological treatise in the strict sense but as an essay that sheds a different light on their field. A similar generosity of mind, I hope, will be displayed by those who will miss in my treatment the larger historical and social context, the linkage between intellectual and social phenomena. Though readers may occasionally get this impression, I certainly do not hold that ideas respond *only* to other ideas. My concentration on their interaction was in large part determined by the need to give focus to a sprawling subject; for the rest, I have been groping toward a certain pattern and logic in the history of ideas, to replace the basic categories of *Geistesgeschichte* with a looser dialogical principle.

III

More concretely, I shall be concerned with the role of music aesthetics in the Romantic revolution, which necessitates a working definition of both *Romanticism* and *revolution*. The most authoritative account of the aesthetic presuppositions of Romanticism, Abrams's *The Mirror and the Lamp*, suggests that the Romantics "pose and answer aesthetic questions in terms of the relation of art to the artist, rather than to external nature" (3). This aesthetic revolution, which replaces mimesis (art in relation to nature) by an expressive theory (art in relation to the artist), is a changeover indicated by the metaphors of mirror and lamp:

> For the representative eighteenth-century critic, the perceiving mind was a reflector of the external world; the inventive process consisted in a reassembly of "ideas" which were literally images or replicas of sensations; and the resulting art work was itself comparable to a mirror presenting a selected and ordered image of life. By substituting a projective and creative mind and, consonantly, an expressive and creative theory of art, various romantic critics reversed the basic orientation of all aesthetic philosophy.[69]

In this perspective expressive creativity is a "spontaneous overflow of powerful feelings" that demands sincerity and adequacy to "the intention, the feeling, and the actual state of mind of the poet while composing" (23). Nature enters into art not via imitation but by means of a "natural" creativity which proceeds "spontaneously, artlessly, and without forethought either of their design or their audience" (83). Hence literature becomes "an index to the artist's personality" (23).

Abrams's reading of Romanticism as spontaneous creativity reinforces the common notion that the movement was unreflective. Yet, as Coleridge has already shown in the *Biographia Literaria*, Wordsworth's occasional sympathy with primitivism and spontaneous creativity was unworthy of his own poetic talent; similarly, Wackenroder's "outpourings of the heart" typify neither German Romanticism nor even Wackenroder's own poetic mode. Abrams slights those reflective and intellectual qualities of Romanticism that recent scholarship has amply demonstrated, but luckily his interpretations are so sensitive to his wide-ranging texts that the book succeeds admirably against the thesis implied by its captivating title.

According to Abrams, music theories actually heralded the emergence of expressive aesthetics, in that British critics regarded music as the first nonmimetic art, and German critics thought of it as the "undistorted expression of the feelings and mental powers of the artist," the "apex and norm of the pure and nonrepresentative expression of spirit and feeling" (22, 50, 92, 94). One stumbles, however, over the concept of "nonrepresentative expression." Can one express without expressing, and thereby representing, something? In the *New Grove* article on expression, Scruton claims that the verb *to express* has an intransitive (nonrepresentative) meaning, but this is not sanctioned by the *OED* nor sufficiently documented in the history of music. In a fundamental sense, expression always represents, and it should therefore not be set up as an alternative to mimesis. Expression is a mode of imitation because, as Krieger says with regard to poetry, it requires an entity preexisting the artwork: "The source of imitation may shift, now coming from within the poet rather than from outside him. But its status as object, together with the poem's subsidiary status, is unchanged" (81). Goodman, coming from a different direction, also defines expression as a species of symbolization or reference but notes that the direction of symbolization in expression runs counter to reference in denotation: a picture painted in gray color "does not denote the color gray but is denoted by the predicate 'gray'" (52). Goodman calls this expressive mode of reference *exemplification*.

What Krieger says about poetry applies still more readily to music. From about 1600 until the last decade of the eighteenth century, it was generally held that the purpose of music was to arouse certain stock passions by the appropriate use of key, meter, rhythm, and other musical elements. While recent scholarship has shown that this

theory of the musical affects never congealed into a doctrine and
never succeeded in establishing an unequivocal relationship between
the standard affects and the elements of music,[3] it remains true nevertheless that musicians and theorists generally believed in the musical representation of the passions. As I shall show, the shift from
this kind of musical representation in the seventeenth and early eighteenth century to what came to be called musical expression in the
later eighteenth century is in no way a movement away from mimesis in Abrams's sense. It was, just the other way around, a move
toward greater verisimilitude in representation, for composers were
now asked to portray finely shaded, individualized, and personal emotions instead of stock affects.

IV

If musical expression is actually a species of imitation—if "lamps" indeed shatter no "mirrors"—then we have to reconsider what the aesthetic revolution was and how music contributed to it. I share the
view that music was a major force in weakening mimesis, but, contrary to traditional interpretations, I do not think that expressive theories, which had mimetic foundations, could accomplish the task. Affect, expressive, or verbal theories were of little use when confronting
the new music, which had no definite representational content. A
better base, I suggest, was provided by the so-called Pythagorean tradition and by mathematical approaches to music in general.

   I shall support this central thesis by sketching a history of mathematical approaches to music, from their origin in Pythagorean
notions of harmony in antiquity, through theories of music as a
mathematical science in the Middle Ages, Renaissance polyphony,
seventeenth-century Pythagorean theories of a musical cosmos, rationalist theories of music in the Enlightenment, to the Romantic
revival of Pythagoreanism. Despite their differences, they are manifestations of a single and continuous tradition that outlived Romanticism and continues down to the computer and serial music of today. Its metamorphoses were brought about by a number of internal
and external pressures, foremost among them the interaction with rival and equally ancient verbal (or rhetorical) approaches to music, of
which affect and expressive theory are but variants. The alternating
dominance, the frequent battles, and the occasional peaceful coexis-

tence of verbal and mathematical approaches to music constitute the history of music theory in my view. Instrumental music aided the resurgence of certain mathematical and Pythagorean notions of music that formed the basis of a new aesthetics in Romanticism. As Spitzer, who comes to the subject from a different angle, rightly remarks, "The Pythagorean concept of world harmony was revived in modern civilization whenever Platonism was revived; and the German word 'Stimmung' is the fruit of one of these revivals" (*Harm.* 3). One may add that *Stimmung* ("mood" but also "tuning") reflects therefore the contribution of both music and Pythagorean mathematics to Romanticism.

Details will be furnished later; at this point I want only to add a few comments and to suggest some historical and theoretical implications. To begin with, what are we to make of the idea of an aesthetic revolution from the perspective of the suggested model? Could it not be objected, for instance, that baroque fugues are more purely musical, more mathematical, as well as older, than classical sonatas and symphonies? Do the lied, the Romantic opera, and frequent mimetic interpretations of instrumental music by Romantics not indicate that the verbal paradigm was not summarily destroyed by the revolution?

Both questions are justified, although they actually illustrate aspects of my thesis. Fugues and other so-called pure musical forms existed, of course, before the triumph of instrumental music in the late eighteenth century, but they were regarded as minor art forms and did not receive broad and original theoretical explanation. Only a combination of theory and practice could produce a major shift in aesthetics. The continuity of the verbal tradition, in turn, shows that the history of music aesthetics, and intellectual history in general, is not constituted of epochs defined by single paradigms. Just as Romanticism was not purely Pythagorean and mathematical, so the eighteenth century was not exclusively verbal and the Middle Ages unequivocally mathematical. In general the flux of ideas on any subject cannot be forced into longer cohesive periods separated by shorter revolutionary upheavals.[4] Models of this kind, whether indebted to the notion of zeitgeist in Geistesgeschichte, Kuhn's theory of paradigms, or Foucault's notion of *epistèmes*, fabricate coherent systems by excluding or ignoring whatever resists coercion and by paying undue attention to ruptures. In a more comprehensive and accurate vision, the homogeneous and cohesive structures of history dissolve into groups of conflicting ideas, resilient competing strands of tradition that reach across the presumed revolutionary ruptures by undergoing frequent transformations but seldom, if ever, disappearing completely. Although it is problematic to enchain discrete historical phenomena by such terms as *development, continuity*, or *causality*, the alternative of irrational ruptures between incommensurable sets of ideas seems no more satisfactory.

V

These methodological and thematic considerations determine the organization of my book. The opening chapter, on the Pythagorean tradition, is followed by three chapters on dimensions of the verbal paradigm: musical rhetoric, affect theory, and musical mimesis. Chapters 5–9 deal with the conflict between the verbal and mathematical traditions in the eighteenth century through the clash between Rameau and the philosophes. An arrangement by authors rather than traditions seemed preferable here, not only because each figure merits separate discussion but mainly because only this approach could highlight the conflict between traditions in individual minds. Rameau, the quintessential mathematician of music, was a composer of operas and a believer in affect theory; Rousseau, d'Alembert, and Diderot upheld musical imitation and the primacy of language, though they frequently went beyond Rameau in the direction of nonrepresentational music. Chapter 10, on the sister arts, attempts to show that, contrary to expectations, comparative studies of the arts and experiments with their union often prepared the ground for the emancipation of music. The chapter on expression attempts to deflate the term by showing that British critics used it in a restricted and by no means antimimetic sense, and that other writers, like Herder, went considerably beyond a theory of spontaneous expression. The central thread of the last three chapters is the link between mathematical and nonrepresentational theories of music. The emergence of that link is the subject of chapter 12, which is followed by a brief chapter on Kant, to show both his debt and his resistance to the mathematics of music. I conclude with Romantic texts with a Pythagorean disposition that give instrumental music its first full recognition.

If texts by poets and thinkers gradually displace the writings of composers and professional music theorists as my presentation progresses, this reflects, I believe, a growing attention in the eighteenth century to the broader cultural questions raised by music, culminating in the resonance that the new instrumental music found in Romantic poetry and poetics. As far as I can see, at no other time in history was the rationale of an art formulated by practitioners of another art rather than by its own practitioners or theorists. The explanation must be that instrumental music concretely demonstrated to poets the possibility of an art beyond language and representation. Having defined the new music as an art independent of language, the Romantics could then paradoxically proclaim music as the paradigm for poetry just because it had emancipated itself from language. The model became useful in Romantic experiments with the musicalization of poetic language not as outpouring or spontaneous overflow of emotions but as something resembling the classicism of Beethoven—the epitome of Romantic music for E. T. A. Hoffmann.

If I am favorably disposed toward the emancipation of music, this is not because I consider pure instrumental music—as an exemplification of abstract art in general—higher or better than word-dependent music. Rather, I believe that the new musical forms and the theoretical justifications engendered by them were beneficial for music as well as all the other arts, because they widened the range of artistic forms and granted the recipient a freer and more active role.

I MUSIC AND MATHEMATICS: THE PYTHAGOREAN TRADITION

The Soul of the Universe is united by 'Musical Concord'.
—Plato *Timaeus* 37a

The association between music and mathematics, probably as old as counting and singing, has throughout history charmed strict rationalists as well as rationalists with a mystic bent such as Plato, Kepler, Leibniz, and Novalis. Today, the strict rationalists include Boulez, Babbitt, and most serial, computer, and electronic composers, whereas the mystic cosmologists include perhaps Stockhausen.[1]

GREECE AND THE MIDDLE AGES

How Pythagoras discovered the mathematical proportions of music is related in Nicomachus's *Harmonikon Enchiridion* of around A.D. 100:

> Once upon a time, while pondering with intense calculation whether it might be possible to devise some kind of instrumental aid for the ears which would be firm and unerring . . . by a miraculous chance, he [Pythagoras] walked by a smithy and heard the hammers beating out iron on the anvil and giving off the sounds that are the most harmonious in combination with one another, except for one pair. He recognized among them the consonance of the octave, the fifth and the fourth. But he perceived that the interval between the fourth and the fifth was dissonant in itself, but was otherwise complementary to the greater of these two consonances. Delighted, therefore, since it was as if his purpose was being accomplished by a god, he ran into the smithy and found by various experiments that the difference of sound was consistent with the weight of the hammers, but not with the force of the blows, nor with the shapes of the hammers, nor the alteration of the iron being forged. Taking precise note of the weights of the hammers and their downward momentum. which was identical, he departed to his home. [Levin 70]

Since Pythagoras's writings have not survived, this Nicomachean version of the Pythagorean legend has become the canonized history of the birth of Greek musical physics and metaphysics.

Pythagoreanism and all other mathematical approaches to music start from the observation that the frequency ratios of the octave, the fifth, and the fourth are 1:2, 2:3, and 3:4, respectively. As Aristotle critically notes in his *Metaphysics*, the Pythagoreans believed "that many attributes of numbers belong to sensible bodies; they posited that . . . attributes of numbers exist in musical notes and in the heavens and in many other things" (1090a). According to Pythagorean metaphysics, harmony infused all aspects of the universe and mirrored itself specifically in the simple harmonic proportions of music.[2] Musical harmony thus expressed the balance of things—of the elements, of the humors in the body, of soul and soma, of the political state, and, especially, of the movements of the heavenly bodies, believed to result in the celebrated "music of the spheres." As first stated in the concluding myth of Plato's *Republic*, each planet emits a tone based on its orbital speed and size that harmonizes with the tones of the other planets: "Up above on each of the rims of the circles a Siren stood, borne around in its revolution and uttering one sound, one note, and from all the eight there was the concord of a single harmony" (617b).

Socrates agreed with the Pythagoreans that music was a science of the cosmos, for "as the eyes are framed for astronomy so the ears are framed for the movements of harmony, and these are in some sort kindred sciences" (530d). As a rational rather than an empirical science, music was regarded as a wisdom that leads the mind from the unstable physical world to the forms and ideas. According to Boethius, the Pythagoreans "measure consonances themselves with the ear, but the distances by which consonances differ among themselves they do not entrust to the ears, the judgments of which are unclear, but to rules and reason—as though the sense were an obedient servant, and the reason were truly a commanding judge" (1.9:58).

Boethius's *Principles* and Cassiodorus's *Institutiones*, both compiled in the sixth century from Nicomachus, Ptolemy, and other neo-Platonic sources, became the musical canon of the Middle Ages. The Pythagorean metaphysics of music readily fitted into the medieval world picture because it eminently satisfied the mathematical, symbolic, and metaphysical disposition of medieval culture. "The heavens and the earth," says Cassiodorus, "share in this discipline of music, for Pythagoras attests that this universe was founded by and can be governed by music" (Strunk 88). This "daughter of Arithmetic" and "theory of concord" was defined in the anonymous *Scholica Enchiriadis* as the "rational discipline of agreement and discrepancy in sounds according to numbers" (Strunk 134–35). The mathematical concept of music became formalized in the medieval division of the liberal arts, which assigned music, together with arithmetic, geometry, and astronomy, to the quadrivium, and the verbal arts of rhetoric, grammar, and dialectic to the trivium.

In the Christianized Pythagoreanism of the Middle Ages, musical harmony continued to have a metaphysical meaning. Isidor of Seville thought that the very universe was "held together by a certain harmony of sounds," and that the heavens were made to move by its modulation (Strunk 94). For Johannes Scotus (Erigena), "the rational relations of different intervals, which, compared to each other, make for the sweetness of music" intimated universal harmony and the divine creative act itself (Handschin 323–24).

Hence the symbolic value of musical numbers in the Middle Ages. Cassiodorus described the Ten Commandments as a "decachord" (Strunk 88), and Jean de Muris set out to demonstrate that music originates from the most perfect number, namely three (Strunk 173–74), while Scotus derived all music from the number twelve. These and other numerological speculations had no empirical foundations, of course, but they structured music just as they structured Dante's cantos and Gothic cathedrals. Unlike Lang (*Music* 41), I think they had therefore an organic relation to musical practice. Furthermore, mathematical and metaphysical interpretations gave music its extraordinary prestige within the scholastic hierarchy.

The prestige granted to mathematical music presupposes, however, its subservience to faith and morality. When Plato elucidates the ratios between notes in the *Timaeus*, he is not analyzing music; he sets out to demonstrate that the divisions of the world soul and the orbital periods of the planets have the same proportions. Music resonates in the soul because it attunes man to cosmic harmony (43 d–e); its delight flows from "an imitation of divine harmony in mortal motions" (80b). Hence harmony is given to us not to engender irrational pleasure, "but as means to correct any discord that may have arisen in the courses of the soul, and to be our ally in bringing her

into harmony and agreement with herself" (47c–d). A further function of music is to harmonize the soul with the body, for, as Boethius says, "The whole structure of soul and body is united by musical
harmony" (Strunk 83). This harmonic tie between body and soul allows the stirring of emotions through music and forms, as we shall
see, the foundation of affective theories of music.

THE RENAISSANCE AND THE BAROQUE

An impressive book by Hollander describes the "untuning of the
sky" between 1500 and 1700, a gradual "demythologizing of musical
esthetics" that allegedly led from Pythagorean speculation to an interest in musical practice as interpersonal communication: "The very
notion of the heavenly harmony changes its function radically in an
age when myths about the music of the spheres can no longer be believed, and when their metaphorical use is no longer permitted in
empirical accounts of the nature of the universe" (145). With the
"untuning of the heavens" the Pythagorean doctrine becomes a literary convention that trivializes former beliefs by making them the
subject of wit (238). A similar fading of Pythagoreanism has also
been noted by Schäfke (*Gesch.* 243) and in Palisca's excellent account
of a "scientific empiricism" in sixteenth- and early seventeenth-
century musical thought. In all these, the musical thinking of the age
is said to have turned from a science of reason into an art of the
senses.

These accounts identify an important force in the ferment of
Renaissance thought. And yet, Palisca's conclusion that "the new
acoustics replaced the elaborate conglomeration of myth, scholastic
dogma, mysticism, and numerology . . . with a far less monumental
but more permanent and resistant base" (137) holds on to a now dis-
credited exaggeration of the scientific revolution. If we look beyond
English poetry and the experimental theorists and composers of music in the sixteenth and seventeenth centuries, we see that Pythagoreanism retained a vigor by incorporating elements of the new science
into traditional cosmology, metaphysics, and theology.

Both the Renaissance and the Baroque are multifaceted in this respect. The former gave a powerful impetus to the empirical discovery
of the world without appealing to mathematics. But Pico, Ficino,
Bruno, Paracelsus, and others also revived ancient cosmological

speculation and were specifically interested in Plato and his Pythagorean mathematics of music. The polyphony of Renaissance music
is essentially "self-contained, autonomous," and, loosely speaking,
mathematical.

The attacks on counterpoint and the growth of monodic music in
the early seventeenth century were balanced by the growth of the
new science, which inevitably enhanced the prestige of mathematics
and its role in music. While the new mathematics largely freed itself from Pythagoreanism, the leading mathematicians of music, from
Descartes, Kircher, and Kepler to Leibniz, Rameau, and Euler never
fully renounced the idea that musical and cosmic harmony were in-
terconnected. As Palisca admits, the impact of mathematical physics
on the empirical study of acoustics was barely felt before the eighteenth century.

Three types of evidence suggest that the mathematical tradition remained a major force in the sixteenth and seventeenth centuries: (1)
the conciliatory attitude that representatives of the new rhetorical approach showed toward it; (2) its reaffirmation by a large and broadly
representative group of musicians; and (3) major new Pythagorean
syntheses, which incorporated a vast range of new, empirical knowledge. The musical literature of that age was remarkable not for its departure from the Pythagorean tradition but for its tenacious adherence to it in the face of a rapidly changing world view.

Zarlino, a leading theorist of the sixteenth century, explicitly reaffirmed that "the subject of music is sonorous numbers" (29), even
though he attributed new importance to language in music. The generation of Vincenzo Galilei and the Camerata went beyond him in
attacking polyphony and developing a rhetoric of music, but it seldom questioned the mathematical foundations and filiation of music.
To be sure, the very name of the new musical style, "seconda prat-
tica," indicated a newly acquired interest in practice, but it was precisely this relative neglect of theory that left the inherited theoretical
base largely intact. And so, Monteverdi could aim at satisfying the
ear and yet "take his stand upon the consonances and dissonances approved by mathematics" (Strunk 50).

Dammann and Schäfke (*Gesch*. 285–89) have amply shown the
dominance of mathematics in a broad range of seventeenth-century
treatises on music, so I shall mention here only four prominent
encyclopedic works of the age with Pythagorean foundations:

Fludd's *Utriusque cosmi historia* (1617), Kepler's *Harmonices mundi* (1619), Mersenne's *Harmonie universelle* (1636–37), and Kircher's *Musurgia universalis* (1650). These works bring together mathematics, new findings in science, legends, dogmas, articles of faith, ancient authorities, and allegorical speculation but ultimately integrate them into a Christianized Pythagorean vision of universal harmony. The synthesis is visually embodied in Fludd's temple of speculative music and cosmic monochord (the universe being represented as a musical instrument played by the world soul), Mersenne's lyre of God, Kircher's organ universe, and Kepler's polyhedra.[3] Within these symbols all four works accommodate a veritable mine of practical observations and inventions: Fludd devotes a whole, profusely illustrated chapter to the military art; Kircher invents listening and sound-amplifying devices for military purposes; and Mersenne produces an invaluable illustrated description of the instruments of his time.

The tension between abstract musico-mathematical order and empiricism is most evident in Kepler's work, the scientific achievement of which cannot be separated from its Pythagorean inspiration. As stated in the dedication to King James, the germinal idea of a Pythagorean and Platonic heavenly harmony informed Kepler's discovery of the law for planetary orbits, and the *Harmonices mundi* was offered to the king in the hope of furthering political harmony. The analogy between the ratios of the aphelion and perihelion of the six planetary orbits and the ratios of the six basic intervals in music was for Kepler a kind of Kantian regulative idea that guided his study of nature, for he was convinced that the heavenly movements were an "everlasting polyphony (intelligible but inaudible) with dissonant tunings, like certain syncopations or cadences by means of which men imitate these natural dissonances." Imitating cosmic harmony, man has "discovered the art of singing polyphonically, which was unknown to the ancients. He wanted to play the perpetuity of cosmic time in a short part of an hour by means of an artful concord of several voices" (315).

Throughout the seventeenth century this Pythagorean tradition coexisted comfortably with the increasingly well-articulated and powerful verbal theories of music, because both the word and mathematics were usually understood as manifestations of reason. Mersenne's treatise includes, for instance, a "Traité de mechanique" with physical and mathematical observations, and a "Traité de la voix et des Chants," in which he correlates music with verbal accent. Kircher defines "numerus sonorus" as the true and formal object of music (45) and the affect aroused as its final purpose (565).

The continuing vitality of mathematical music is also evident in the emergence of the *ars combinatoria* as a compositional method. In the words of Mersenne, who treated it first, "The ordinary rules of combinations teach how many songs can be made out of a certain number of notes, provided that one always retains the same number of notes and one does not repeat the note two or more times" (*Harm. univ.* "Traité de la voix et des Chants" 107). The idea led Mersenne to prepare extensive combinatorial-compositional tables of sounds (107–58) and Kircher to construct a composing machine, the "musurgia mirifica." These apparently naive attempts at a mechanical construction of complex structures from simple elements are versions of the Leibnizian *ars inveniendi*, which Foucault has rightly posited as the conceptual background of the "classical age."[4] The same principle underlies serial music today.

JOHANN MATTHESON

The writings of Werckmeister around 1700 were probably the last distinguished expositions of a Pythagoreanism that was increasingly threatened by the growth of empiricism. The decisive empiricist assault was carried out by Johann Mattheson, who has been hailed as the major theorist of affects, though in my opinion, his originality lies more in turning against the mathematicians of music.[5]

Mattheson, a lifetime resident of Hamburg, started his career as a singer and composer at the Hamburg opera, which had its heyday during his youth, but he left in 1705 to become tutor and from 1706 onward secretary in the house of the English Resident in Hamburg —positions that assured him financial independence.[6] In 1715 he became, in addition, director of music at the cathedral in Hamburg and shocked the orthodox by using for the first time a female soloist at his inaugural. Mattheson also edited Germany's first "moral weekly," *Der Vernünfftler* ("The Man of Reason") (1713–14), which was expressly modeled on the *Tatler* and the *Spectator*, and its first music periodical, the *Critica Musica* (1722–23, 1725). These and other activities indicate the range of Mattheson's talents, but his lasting fame is based on his work in music theory, which he started at the ripe age of thirty-two with a resolute blow to Pythagoreanism in *Das Neu-Eröffnete Orchestre* (1713).

Mattheson has at times been seen as a representative of French neoclassicism and rationalism, but this is mistaken, even if we recognize that he adopted some ideas from Descartes, Brossard, Jean-Baptiste Rousseau and others. His model philosophers, Bacon and Locke, came from the British empirical tradition, and his own method of argumentation was critical and inductive rather than deductive, anticipating thus the method of Lessing rather than that of Gottsched. As Forchert has pointed out, Mattheson's knowledge grew out of polemics with others; he aimed "much more at the weakening of opposing positions than positing his own" (200). This is one reason why his ideas never crystallized into a coherent doctrine, why scholarship today has so little difficulty in demonstrating that Mattheson's system, patched together from his polemics, is rent with inconsistencies and contradictions. For me, the more exciting and interesting part of his legacy lies not in the disparate parts of the system he aspired to construct but in his attempts to demolish the systems of others, not in his *summa, Der vollkommene Capellmeister* (1739), but in the early polemics against the Pythagorean tradition.

The very title of Mattheson's first book, *Das Neu-Eröffnete Orchestre* (1713), announces that its author, who came from the world of opera, wishes to speak to the amateur public beyond his learned colleagues, though the subtitle addresses this "galant" audience with a baroque involution: "Universal and thorough Manual, how a Galant Person can acquire a Complete Notion of the Sublimity and Dignity of Noble Music, shape his Taste accordingly, understand the Technical Terms, and skillfully discourse about this Excellent Science."

Dilettante readers expecting merely tidbits for scintillating conversations in salons were surely disappointed, however, for Mattheson's treatise was much too learned and philosophical for their purposes. It is a debunking of abstract theorizing and an empiricist attack on the rationalist premise that musical harmonies reveal immutable cosmic laws. If music is divine, rules give us merely an earthly idea of this elusive subject, and they, like our perception of the heavenly constellations, must change. Since everything in the mind must come through the senses, all science originates in perception, and all rules must follow the alternation of conjunctures and circumstances (3–4).

The ear is the only channel through which music "penetrates into the innermost soul of the attentive listener" (126–27), hence mathematical studies of music, combinatorial composition (105), and numerology (109–10) are misguided.

The rationalist position was revindicated in the wonderfully entitled *Ut, Re, Mi, Fa, Sol, La Tota Musica et Harmonia Aeterna, oder Neu-eröffnetes, altes, wahres, eintziges und ewiges Fundamentum Musices, entgegen gesetzt Dem neu-eröffneten Orchestre* (1715) of a certain Buttstett. Unfortunately, this "Newly-Opened old, true, unique and eternal Fundament of Music" is merely a pastiche of quotations from venerable Pythagorean authorities, which controverts the very principles of rationalism.

Mattheson's *Das beschützte Orchestre* (1717) responded to some particulars in Buttstett's book, but his substantive answer is contained in the third installment of the series, *Das forschende Orchestre* (1721), which moved beyond the quarrel to an even more general attack on the mathematical tradition. Repeatedly invoking Bacon, the acoustical researches of Sauveur, and Locke's denial of innate ideas, Mattheson posits the sensual origin of all knowledge and the fallibility of reason: empty thoughts are more dangerous than blind perceptions (140, 146). Mattheson can suggest, courting sensualism, therefore, that the senses are fused with the spirit: "The soul is what sees, hears, smells, feels, and thinks through the senses" (96), and, in turn, the senses are a property of the soul and as such immortal (105). Hence the body is no prison of the soul (108–09) but God's gift to enhance the enjoyment of life. "Honesta voluptas" in the Cartesian sense (see p. 49) is therefore the genuine aim and purpose of music:

> My theoretical and practical principles in music came from experience, through the senses; my guideline is to honor God and serve human pleasure and well-being; my fundament is nature, and my purpose in music (qua music) is and remains eternally to move the sense of hearing resident in the soul as the best judge in this matter. [449–50]

Such praise of the senses necessarily leads to sharp attacks on the excesses of the mind and the abuses of mathematics. From the empiricist perspective, numbers and harmonic relations are not manifestations of a metaphysical order but merely abstractions from physical experience. Invoking Bacon, Mattheson demands that mathematics serve experience and be limited to technical application (249 ff.), because its unwarranted extension furthers hubris, the intellectual conceit of a self-sufficient mind. The source of moral corruption is not the flesh, but, as for Malebranche, the "most inward part of the soul," the overreaching intellect. "Sense-less" ratiocination alone is truly irrational (119–20).

Since the arts originate in experience rather than in philosophy or mathematics (246), music must find new empirical foundations and cannot be understood as a Platonic anamnesis of a divine harmony. None of "the most famous and gallant composers . . . ever improved their work by drawing even a single line with a compass" (276), and scholars of mathematics in music remain incompetent composers unless they learn about people and their feelings. Mathematical physics helps to design instruments or buildings but remains a servant and a tool, and cannot become the foundation or cause (176–78). Mathematicians are "apothecaries of music" (228), who merely administer prescriptions.

Mattheson's anti-mathematical tirade culminates therefore in an intensification of Bacon's demand that mathematics and logic serve physics: let us "throw out the handmaid [mathematics] together with her son [number]" (253), for no self-respecting poetic musician "is going to seek the principle of his science, the origin, fundament, and ground rules of his art in sordid, miserly, and paltry arithmetics" (255). "My pious numerosissime domine Mathematicotere, you are far from being that hero you may have been under the Pythagorean regime!" (277).

I find this temperamental but by no means unsophisticated exercise in demolition historically more important than Mattheson's later attempt at constructing his own edifice, though one must admit that its passages of vigor and clarity alternate with prolix pages where Mattheson, stung by Buttstett's charge of dilettantism, marshals troops of venerable authorities in support of his case. The weight of testimony ironically undermines his attack on pedantic erudition and forces him to swerve from his original program of a "galant" learning. These blemishes notwithstanding, *Das forschende Orchestre* is a landmark.[7]

And yet, while Mattheson's early writings exposed the weaknesses of Pythagoreanism, neither these nor his later crusades could stamp out mathematical approaches to music, which gradually renewed themselves by jettisoning the accumulated burden of tradition. Ironically, just a year after Mattheson had buried Pythagoreanism, it was reborn in Rameau's epochal *Traité de l'harmonie*. Mattheson instantly recognized the new enemy, but he could no longer play a leading role in the battle that Rameau's theory unleashed in the 1750s.

2 MUSIC AND LANGUAGE

Orators and musicians have . . . fundamentally the same purpose, namely to master the hearts, to rouse or calm the passions, and to set the listeners now in this now in that affect.

—*Quantz* 100

Musical pieces of a certain length . . . share with actual speeches the rules of order and the arrangements of ideas.

—Forkel *Gesch.* 50

The full emancipation of music from language is a relatively recent development in the Western tradition. The variety of their historical relationships, on the other hand, is a vast and complex subject, which I shall try to illustrate here only by means of select examples.[1] My aim is twofold: first, to indicate a tradition descending from Plato that advocated a subordination of music to words for further moral and religious ends; second, to sketch the rhetorical link between music and language. Both of these aspects became central in eighteenth-century debates.

THE VERBAL DOMINATION OF MUSIC

The Greek concept of *musiké* covered both music and language, because music was based on the invariable length and pitch of Greek syllables. No comparable musical imitation of words is possible in the modern European languages, because in these the length and pitch of a syllable depend on the particular semantic emphasis it receives in context. The tie between Greek language and music did not allow the development of complex, multilayered musical textures, and the instruments accompanied the voice in unison or with minor deviations. The aulos, a wind instrument, imitated the voice and intensified the frenzy at Dionysian rites, while the lyre was Apollo's instrument, designed to create soft, lyrical consonances in imitation of cosmic harmony.

However, toward the end of the fifth century B.C. a musical revolution gradually destroyed the unity of musiké and "broke the old associations of poetic and musical forms. Instrumental improvisations, with sound effects imitating nature, overshadowed the vocal part that had dominated. . . . Music, though widely enjoyed, lost its cultural prestige and . . . was left to professional virtuosos of high technical skill" (*Harv. Dict* 352). Plato bitterly resisted the new music because he thought that only the unity of musiké and the dominance of language could assure music an ethical and educational function. One may pointedly say that ethical considerations led Plato to favor word-dominated music to a mathematical music that offered insight into cosmic harmony—though the True and the Good were inseparable for him, and the cognitive grounds were ultimately ethical as well.

Book 3 of the *Republic* subordinates harmony and rhythm to speech (398c–d), and prohibits the use of four modes because they demoralize. The remaining modes are acceptable because the Phrygian imitates "the utterances and the accents of a brave man who is engaged in warfare," while the Dorian is for men engaged "in works of peace" (399b). Music, unlike poetry, survives Plato's moral scrutiny "because more than anything else rhythm and harmony find their way to the inmost soul and take strongest hold upon it, bringing with them and imparting grace, if one is rightly trained" (401d–e). The perfect musician "blends gymnastics with music and applies them most suitably to the soul" (412).

Plato's benign attitude changed, however, when he observed that

> an unmusical license set in with the appearance of poets who were men of native genius, but ignorant of what is right and legitimate in the realm of the Muses. Possessed by a frantic and unhallowed lust for pleasure, they contaminated laments with hymns and paeans with dithyrambs, actually imitated the strains of the flute on the harp, and created a universal confusion of forms. Thus their folly led them unintentionally to slander their profession by the assumption that in music there is no such thing as a right and a wrong, the right standard of judgment being pleasure given to the hearer, be he high or low. By compositions of such a kind and discourse to the same effect, they naturally inspired the multitude with contempt of musical law, and a conceit of their own competence as judges. [*Laws* 700d–e]

The sound of the "musical sweetmeats" in the "popular, cloying" music (802c–d) that flooded Athens and "corrupted its youth" so disheartened the aged philosopher that for moral reasons he came to demand stricter mimetic rules. In books 2 and 7 of his late dialogue, the *Laws*, the instrument of knowledge became a dubious weapon that may serve evil as well as good causes; the doctrine that all music is "representation and portraiture" (668b) is forged to combat the "blasphemy" that music is to be judged by the pleasure it gives (655d). If music must be right, not pleasurable, the composer must know "what the object reproduced *is*, next, how *correctly*, third and last, how *well* a given representation has been effected, in point of language, melody, or rhythm" (669a–b). Plato's long list of errors includes the attribution of words, rhythms, or melodies to the wrong sex, social class, or animals, and culminates in the gravest offense of destroying the harmony among the constituent parts of musiké:

> [The poets] divorce rhythm and figure from melody, by giving metrical form to bare discourse, and melody and rhythm from words, by their employment of cithara and flute without vocal accompaniment, though it is the hardest of tasks to discover what such wordless rhythm and tune signify, or what model worth considering they represent . . . the use of either as an independent instrument is no better than unmusical legerdemain. [669d–670]

A profound shift has taken place. While Plato still believes that music can reveal the harmony of immutable forms and ideas, the separation and wanton abuse of words, rhythm, and melody signal to him that music is not intrinsically harmonious but a corruptible social instrument. In the absence of verbal control, music will ignore reason and appeal to the baser emotions. Since music no longer self-evidently reflects metaphysical truth, beauty, and harmony, but reproduces "the moods of better and worse men" (798d), imitation must strictly be enforced for social and political reasons. Select wise judges over fifty ought to interpret the legislator's will (802b–c) and, following the Egyptian model, permit alterations in the canon only for serious reasons (657a–b). Music could still be used to rouse the emotions for proper moral or religious ends, but Plato was now keenly aware that passionate music could work at cross-purposes with those ends, and he insists that music be accompanied by words. Most eighteenth-century defenders of imitation and enemies of pure instrumental music echoed him.

   That the medieval church, in spite of its deep involvement with music, had similar concerns, is perhaps nowhere more evident than in the writings of one of its greatest figures, the one who comes closest to

Plato in adopting a strict rational and moral position in spite of his poetic temperament and sensitivity: St. Augustine. In his treatise *De
Musica*, written shortly after his conversion, he is eager to prove that
music is a science that appeals to reason, and he is therefore contemptuous of those intrumental artists who play merely for the senses
without knowing anything about the principles of their science. But
a famous and moving passage in his *Confessions* reveals how sensitive
St. Augustine was to the seductive powers of music. Vacillating between "dangerous pleasure and tried soundness," at times he desired
"that every air of the pleasant songs to which David's Psalter is often
used, be banished both from my ears and those of the Church itself,"
or, at least, that psalms be recited "with so slight an inflection of
voice that it was more like speaking than singing." At other times he
felt that the mind was "more devoutly and earnestly elevated into a
flame of piety by the holy words themselves when they are thus sung,
than when they are not." One was to be moved "not by the singing
but by what is sung," and this required ceaseless vigilance against the
seductions of music. Singing was most useful to those weaker minds
whom words alone could not reach (10.33:172). St. Basil and St. John
Chrysostom adopted similar cautious justifications of devotional
singing.

The religious doubts persisted beyond the Middle Ages. Calvin's
Geneva Psalter admits that songs have "great force and vigor to move
and inflame the hearts of men to invoke and praise God," but warns
that music "should not be the occasion of our giving free rein to disso-
luteness or of our making ourselves effeminate with disordered pleasures and that it should not become the instrument of lasciviousness
or of any shamelessness." Music has "a secret and almost incredible
power to move our hearts in one way of another" (Strunk 346–47).
The Council of Trent, on the Catholic side, decreed that music in the
church must be uplifting and the words sung in liturgy must be clearly
intelligible, not obscured by the music. Finney has shown that the use
of ecstatic music in service was continuously debated throughout the
Renaissance and the seventeenth century.

MUSIC AND VERBAL INTONATION

The first major secular attacks on the musical obfuscation of the text in
polyphony were launched in the last decades of the sixteenth century

in Italy. Starting in 1573, the poet Ottavio Rinuccini, Vincenzo Galilei (father of Galileo), the musicians Jacopo Peri and Giulio Caccini, and others regularly gathered in the palace of Giovanni de Bardi to advance musical learning and to experiment with new styles. As Palisca has shown, Galilei adopted from the humanist Girolamo Mei a monodic and expressive notion of Greek music and brought it to bear upon the writings and compositions of the Camerata, which set out to create a humanistic music dominated by language and voice.

Galilei's *Dialogo della musica antica e della moderna* (1581) alleges that instrumental sounds produced by simple pieces "of hollow wood over which are stretched four, six, or more strings of the gut of a dumb beast" cannot match the dignity of the voice (Strunk 313). Furthermore, unequal rhythms, melodies, and tempos, or the mingling of voices in polyphony impede communication. Modern polyphonic singing is "absurd" and offers vacuous pleasure. Counterpoint subjects "reason to sense and form to matter, and truth to falsehood." The rules of harmony are useful to delight and "tickle" the ear, "but for the expression of conceptions they are pestilence," because the mind, "bound by the snares of pleasure thus produced, is not given time to understand, let alone consider, the badly uttered words" (Strunk 311–15). Polyphonic composition must be replaced by a monodic style, because "truth is a unity," and only an uncluttered voice can communicate clearly.

Galilei protests the subjection of "reason to sense," but he is equally suspicious of the intellectual pleasures in polyphony and counterpoint that have "little value for expressing the passions" (Strunk 315). Music should not use clever allegories, paint bitterness or savagery with dissonant chords, imitate natural sounds or motions, and, above all, should not paint with the lines and shapes of notes in the score (Strunk 315–16). To imitate language in music means to revive the ancient imitation of intonation:

> When the ancient musician sang any poem whatever, he first considered very diligently the character of the person speaking: his age, his sex, with whom he was speaking, and the effect he sought to produce by this means . . . [he] then expressed in the tone and with the accents and gestures, the quantity and quality of sound, and the rhythm appropriate to that action and to such a person. [Strunk 319]

> [composers ought] to observe, when one quiet gentleman speaks with another, in what manner he speaks, how high or low his voice is pitched,

with what volume of sound, with what sort of accents and gestures, and with what rapidity or slowness his words are uttered. [Strunk 318]

Thus Galilei wants to characterize people by imitating in music their typical intonation. The contrapuntists failed in this rhetorical enterprise because they know not "how to express the conceptions of the mind and how to impress them with the greatest possible effectiveness on the minds of the listeners" (Strunk 312).

Galilei no longer considers, then, music as an incarnation of divine *logos*, for he wants to imitate ordinary speech to communicate human feelings and attitudes. He and the members of the Camerata have justly been called "musical humanists," both because they wished to resuscitate ancient music and because they sought a music centered on man.

Of course, a revival of ancient music had to face all but insurmountable obstacles, because, contrary to the situation in literature, no significant pieces of ancient music survived. As D. P. Walker has shown, the musical humanists were as a result deeply divided about whether ancient music could be resuscitated, and if so, by what means. Galilei's radical views were not shared by everybody, but they were a strong force in fomenting experiments with a new, expressive madrigal style, which, in turn, gave rise to the first operas around 1600. As Peri explains in the introduction to his *Euridice* (performed October 1600, printed 1601) in direct reference to the Aristoxenian distinctions (see below, chapter 3), he attempted to steer a middle course between singing, which slowly moved from one distinct and sustained note to another, and speech, which rapidly and continuously glided in pitch. In the new style, the harmonic accompaniment moved in accord with the affects, but generally slowly, while the voice was allowed to pass freely over dissonant notes on unstressed syllables and join the harmony on stressed ones:

I knew likewise that in our speech some words are so intoned that harmony can be based upon them and that in the course of speaking it passes through many others that are not so intoned until it returns to another that will bear a progression to a fresh consonance. And having in mind those inflections and accents that serve us in our grief, in our joy, and in similar states, I caused the bass to move in time to these, either more or less, following the passions, and I held it firm throughout the false and true proportions [consonances and dissonances] until, running through various notes, the voice of the speaker came to a word that,

being intoned in familiar speech, opened the way to a fresh harmony.
[Strunk 374]

This early rhetorical style in opera was carried to its apogee in the
music of Monteverdi. Slowly, however, the more melody-centered
arias came to dominate Italian opera, and the rhetorical style became
restricted to the recitative sections. In the new standard "division of
labor" the arias displayed the affects while the recitative explained
the action and provided "transitions from one passion to another"
(Krause *Poesie* 233). As late as 1779, Lepileur defined recitative as that
part of opera "which has no passions to paint and which requires
therefore only the inflection of the voice needed to recount the facts"
(89).

Though I cannot give an account of the development and variety
of recitative, a few words about the French rhetorical tradition are
necessary, both because it indicates a different relation between music and language and because it became a central issue in eighteenth-
century French debates about music. Italian attempts to revive a musical style suited to ancient tragedy paralleled Baïf's experiments
from 1567 onward to write quantitative (as against stressed) verse
in the vernacular. The new quantitative *vers mesuré* was set to music
(*musique mesurée*) by Baïf's friends in the Académie de poésie et de
musique.

These experiments in Baïf's Académie played an important role in
the development of French *récit*, which was more melodic and less
declamatory than Italian recitative, though it attempted to follow
faithfully the rhythm, accents, and intonation of French. In the classic example, which was to become the center of controversy between
Rameau and Rousseau, the heroine of Lully's *Armide* (1686) intends
to kill the sleeping Renaud but ends up punishing him with love for
her. The music expresses the fluctuating emotions with frequently
changing meter, but, in contrast to Italian recitatives, the modulations are simple, and the vocal line is shaped as much by musical considerations as by the verbal intonation. For Rousseau, it was a misbe-
gotten bastard: "If one takes it to be a song one finds in it neither
meter, nor character, nor melody; if one wants it to be a recitative
one finds in it neither nature nor expression" (*Ecrits* 321).

The experiment of imposing ancient quantitative meter on modern
languages was doomed to failure, though it remained a cherished

idea of those who favored the ancients in the renewed debates between partisans of the ancients and the moderns. Isaac Vossius's treatise *On the Singing of Poems and the Power of Rhythm* (1673) forcefully
argued, for instance, that the shift from quantitative to accentual meter led to a decline in the art of singing. According to Vossius, "In a
genuine song, rhythm has more force and effect than words," and
"proper scansion" is therefore indispensable (46, 97). The increasing
role of words and the greater philosophical sophistication of modern
languages are responsible for the decline of music (97).

Vossius's lament that the sharpening of reason led to the dwin-
dling of verbal musicality anticipates Rousseau and Nietzsche, but
most eighteenth-century thinkers and musicians, Rousseau included,
did not believe that one could simply reintroduce quantitative meters in poetry, and the alternative, of indicating verbal accent by the
length of notes, did not fare much better.[2] The role of classical prosody in music became restricted to sporadic attempts to assign affects
to the classical feet and to employ these directly in musical rhythm.
According to Serauky, Kuhnau and J. S. Bach made conscious use
of spondaic and trochaic passages to illustrate corresponding affects.
"Sound feet" were for Mattheson the smallest units of musical
rhythm to possess affective character (*Capellm.* 160–70).

While the idea of a classical prosody in music failed, the seventeenth and eighteenth centuries remained preoccupied with the musical imitation of intonation, and they developed special rules not only
for the correlation of verbal accent and musical rhythm, but also for
imitating phrasing and punctuation.[3] Verbal clauses, for instance,
were not to be interrupted by long musical pauses, and they were to
be terminated with cadences appropriate to the punctuation.

Recitative was frequently criticized, of course, by the harmonists and the mathematicians of music. As Hawkins wrote, "Musical
sounds do not imitate common speech; and therefore . . . recitative can in no degree be said to be an improvement of elocution"
(XXXIII). But even rhetoricians of music had to admit that the conflicting demands of melody and intonation created serious problems
for recitative. Addison pointed out in the twenty-ninth issue of the
Spectator that "Recitative Musick in every Language should be as different as the Tone or Accent of each Language." This would make
operas more comprehensible but, as Scheibe noted later, limit the
freedom of melodic invention. Rousseau explicitly invoked Addi-

son's principle in the *Lettre sur la musique française* (*Ecrits* 306–09)—
chastising thereby the Lullists for deviating from the French intonation that he found otherwise inferior—but by the time of the *Dictionnaire* he had perceived an irresolvable conflict between modern
accent and melody: "The Greeks could sing while speaking; but we
have to sing or speak, we cannot do both at the same time" (art. "ré-
citatif"). Rousseau was so fearful of the encroachment of intonation
on melody that for the expression of shifting passions he preferred
sophisticated harmonic transitions and modulations to recitatives. As
we shall see, he reacted in a similar manner to Gluck.

During the second half of the century, enthusiasts of recitative
dwindled, and even Algarotti, who considered it the "most essential
part of the drama" (59), wanted to cleanse it. Burney observed in 1773
that everybody was "tired and disgusted" with recitative (*Germ.* 2:
159). One reason for this was that recitatives had become formulaic
and had lost their earlier expressiveness; the other may well have
been that musical subservience to the words no longer seemed a worthy aim to pursue. Though recitative lingered on for a few more decades, it went into a long hibernation with the advent of Romantic
music. Its fading signaled the demise of word-oriented music toward
the end of the eighteenth century.

This decline of recitative paralleled the emergence of arguments
that a strict musical imitation of poetic prosody was impossible. Two
instances were being mentioned with particular frequency by the second half of the century. First, music set to the prosody of one language would not fit translations, and secondly, the metric pattern of
poems frequently varied from stanza to stanza and could not be captured by a strophic setting. Marpurg, who still insisted that single-
stanza songs be set in strict observance of "the declamation of each
comma and word," gave almost complete freedom therefore in setting poems of several stanzas (*Briefe* 1:169–70), and he recommended
that odes be set according to affect rather than meter (2:78). The
gradual separation of musical rhythm from poetic meter finally led to
Romantic "through-composed" songs. Musical syntax also emancipated itself gradually, and by the time of Forkel the term *musical period* had come to refer not to underlying verbal phrases but to structures intrinsic to music itself (*Gesch.* 42).

In retrospect, the idea of a musical imitation of verbal intonation
failed because it demanded a perfect correlation between music and

language, just as poetry itself failed when words were required to conform exactly to an abstract metrical skeleton. As poets came to value the affective tension between scansion and accent, so too, Romantic composers came to exploit clashes between poetic accent and musical beat. Toward the end of the eighteenth century the liberalization of music and poetry ran parallel, and, once music developed its own prosody and syntax, a new kind of cooperation between the two arts became possible.

RHETORIC AND MUSIC

In its most general sense, rhetoric is the art of persuasion. If music is given an educational task or the task of arousing feelings in the listener, as was the case with Plato, St. Augustine, and Galilei, one may treat it under the heading and according to the principles of rhetoric. While this is, indeed, a frequent practice in historical scholarship, I prefer not to regard the cases above or the theory of affects discussed in the next chapter as instances of musical rhetoric, because rhetoric is both narrower and broader than those cases warrant: narrower, because it contains a set of specific means and instructions, and broader, because in its most developed form it embodies a humanistic ideal. Plato had a definite dislike of rhetoric, because he saw it as the art of the sophists; Galilei seems to have had no interest in the techniques of rhetoric; my reasons for separating musical rhetoric from the theory of affects I shall explain at the beginning of the next chapter.

The application of rhetoric to music was most intense and widespread in the seventeenth and eighteenth centuries, though the roots of their intertwining go back to antiquity, particularly to Quintilian's *Institutio oratoria* (ca. A.D. 95), which seems to have been the first work to draw an explicit analogy between music and rhetoric, by describing the rousing power of martial instruments and the solace drawn by galley slaves from singing. Quintilian argued that the study of music can help to refine the modulation, tone, rhythm, and inflection of an orator's voice. Gaius Gracchus, for instance, allegedly stationed a pitch piper behind himself, "whose duty it was to give him the tones in which his voice was to be pitched" (173). Such examples show that music helps language to persuade and to transport the listener into the desired emotional state.

Isidore of Seville's *Etymologiarum* is one of the key documents indicating that the rhetorical approach to music was kept alive in the Middle Ages, even though the two belonged to different categories within the system of the liberal arts:

> Music moves the feelings and changes the emotions. In battles, moreover, the sound of the trumpet rouses the combatants, and the more furious the trumpeting, the more valorous their spirit. Song likewise encourages the rowers, music soothes the mind to endure toil, and the modulation of the voice consoles the weariness of each labor. Music also composes distraught minds, as may be read of David, who freed Saul from the unclean spirit by the art of melody. The very beasts also, even serpents, birds, and dolphins, music incites to listen to her melody. But every word we speak, every pulsation of our veins is related by musical rhythms to the powers of harmony. [Strunk 94][4]

The rediscovery of Quintilian's *Institutio oratoria* in 1416 led to a revival of interest in rhetoric, its widespread introduction into school curricula, and a closer connection between rhetoric and music. Following sporadic attempts in the sixteenth century, a systematic application of rhetoric to music was initiated with the works of Joachim Burmeister in the early years of the seventeenth century. Burmeister's work, which was followed by a long line of systematic German treatises throughout that century and the next, forms the basis of a baroque musical rhetoric that was not restricted to Germany.[5] As Buelow states in the *New Grove* article on "Rhetoric and Music":

> Beginning in the 17th century, analogies between rhetoric and music permeated every level of musical thought, whether involving definitions of styles, forms, expression and compositional methods, or various questions of performing practice. Baroque music in general aimed for a musical expression of words comparable to impassioned rhetoric or a *musica pathetica*. The union of music with rhetorical principles is one of the most distinctive characteristics of Baroque musical rationalism and gave shape to the progressive elements in the music theory and aesthetics of the period. . . . Nearly all the elements of music that can be considered typically Baroque, whether the music be Italian, German, French or English, are tied, either directly, or indirectly, to rhetorical concepts. [15:793−94]

Due to the decline of rhetoric at the end of the eighteenth century, this body of learning behind baroque music became buried; system-

atic efforts to unearth it were undertaken first by German scholars in
the early decades of this century.[6] These early studies often exagger-
ated the general possibilities of a musical rhetoric, however, and the
present revival of interest in the rhetoric of the arts has complicated
the issue even further. How problematic the whole issue still is I shall
discuss at the end of this chapter, once I have outlined the main ideas
of musical rhetoric.

What, then, were these ideas? We may roughly divide them into a
rhetoric of composition and a doctrine of musical figures, though
one must add that the application of figures is in fact central to the
decoratio phase of composition. It will be most convenient, therefore, to discuss seriatim how the five traditional phases of speech
writing (*inventio, dispositio, elocutio, memoria,* and *actio*) were applied
to composition.

Invention was the most important but also the most intractable dimension of rhetoric, for its teachability was always doubted. Most
musical rhetoricians admitted that invention ultimately eluded for-
malization yet gave it a try, for guides to invention were useful in
an age in which compositions, like sermons and speeches, had to be
prepared routinely, for specific celebrations. Thus, for instance, seventeenth-century authors compiled long catalogues of musically
paintable words, and composition then became a combinatorial as-
semblage of such musical paintings. In his first work Mattheson had
made fun of those who believed that invention could be taught, but,
as Arlt has shown, by the time of the *Vollkommene Capellmeister* the
rebel had turned conservative: he now offered "aids" to the imagination and prided himself on giving the first systematic discussion of
melodic invention (*Capellm.* 133). Since genius was not yet required
for creativity, it was perfectly legitimate to make ingenious use of
traditional materials instead of inventing something original,[7] and
young composers were advised to exercise their imagination by recording what they had heard. Mattheson generously allowed "bor-
rowings" if one repaid "with interest" (*Capellm.* 57, 131) and suggested that even an original melody ought to contain a commonplace
"known to the whole world" (142). Marpung considered the imitation of masters a legitimate "sort of theft" (*Beytr.* 3:45–46).

Heinichen suggested that words and phrases in a text were *loci
topici* suitable for musical elaboration: if the loci allow all possible
arguments about a philosophical thesis, they can also offer all possi-

ble musical inventions and expressions corresponding to a given text (88). If the passage was dull, the music could elaborate on its antecedents, circumstances, and consequences. This way, experienced masters could set a text "five, six, and more times, no aria being in the least similar to the one in the previous composition." Scheibe allowed even less freedom in composition, for he thought that only the main theme should be invented, and that the rest should be derived from that premise. Once the original idea was settled on, the rest was just stylistic elaboration (82).

Disposition, the second phase of composition, was, according to Mattheson, "a neat arrangement of all parts and details in the melody, or, in a complete melodic composition, almost the way one arranges and draws a building, making a sketch or a plan of it, in order to show where a hall, a parlor, a chamber, etc., should be placed" (*Capellm.* 235).[8] These rooms of a musical building included the rhetorical introduction, report, discourse, corroboration, confutation, and conclusion, though Mattheson refrained from insisting that each promenade include all rooms. As the affective unity of music loosened, the importance of disposition increased, and, by the time of Quantz and C. P. E. Bach, it included the introduction of complementary and contrasting secondary affects. This expanded notion of disposition allowed Forkel, a generation later, to cling to the outdated language of musical rhetoric in accounting for the developmental sections in the new sonata movements. The function of such developmental sections, he thought, was to analyze the main affect, to introduce supporting affects, to cast doubts on it by means of opposing affects, and, finally, to reinforce and unify them (*Gesch.* 50).

The heart of compositional rhetoric was the use of musical figures in the decoratio phase. Figures in this sense have nothing to do with embellishing trills and mordents, for they are an integral part of the harmonic and melodic structure. As Scheibe says, "Just as the best decoration of poetic expressions consists of tropal, indirect, and figurative words and idioms, so too, in the case of musical expressions, the task is . . . to raise them by embellishing, changing, and enlivening them" (642).

The large number of rhetorical figures, their divergent and often inconsistent application to music, and differences among scholars as to their classification make it impossible to survey here this curious field.[9] However, I want to give some illustrations of the different functions that figures may play in musical textures. A large class, perhaps the largest, can be placed under the generic heading of *hypotyposis*, the figure of vivid description. In the chapter on imitation I shall discuss the problems and questions that musical hypotyposis raises; here I merely wish to distinguish between those kinds of imitations that were primarily visual and thus required familiarity with the score and those that were fairly obvious from listening only. Thus, Burmeister translated the rhetorical *hyperbole*, the means of exceeding or exaggerating the normal or probable, by placing a note or notes outside the range of the stave, on supplementary lines. A musical example of it may be found in Kuhnau's sonatas on biblical histories. Kuhnau, Bach, and others routinely used imitations of the second type, for instance *anabasis* (see Ex. 1) and *catabasis* to represent ascent and descent respectively. Kuhnau illustrates the flight of the Philistines after Goliath's death with a fugue of rapidly moving notes, which is actually a pun: the figure of *fuga*, used to represent flight, need not employ a fugue at all (Ex. 2).

Moving from hypotyposis, a representation of external objects and events, to the representation of affects, we find the widespread use of the *passus duriusculus* (see Ex. 3), the expression of grief by means of descending minor seconds. A similar effect was assigned to skips by large dissonant intervals, the *saltus duriusculus*. Doubt, *dubitatio* (Ex. 4), was represented by tonal ambiguity, and a similar state of confu-

Example 1.
Anabasis in J. S. Bach's Cantata no. 31, "Der Himmel lacht." The rising of the soul and the resurrection of Christ are set to steadily rising notes.

Example 2.
Fuga in Kuhnau's *Biblical* Sonata no. 1. The flight ("fuga") of the Philistines after the fall of Goliath is illustrated by a rapid fugue.

Example 3.
Passus duriusculus in J. S. Bach's *St. Matthew Passion*. The descending half-steps in the bass of the chorale "O Mensch bewein dein Sünde gross" express grief.

sion could also be expressed by notes describing a circular motion, *circulatio* (Ex. 5), used also to represent circular physical movement.

In addition to representing physical or psychological matters, musical figures could also portray or underscore aspects of language. Thus, for instance, *exclamatio* (Ex. 6) was represented by jumping to a higher note in a variety of ways, *interrogatio* (Ex. 7) by a rising sec-

Example 4.
Dubitatio in J. S. Bach's *St. John Passion*. The unexpected terminal modulation from D minor to C major in the arioso "Mein Herz" expresses the uncertainty contained in the last question, "Was willst du deines Ortes tun?"

ond or sixth, and *abruptio*, a sudden breaking off, by a general pause or unexpected silence. Of course, the musical figures that underscore verbal intonation ultimately express emotions, and all the figures may be said to enhance the impact of music on the listener. But they are equally important as means of representation, as I shall show in the chapter on musical imitation.

The two final phases of the rhetorical process need not concern us much here. Memoria, the memorization of the work, was hardly discussed. Actio, performance, became the subject of a burgeoning number of manuals in the second half of the eighteenth century, as exemplified by the works of Quantz, C. P. E. Bach, and Leopold Mozart. Though these manuals were in many respects still indebted to rhetoric, their focus on practice and their catering to a wider, amateur audience precluded a scholarly treatment of the learned lore of rhetoric. C. P. E. Bach's famous advice that "one must play from the soul and not like a trained bird" (105) surely did not encourage the study of musical rhetoric.

Example 5.
Circulatio in J. S. Bach's Cantata no. 131, "Aus der Tiefe rufe ich, Herr, zu dir." In the
duet "So du willst," the fear ("dass man dich fürchte") is expressed by undulating
notes.

This all too sketchy overview may offer enough material to raise
two fundamental questions about musical rhetoric: its relevance to
the music of the seventeenth and eighteenth centuries and its general
value as an approach to music.

Responding to the first question, I find myself between Buelow's view that the "union of music with rhetorical principles is
one of the most distinctive characteristics of Baroque musical rationalism" (*New Grove* 15:793) and Vickers's skepticism, which questions
"whether composers ever actually set out to imitate specific figures of

Example 6.
Exclamatio in J. S. Bach's *St. Matthew Passion.* The upward jump of a sixth in the aria "Erbarme dich" (Have mercy) accentuates the desperateness of the cry.

Example 7.
Interrogatio and *congeries* in J. S. Bach's *St. Matthew Passion.* The question "Bin ich's?" (Am I [the one who betrayed you]?) is indicated by an upward jump and is repeated in all voices of the chorus.

rhetoric." Vickers suggests that "this whole enterprise was of more use to critics . . . than to creators" (41). Yet, Kuhnau, Mattheson, and other rhetoricians of music applied their theories to composition, and, more important, there is now strong evidence that even major composers consciously used rhetorical principles while composing. Birnbaum, a friend of Bach, stated that Johann Sebastian knew "so perfectly the role and the advantages of rhetoric in working out a musical piece that one not only listens with full pleasure when he explains the similarity and agreement between the two, but one admires also their skillful application in his works" (Scheibe 997). A growing number of studies—among them Ursula Kirkendale's recent article, in which she claims that Bach's *Musical Offering* was painstakingly patterned after the *Institutio oratoria*—demonstrate the practical use of rhetoric and figures in the music of the age. On the skeptical side one must note that the application of rhetoric to music seems not to have created new musical forms; it merely labeled and perhaps highlighted existing ones. Hence the appearance of a figure in a piece of music does not ipso facto prove that the composer relied consciously on rhetoric, especially not toward the second half of the eighteenth century, when figures and rhetoric had become rather esoteric subjects. Hence many unanswered questions remain.

Musical rhetoric was the most concerted effort in history to apply verbal principles to music. Since I believe that the emancipation of music toward the end of the eighteenth century opened up new possibilities for music as well as for poetry, I tend to agree with Vickers that the influence of rhetoric "did not always assist the development of specifically musical resources" (40). Yet, one needs language and linguistic metaphors to talk about music. It may well be that Burmeister and his followers made errors, were confused, or lacked the necessary imagination when they tried to find musical equivalents for rhetorical figures, and Vickers is surely right in insisting that all comparisons of the arts are made at the peril of overlooking their differences and that one cannot translate terminologies mechanically. But, if it should be the case that the glory of seventeenth- and eighteenth-century music partly derives from the deliberate employment of musical figures as a code, then confusions and mistakes in their translation are hardly relevant, no matter how irritating they may be for historians and theorists, who ask for a clear and efficient terminology. All art needs codes for structuring, but the correctness or provenance of these codes matter very little, especially in music. We should, therefore, accept musical rhetoric as the code for some important music in the seventeenth and eighteenth centuries and yet judge the thrust of the theoretical effort from our vantage point as mistaken. Musical rhetoric became problematic only when it claimed exclusive rights to music theory and resisted the development of pure instrumental music.

There is an even more general theoretical dimension to this question. Vickers has clearly demonstrated that "the musical application of a figure is always more limited than its rhetorical function" (41), because it inevitably translates semantic content into musical form (33, 34, 40), one that is frequently vertical and harmonic rather than horizontal (36). If we match the metaphoric adaptations of musical rhetoric against rhetoric proper, the impoverishment seems undeniable. But is this not the case with all metaphorical adaptations of a term? The demand that all the original connotations of a term be relevant in the new context is clearly impossible to satisfy. We should ask rather whether the term has a specific function and, perhaps, a new dimension of meaning in the new context. Whether this is the case with musical rhetoric I am not prepared to say, but I would plead that we consider all aspects of the issue.

3 MUSIC AND THE AFFECTS

"Affectus" was originally a translation of *pathos* and designated an externally induced emotional state. Theories of the affects in the arts describe how to encode the emotions and how the codes induce emotions in the recipient. Since affective music wishes to persuade its listeners, it may be said to rely on rhetoric; musical rhetoric is, in this sense, a means of achieving affective ends. Thus Buelow defines the "doctrine of the affections" as an aesthetic concept in baroque music "originally derived from Greek and Latin doctrines of rhetoric and oratory" (*New Grove* 1:135); and again, even more clearly: "The concept of the Affections arises in baroque musical terminology as part of the rhetorical concepts these composers and theorists adopted so earnestly" (*Bibliography* 250).

Thanks largely to Buelow's recent work, it has become evident, however, that, contrary to the views of Kretzschmar, Schering, and others, baroque ideas on the affects never crystallized into an *Affektenlehre*, a consistent doctrine of the affections. Precisely because I agree with Buelow that ideas on affects remained vague, I believe we should separate them from rhetorical notions, which, in spite of some confusions, have much greater specificity and precision.

There are a host of other reasons as well for distinguishing between musical rhetoric and the theory of affects. While all affect theorists thought that music ought to arouse specific emotions in the listeners, many of them, including Aristotle, Descartes, Kircher, and Rameau, had little interest in relating music to language—a sine qua non for being a musical rhetorician. This also explains why variants of affect theories persisted throughout the nineteenth century, whereas rhetoric had all but disappeared by then. The imitation of language is central to musical rhetoric, but it is marginal to affect theories of music, which use language only inasmuch as they rely on verbal definitions of affects. As I shall show, the correlation of emotions with keys, intervals, meters, instruments, and other dimensions of sound actually aims at short-circuiting language. Finally, as I indicated in the previous chapter, not all the musical figures have emotive functions. The figures of hypotyposis primarily represent or paint, and many among them appeal to the imagination and wit rather than to the emotions. As Bukofzer (*Allegory*) has argued, baroque musical figures are often intellectual.

An outline of a history of musical affects should start with Aristotle rather than Plato. The latter wanted to subordinate music to language, because he feared the destructive passions unleashed by pure music. He insisted therefore that rhythm and melody be accompanied by words, even at Dionysian festivals. Aristotle developed his music theory in answer to Plato by focusing more on the affects than on words, and to a degree he emancipated music from language by stressing its beneficial and cathartic effects. Similarly, he responded to Plato by turning from the metaphysics of proportions to empirical questions, and on these grounds he challenged the Pythagoreans to demonstrate the audibility of spherical music (*De coelo* 290).

But Aristotle's *Politics* shows that music loses much of its educational value by surrendering the cognitive power of Pythagorean harmony. Since music is less instructive than the other three basic subjects—reading-writing, gymnastics, and drawing—and people usually turn to it for pleasure rather than edification, Aristotle must find a broader rationale for it.

Chapters 5 and 7 of the *Politics* recommend music as having the power to amuse, relax, release the emotions, and cultivate the mind. In contrast to Plato, Aristotle encourages the use of pure instrumental music to express and to whip up the passions, for "Dionysiac frenzy, and all such agitations of the mind, are more naturally expressed . . . by an accompaniment on the flute" (1342b); flutes and lyres "provide us with images of states of character—images of anger and of calm; images of fortitude and temperance, and of all the forms of their opposites; images of the other states—which come closer to their actual nature than anything else" (1340a).

Aristotle actually had little interest in musical imitation, and he departed from Plato also by shifting his attention from musical representation to the arousal of passions and the psychology of listening. "The modes and rhythms of music have an affinity with the soul, as well as a natural sweetness" he says (1340b), but the "affinity with the soul," whereby music can rouse the passions, is more important to him than the Pythagorean "natural sweetness." The flute, so ill-suited to the education of young people, may justifiably be used as a power to excite and release an emotion that "does not express a state of character, but rather a mood of religious excitement; and it should therefore be used on those occasions when the effect to be produced on the audience is the release of emotion (katharsis), and not instruction" (1341a). Flute playing can thus be of value without representing passions or instructing.

Aristoxenos, a student of Aristotle, carried this emancipation of music a step further, by treating the materials of music for their intrinsic value rather than in relation to the cosmos, language, or the emotions. But he did not carry it with equal force in all directions and distinguished himself primarily as a foe of the Pythagoreans, who "introduced extraneous reasoning and rejected sense data as inaccurate and fabricated." Aristoxenos promised to anchor his claims in the phenomena themselves, by starting with accurate sense observations. The musician "cannot deal successfully with those questions that lie outside the sphere of sense perception altogether" (188–89), and since the mind can only treat sensations that are correctly registered, musicians must have a good ear. Aristoxenos offered, accordingly, a nonmathematical treatment of acoustics. Starting from the premise that speech glides while singing leaps between stable sounds, he analysed the ear, the instruments, and the range of voices, as well as the minimal and maximal intervals they can produce or perceive: "What the voice cannot produce and the ear cannot discriminate must be excluded from the available and practically possible range of musical sound" (175).[1] This empirical, antimetaphysical bent made Aristoxenos into the leading authority of the *musici*, who opposed the Pythagorean *canonici*, or "harmonists."

Thus Aristotle's and Aristoxenos's battle with Pythagoreanism was accompanied by a minor attack on verbal approaches to music: Aristotle departed from Plato precisely by approving wordless, instrumental music, whereas Aristoxenos separated gliding speech from the sustained notes of music. The latter is particularly important to note in view of Aristoxenos's later reputation as a champion of word-oriented melodies. The prestige of the musici revived as Renaissance empiricism gained ground against the waning tradition of Pythagoreanism, and by the early eighteenth century Brossard, Walther, and others were hailing Aristoxenos as the first to study acoustics empirically as well as as an advocate of melody. Mattheson proudly brandished the title "Younger Aristoxenos." Only when the eighteenth century reinterpreted Aristoxenos's attack on Pythagoreanism as a defense of melody against harmony did his theory come to appear verbal.

THE AFFECTS IN THE SEVENTEENTH CENTURY

Ancient affect theories were closer to rhetorical theories than to Pythagoreanism. I shall now try to show that this was not the case with sixteenth- and seventeenth-century affect theories, and that one should therefore actually distinguish two phases in their modern history: in the first, terminating roughly with Mattheson's attack, they coexisted with Pythagoreanism, whereas in the second, they coopted rationalist, empiricist, rococo, and neoclassical notions of imitation and came closer to rhetoric. Hence also, eighteenth-century symbiosis between affect and rhetorical theories had historical rather than logical foundations, and their intrinsic differences became evident again with the advent of Romanticism, which was a death knell for rhetoric but required only adaptation from affect theories.

Seventeenth-century affect theories modified the Pythagorean notion of harmony by permitting transitional imbalances, extreme tensions, and dissonances. The representative of this new, affective music was no longer Orpheus, who pacified beasts and men through the power of secret harmonic numbers, but Timotheus, Dryden's and Handel's legendary musician at Alexander's feast, who roused and calmed the king's ire at will. The interest in transitions from one passion to another furthered the use of dissonances.

Nevertheless, the new concern with the affects and transitions between them did not constitute as yet a shift from imitation to expression, as Hollander (173) claims. Seventeenth-century music could not yet "pierce" listeners and engender in them a desired feeling (201), because the affects represented in music were still conventional categories anchored in natural philosophy rather than subtle romantic moods. As Bukofzer says, baroque composers wrote music that corresponded to stereotyped, static mental states, having at their disposal "a set of musical figures which were pigeonholed like the affections themselves and were designed to represent these affections in music" (*Baroque* 5). This verbal standardization of the affects precluded the emergence of musical self-expression, as Hollander's own excellent reading of seventeenth-century English poems shows: Timotheus, St. Cecilia, or the lover's flute charm the listener into stylized rather than personalized emotions—a "figurative ecstasy" in Philip Ayres's "On Cynthia Singing a Recitative Piece of Music," and a "figurative enthusiasm" in Crashaw's "Musicks Duell" (Hollander 185, 235–36).

Affect theories emerged from seventeenth-century philosophy and psychology, but they were also indebted to the hermeticism and ancient cosmological speculation that Cardanus, Ficino, Agrippa von Nettesheim, Paracelsus, and Giordano Bruno had revived in the Renaissance. The analogy between the elements, the humors, and the temperaments was adopted not only by Fludd and Kircher but also by thinkers of a more Cartesian bent. The particular contribution of the seventeenth century was to reformulate these analogies in terms of new, mechanistic models for the circulation of the blood and other physiological processes.[2]

Kircher, for instance, defined the four traditional temperaments in terms of not only the humors but also the temperature and humidity of their fine vapors, the so-called animal spirits, which were believed to circulate in the nerves at speeds dependent on the momentarily dominant affect. The animal spirits, or "inner air," depended therefore on the humors but could also modulate their composition according to impulses from the soul or the environment. The agitation of the spirit in listening to music was then directly correlated with the intensity of vibrating air and the affinity between the music and the listener's temperament:

> Melancholic people like grave, solid and sad harmony; sanguine persons prefer the hyporchematic style [of dance music] because it agitates the blood; choleric people like agitated harmonies because of the vehemence of their swollen gall; martially inclined men are partial to trumpets and drums, and they reject all delicate and pure music; phlegmatic persons lean toward women's voices because their high-pitched voice has a benevolent effect on phlegmatic humor. [1:544]

Each temperament resonates therefore to the corresponding musical characteristics. The closer the ratio of harmonies to the natural circulating frequency of the animal spirits, the better air and animal spirits harmonize, intensifying thereby the aroused affect. Basically, expansions or accelerations of the animal spirits produce symptoms of joy, their contractions or decelerations sadness. The humors and their mixtures are controlled by the spirits via the brain and the imagination (2:211), but Kircher does not explain how the animal spirits mix and produce the humors, how the humors affect the soul, or how the mixtures of the humors produce various affects.

The basic model developed by Descartes in the *Musicae compendium* (his first work, written in 1618 but published only posthumously in 1650) is very similar. Like Kircher, Descartes believes that music pleases if the temperament of the listener resonates with it (4): slower tempos rouse the "sluggish emotions" of languor, sorrow, fear, and haughtiness, whereas the faster ones generate liveliness and joy (9). But since one must first know which passions music can arouse and only then can show "which pitches, consonances, meters, and other elements would rouse these" (68), the details are left for later. Such an analysis of the passions was indeed carried out in Descartes's last work, *Les passions de l'âme* ("The Passions of the Soul") of 1649, but by that time the point about music had apparently become moot for him. Descartes contributed, then, in a twofold way to music theory, with works that were published almost simultaneously, though they were written one at either end of his career: the *Compendium* is a mathematical study of acoustics and harmony which shies away from the subjective side of music, whereas the treatise *The Passions* analyzes the physics and physiology of affects without explaining their pertinence to music.

That Cartesian affect theory had a greater affinity with Pythagoreanism than with rhetoric, is an illustration of my thesis. Descartes, to be sure, was contemptuous of Pythagorean speculation, but he applied mathematics to the study of consonances and dissonances, and he seems to have had no interest in rhetoric and the musical imitation of language. Hence the *Compendium* opens with the statement that the mathematical analysis of music must explain its affective purpose, namely, how music pleases and arouses various affects in its listeners.

Nevertheless, mathematics and the affects do not dovetail in Descartes's theory. His basic assumption is that harmony in anything increases as the differences between constituent parts decrease and the organization tightens (4). For music, the parts are the individual notes, and the differences between them become the mathematical ratios of chords; the closer the ratio of a chord is to unity, the higher its degree of consonance, or harmony. But while Descartes believes that greater harmonies are more pleasing, he stops short of claiming that harmony alone determines musical pleasure and admits that the senses may override mathematical considerations. Thus, although the ratio of the fourth immediately follows the ratios of the octave and the fifth, he thinks that this "unhappiest of consonances" gives no pleasure and ought to be banished from melodies (24).

Passages in Descartes's correspondence with Mersenne suggest that he was indeed quite uncertain about the relation between mathematical harmony and the affects. In a letter of January 1630 he distinguished mathematically definable, objective consonance from the subjective pleasure of the listener:

> Calculation merely serves to show which consonances are the simplest, or, if you wish, the sweetest and most perfect, but they are not, on that account, the most pleasant; and if you carefully read my letter, you will not find me saying that this calculation should make one consonance more pleasant than another, for on those grounds the unison would be the most pleasant consonance. But to determine what is most pleasant we have to know the listener's disposition (*capacité*), which varies, like taste, from person to person. [*Corresp.* 111]

When Mersenne kept pressing the issue, Descartes had to confess that he had no answer, for the choice between consonances was like preference between fruits and fish (*Corresp.* 123). The simplicity, harmony, and "sweetness" of a consonance was distinct from its "agreeableness," for "there is no absolute way of determining that one consonance is more agreeable than another. . . . But one can say with certainty which consonances are the simplest and most harmonious, for this depends only on whether they unite better and approach unison more closely" (*Corresp.* 205). As an earlier letter explains, beauty and pleasure have no objective criteria, for "what generates in some a desire to dance may induce others to weep. For this results only from the excitation of ideas that exist in our memory; in those who previously enjoyed dancing to a certain song, the desire to dance will be rekindled as soon as they hear something similar" (*Corresp.* 127–28).

The passage exposes the fundamental Cartesian problem of how to coordinate the soul with the world, but it is wisely reticent about giving mathematical criteria for musical pleasure or establishing objective links between affects and musical materials. In contrast to Kircher, Steffani, Euler, and other mathematicians of music, Descartes would not postulate that the affects follow from the mathematical bases of harmony. Physical consonances are measurable universal relations, whereas beauty and pleasure depend on innate temperament, personal history, and environment. Descartes even hints at an association theory of music, by noting the role of time and memory in pleasure.[3]

His reticence notwithstanding, Descartes became a key figure in the history of affect theories through his treatise on the passions, which distinguished itself not so much by the novelty of his treatment as by its defense of the passions.[4] For him the passions are "perceptions or modes of knowledge which are in us." Whereas actions come "directly from our soul and seem to depend on it alone," and intellectual ideas are caused solely by the soul (art. 29), passions are passive because "they always receive their character from the things they represent" (art. 17). The role of the passions is to stimulate the soul to enhance those actions that maintain or perfect the body (art. 137); thus passions can actually help to bring the body under control. Hence the treatise clears the passions of charges of sinful sensuality and advocates their domestication rather than their suppression. Excessive or misdirected passions lead to sin, but "even the weakest souls can acquire absolute reins over all their passions" (art. 50) in order to reinforce and perpetuate worthwhile thoughts in the soul (art. 74). The principal utility of properly guided and instructed desire is to help us toward virtue and the well-being of the body. The customary fault is not to desire too ardently but to have a deficient desire for the good (art. 144).

Descartes's legitimation of the passions helped to induce a change in perspective, and his scheme of six primitive passions with thirty-five combinations was an improvement on both the medieval system of "concupiscible" and "irascible" passions and the theories of Mersenne and Kircher, which used inconsistent sets of categories. Descartes also recognized that passions, as well as their symptoms, were overdetermined: a passion could be engendered by several different external causes, and a symptom could manifest different passions.

Buelow is probably right that the *Passions* was "perhaps the single most influential philosophical work of the seventeenth century in relation to musical theory and aesthetics" (*Bibliography* 252). Yet this influence was not wholly salutary. Though more flexible, Descartes's scheme of the passions shared the weakness of all such theories, namely, that of freezing complex and fluid psychological processes into a few fixed categories. As an empirical-scientific description of how the passions work, it was a failure, and inasmuch as it furthered speculation about the impact of music on the real feelings of real people, it guided thinking about music *reception* in the wrong direction.

But if we consider the Cartesian theory of the passions, like the musical figures, as a conventional code of *representation*, then we may ask how this vocabulary gave music form and structure. For, as so often happens, "faulty" science and philosophy could support good art: though the Cartesian categories of passion were logically and empirically ill founded for a scientific theory of musical affects, they could become labels for units of music or emotional states of characters on stage that made no pretence at psychological realism. The abrupt change from one static passion to another, which is all that the Cartesian model allows, corresponds exactly to the baroque practice of representing a series of static depersonalized passions. In Lully's and Quinault's *Armide*, for instance, the whole plot is determined by a series of emotional reversals, a repeated fluctuation between love and hate, between Armide's magic charm and her opponents' desire for martial glory. The inversions are so frequent and violent that only magic can make them "plausible." One function of the *merveilleux* in baroque opera was to allow such abrupt transitions from one affect to the next. A similar contrast of affects is at work in baroque suites and concerti. As Georg Muffat says in the introduction to his new, Italian concerti (1701):

> At the direction *piano* or *p* all are ordinarily to play at once so softly and tenderly that one barely hears them, at the direction *forte* or *f* with so full a tone, from the first note so marked, that the listeners are left, as it were, astounded at such vehemence. . . . For by exactly observing this opposition or rivalry of the slow and the fast, the loud and the soft, the fullness of the great choir and the delicacy of the little trio, the ear is ravished by a singular astonishment, as is the eye by the opposition of light and shade. [Strunk 451]

Of course, Descartes's *Passions* was just the standard work on a topic that concerned the whole age; while it illuminates baroque musical structure, we need not assume that either Quinault or Muffat relied on it literally.

MUSICAL AFFECTS IN THE EIGHTEENTH CENTURY

I have tried to show that seventeenth-century treatments of the affects in music remained intertwined with Pythagorean mathematics. In the eighteenth century, partly but certainly not exclusively as a result of Mattheson's attacks on the Pythagorean tradition, the relationship between Pythagoreanism, affect theories, and musical rhetoric became more complex. Mathematicians of music, like Rameau, Mizler, and Euler, continued to believe that the purpose of music was to arouse the affects, but theories of the affects now interacted more closely with musical rhetoric.

The major theorists of the affects, Mattheson, Scheibe, Marpurg, Krause, and Sulzer, agreed that music ought to represent and arouse the emotions, but they differed on the theoretical and practical implications of this minimal credo, and they placed different values on theorizing. Mattheson, who is usually cited as the clearest exponent of the Affektenlehre, professed an aversion to theory, although he advocated the study of nature, philosophy, morality, and rhetoric. If music was to serve "the glory of God and all virtues," and if the virtues were to be approached in the Cartesian manner by means of the passions, the arousal of the affects had to be the means and the end of music. Sick passions must be "healed, not murdered" (*Capellm.* 15); praiseworthy affects must be displayed, for without them music "is nothing, does nothing, is worth nothing" (146). Hence a "perfect familiarity with the emotions—surely not to be measured out with a mathematical yardstick" (pref. 19)—was a sine qua non for the composer.

The appearance of Scheibe's *Der critische Musicus* (1738–40) in Hamburg and of Mizler's *Neu eröffnete Musikalische Bibliothek* (1739–54) in Leipzig represented a new phase in the history of affect theory. Scheibe and Mizler, both students of Gottsched, wanted to train learned musicians and listeners. But Mizler followed the Leibniz-Wolffian mathematical strain in Gottsched's critical thought, while Scheibe was indebted to Gottsched's rhetoric. Following his mentor, Scheibe believed that "we cannot go wrong in choosing intellect and nature as the sole judges in musical matters" (38), and this premise led him to condemn speculation, including the intellectual excess and surfeit of counterpoint (97–98) that he detected in the music of J. S. Bach. He praised Bach as a great organist but thought that his works were spoiled by an unnatural and turgid style, due to an excess of artifice (96–97).[5]

The same norms of intellect and nature were so dominant in the Berlin of Frederick the Great that the disappointed Burney, finding there only the aged Graun and Quantz, thought it was "formed so much upon one model" that it precluded "all invention and genius"; His Majesty allows "no more liberty in that [music] than he does in civil matters of government (*Germ.* 2:231, 235). Indeed, Frederick the Great reportedly walked out of a Gluck performance that sounded to him like a confused jumble. Burney also noted that Berlin had a plethora of critics and theorists, "which has not, perhaps, either refined the taste, or fed the fancy of the performers" (*Germ.* 2:225). Actually, much of the theorizing in Berlin—for instance, the manuals of Quantz and C. P. E. Bach—was intended to aid the performer, but Burney was certainly right that Berlin was teeming with music theorists, most of them adherents of the Affektenlehre. Among them were Marpurg, editor of the *Beyträge*, and members of the *Montagsklub*, a loose gathering of professional musicians and amateurs. Members of the latter included the poet-theorist Ramler; the lawyer Krause, who founded the first Berlin school of Lieder and wrote *Von der musikalischen Poesie*; the theoretician Kirnberger, a student of J. S. Bach; and Rellstab, a composer of songs.

In the last phase of affect theory, marked by the works of Sulzer, Heinse, and Schubart, intellect no longer functioned as a norm, and faithfulness to nature gradually came to mean an individualization of the represented emotions. The new dictum that "music works neither for the intellect, nor for the imagination, but merely for the heart" finds paradigmatic assertion in Sulzer's dictionary of the arts (art. "Mahlerey").[6]

Theorists of the affects attempted to assign emotional value to the basic musical materials and forms, including intervals, keys, styles, meters, and rhythms, but they disagreed on the most fundamental definitions and categorizations, and their efforts were usually half-hearted. Nevertheless, instead of prematurely demolishing the myth of an Affektenlehre, we will consider three separate questions: (1)

Did seventeenth- and eighteenth-century theorists associate music with the affects? (2) Did they *intend* to construct a theory of affects? (3) Did they succeed?

The answer to the first question must be a categorical yes: virtually all musicians and theorists of the seventeenth and eighteenth centuries thought of music in relation to the affects. They surely believed also that a theory of them was at least possible, though they tended to abhor doctrines. A pedantically rigid treatment like Junker's *Tonkunst* (1777) received a scathing review from Forkel (*Bibl.* 3:244). But if nobody seriously set out to construct a theory, this was due to temperament and lack of perseverance rather than fundamental doubt about its feasibility. This, I believe, was the case with Mattheson. As several of the essays in *New Mattheson Studies* show, he was an eclectic critic rather than a systematic thinker. Though he used the term *Affektenlehre* seldom and then in a restricted sense only, he surely believed in the possibility of such a theory, however half-hearted he may have been in constructing one himself.

With this in mind, we may briefly consider the theories of musical affects and their relation to keys, intervals, styles, meter, and rhythm. There was, to begin with, the problem of the affects themselves. Monteverdi followed "the best philosophers" in identifying anger, moderation, and humility (or supplication) as the principal ones, and he was interested in reviving a style, the ancient *stile concitato*, that corresponded to the first of these affects. Descartes, in turn, assigned a special place to "admiration," a virtue others neglected. Eighteenth-century authors were still more casual about specifying the musical passions, and even the exhaustive lists of Mattheson, Krause, and Marpurg disclaimed authority. Mattheson, for instance, found enumeration tedious (*Capellm.* 16), and although he insisted that composers be exact in representing the affects, he soon excused the paucity of his practical guidance by claiming that no book could plumb the "unfathomable sea" of the affects. It was best to leave the subject to the natural sensibility of each person (19).

A comparison of the treatment of hope by Mattheson, by Marpurg, and in the Braunschweiger music journal *Der musikalische Patriot* (1741–42) reveals how meager the results were:

> Hope is an elevation of the soul or the spirits; but despair is their full depression; all these are things that can be very naturally represented with

sounds, especially if the other modalities (above all meter) contribute their part. [Mattheson *Capellm.* 16]

[Hope is] a happy representation to ourselves of that good which we are going to possess soon. The speech and the voice of a hopeful person is firm (*gesetzt*), manly and meanwhile somewhat proud; and if the probability of the expected good is very high, it is permeated with a jubilant tone. Hope produces pleasant motions in the blood and the nerve fluid which intensifies with the hope. [*Patriot*, as quoted in Mizler 3:1:152]

Hope is delight at something good that we believe we are going to share. It is expressed with manly, somewhat proud, and jubilant melodies. A very high degree of it is confidence. [Marpurg *Beytr.* 3:273]

The vagueness of such definitions prevented their useful application to music. Let us take first the intervals, on which harmony, melody, and key depended. The metaphysical premise of the seventeenth century was that consonances made people happy because they were easy to grasp, whereas dissonances were far removed from perfection and therefore "of a sad and somewhat confused nature" (Werckmeister *Hodeg.* 84). Hence major triads are happier than minor ones (81), and neighboring, dissonant sounds induce sadness, disorder, inertness, or melancholy. The corresponding physiological argument asserted that the expansion of the animal spirits in joy should be expressed by "large and expanded intervals" (*Capellm.* 16). On such grounds the major third was generally believed to be manly and joyful, the minor third sad and soft.

No such consensus existed for the other intervals, in part because of the changing values attached to dissonance, in part because monodic styles furthered new, horizontal and melodic interpretations of intervals. While descending half-steps—often extending over the interval of a fourth: "lamento bass"—had earlier functioned primarily as powerful expressions of sadness, Quantz considered neighboring tones played legato to have a caressing and tender character (108). He asked for a balanced, gracious, and pleasurable music in which disagreeable, repellent, or terrifying baroque dissonances appeared only transitionally, when the music shifted from one affect to another or when the listeners had to be jolted from their comfort to prevent boredom: "The harsher the dissonances the more pleasing their resolution. Without this mixing of pleasing and displeasing harmonies music would have no means to arouse the passions suddenly and to calm them again suddenly" (227). Such transitions became more frequent, and Quantz pleaded for a rapid alternation of moods, "a different affect in each measure" so to speak (108). C. P. E. Bach went a step further by reaffirming the importance of dissonances and recommending that in general they be played louder than consonances, for "special flights of thought that are meant to arouse intense feelings must be given strong expression" (115). Such rapid shifts in taste prevented crystallization of a consistent doctrine of dissonance.

The assignment of affects to keys was complicated by a long-standing confusion of the Greek *harmoniai* with the church modes.[7] The modern system of keys, which emerged in the seventeenth and eighteenth centuries, reduced the variety of the classical and church modes to the minor and major scales, leaving open the question of whether each key had an affective identity. Whereas Gaultier set each song of his *La Rhétorique des Dieux* (1672) in a different mode to excite a different passion, J. S. Bach, in writing a prelude and fugue for each key in *Das wohltemperierte Klavier* probably did not intend to assign a different affective character to each. His frequent transcriptions suggest that he had no strong belief in the affective character of keys, and he may well have agreed with Heinichen that "all keys or musical modes without distinction are suited to expressing many and opposing affects" (83).

While Mattheson's *Das Neu-Eröffnete Orchestre* assigned affects to keys, his later *Capellmeister* admitted that "no key can be so sad or happy in and of itself that it could not set an opposite" affect (68). Scheibe concurred but suggested that keys may acquire affective meaning through custom so that tonality, after all, may determine "the nature and the style of the song one wants to write." Among the later writers only Schubart attempted to establish a correlation, but his pedantic enumeration contrasts oddly with his agitated style and must have seemed dated when it appeared belatedly in 1805. In sum, attributions of affects to keys were hardly systematic.

Styles could not be correlated well with affects, because there were too many ways of classifying them: by historical periods (ancient and modern), nations, place of performance (church, theater, chamber), or the rhetorical categories of high, middle, and low. The multiplicity of perspectives is evident in Brossard's influential definition: "[Style is] the manner in which each individual composes, plays, or teaches; and these diverge according to the genius of the author, the country, and the nation, as well as according to the material, the place, the time, the subject, the expression, etc." (entry "stylo").

As Palisca has shown, Mattheson struggled to create some order in this chaos but with little success (*Style class.* 414, 422). In fact, clear distinctions within these classifications gradually broke down in the course of the eighteenth century, and the affective characterization of styles became a nebulous subject.

On meter and rhythm there seems to have been a general, if rather vague, agreement: faster music suggested anger, excitement, belligerence, or happiness, whereas slower music intimated sadness, love, desire, or yearning (Kepler 174). Composers were expected to select their meter and rhythm according to the dominant affect of the piece (Kircher 1:578). Yet, a category that included both anger and happiness was much too broad, and theorists gave little further help to those in need of guidance. Mattheson, for instance, thought that metric units were based on the heartbeat but, after attempting in *Das Neu-Eröffnete Orchestre* (76 ff.) to translate different throbbings into different affects, he gave up and concluded that the choice of meter was mostly a matter of instinct (172–73).

Because of difficulties in assigning affects to meters and rhythms, language was often invoked, especially in the case of instrumental music. Mattheson described the dance forms (*Neu-Eröffn.* 185 ff. and *Capellm.* 208, 224–33), but his descriptions, apart from his stipulations of tempi and rhythms, remained remarkably vague. The essence of the *Passepied*, for instance, "comes fairly close to lightheartedness," and the English *Gigue* represents "a heated and transitory zeal, and anger that quickly passes" (*Capellm.* 229, 231). Though often cited, such characterizations do not belong to the heart of Mattheson's treatise and certainly do not constitute a theory of musical affects.

Mattheson distrusted the popular affect designations, such as adagio and allegro, and his skepticism was shared by Quantz and C. P. E. Bach, though Quantz considered such terms as the prime indicators of affect (108). Krause was so dissatisfied that he proposed a long list of new, German terms, including *glattgleitend* ("smoothly sliding"), *edelmütig* ("noble-minded"), and even "sigh of a lover," or "praising the beloved's first friendly demeanor" (Marpurg *Beytr.* 3:534). One wonders whether Krause had any particular music in mind; at any rate, he apparently wished to move beyond the traditional idealized categories toward individualized sketches of mood.

One must agree with Buelow therefore that these inconsistent and

vague categories do not constitute a doctrine. Was the whole enterprise fundamentally misconceived, as advocates of "absolute music"
claim? Or could a theory yet be developed that profited from the
mistakes of the eighteenth century, as Kretzschmar and, more recently, Kivy have argued?

Most eighteenth-century writers thought that sounds and affects
were linked by natural laws. Kivy, somewhat reluctantly, surrenders
this idea of a natural tie by suggesting that the expressive power of
music derives from its resemblance to other emotional expressions,
such as gesture, posture, and, above all, speech (26). According to
Kivy, "to 'emote' over music is, in part, to hear what, by association,
one's musical culture conditions one to hear" (136). Thus, to offer my
own example, just as we use a now dead metaphor to express sadness
in saying "I am down," a downward movement of musical notes
expresses sadness. Kivy tends to believe that all conventionally
established emotional meanings originated in a perceived analogy of
"contours" (e.g., line downward) (83), but this notion of an original
"isomorphy" is highly questionable. What, for instance, would be the
contour of a key?

That musical forms often come to exemplify emotions (or, for that
matter, thoughts and objects) metaphorically seems plausible. While
purists may urge us to listen differently, it is probably the way most
people respond to music. But Kivy's theory is both historically vulnerable and theoretically in need of further development. Few
people will, for instance, find in Mattheson the legacy that "music,
in many respects, resembles our expressive behavior" (52). Even more
problematic is Kivy's strategy of setting up two radical eighteenth-
century positions in order to locate his own view between them.
According to what he calls the "normal" view, music would come
to the text repleat with its expressive properties (an affect theory
completely cleansed of verbal references?), whereas according to Hiller's view, as Kivy sees it, music has no affective qualities and comes as
a formless, protean "clay" upon which the text imprints emotional
values of its own. Kivy himself holds that music expresses generally
recognizable broad categories of emotion, which a text particularizes
by imparting intentionality to it (103–04). But this was precisely
the "normal" view of the eighteenth century;[8] what Kivy calls
"normal" and what he attributes to Hiller barely have historical foundations.

On the theoretical level, I am inclined to attribute less objectivity to the affects than Kivy does. While he admits that the meaning of musical forms may vary "horizontally," from culture to culture, he tends to ascribe to them temporally impervious objective meanings in a single culture: "Within certain limits of a given musical culture, like that of the West, emotive descriptions founded on expressive musical 'conventions' are as 'objective' as the conventions themselves, as defensible as any statements can be whose truth relies upon the truth of a psychological generalization; and as respectable" (135). The eighteenth-century affect theories of music—probably the most concerted effort in history to construct an objective dictionary of affects in an art—do not bear out this optimistic contention, and if we look at a larger span of Western music history, the differences with regard to emotions in music become sharper. Surely, much of what the eighteenth century considered harsh and dissonant appears pleasing and harmonious to us, whereas many conventionally and rhetorically established musical meanings no longer speak to us because we have become ignorant of the relevant conventions. Hermeneutic theory is surely right in suggesting that the appreciation of art always involves a fusion of horizons: our perception of baroque form is shaped by our own cultural horizon, and the development of modern sonorities has washed out the meaning of most conventionally defined baroque affects.

To state categorically, as Kivy does, that in the arias of Gluck's Orfeo and Mozart's Cherubino the music ill fits the text is to assume an unequivocal notion of what music means and what meaning may fit what text. Though Kivy has a more subtle approach to musical meaning than the eighteenth-century theorists he considers, he nevertheless believes that we can have intersubjective agreement on the emotional meaning of musical form. I tend to agree rather with Newcomb, that "the requirement of a strictly rule-governed semantic [in music] . . . must go." Music is not expressive and mimetic in the sense that it sets out to translate a preexistent meaning. The essential nature of musical meaning "is created by music itself and exists in its own terms. Language may attempt to give an example of this meaning by bringing the structural patterns of music into relation with other aspects of our experience; this is the enterprise of expressive interpretation. But to do this is not to identify a preexistent verbal meaning, which music only realizes. The verbal conceptualization is

secondary, coming after and illustrating the primary musical meaning. Hence to search for close intersubjective agreement in such verbal descriptions is fundamentally mistaken" (629–30).

Precisely. And if we look for the historical roots of such a conception we shall not find it in rhetorical or affective theories of music,
nor what the later eighteenth century called musical expression. We
shall find it, rather, in Kant's notion of "aesthetic ideas" and, fully
formulated, in Romanticism.

4 · PROBLEMS IN MUSICAL IMITATION

MIMESIS IN THE ARTS

Rhetorical approaches to music survived the decline of the baroque and extended into the Enlightenment, whereas associations between music and the affects continued into Romanticism and beyond, defying standard periodizations. However, the social, intellectual, and artistic upheavals of the eighteenth century shifted both the focus and the context of music theories. The gradual strengthening of verbal approaches in the seventeenth and early eighteenth centuries not only weakened music's association with mathematics but also accelerated its integration into what Kristeller calls "the modern system of the arts." The increasing force of this inter-art context may be sensed in a statement of Addison which subordinates the demands of the separate artistic media to the common laws of "sense and taste":

> Musick, Architecture and Painting, as well as Poetry and Oratory, are to deduce their Laws and Rules from the general Sense and Taste of Mankind, and not from the Principles of those Arts themselves; or in other Words, the Taste is not to conform to the Art, but the Art to the Taste. Musick is not design'd to please only Chromatick Ears, but all that are capable of distinguishing harsh from disagreeable Notes. [*The Spectator*, April 3, 1711]

We can observe the development of a common aesthetic denominator in the comparative art studies of Dubos and Batteux, and in the appearance of aesthetics as a philosophical discipline with Baumgarten's *Aesthetica* (1750–58). One of its consequences for music was the reappearance of imitation as a central theoretical concept. Mimetic theories of music have existed, of course, since antiquity. Though questioned by Patrizi (Weinberg 765 ff.) and others in the Renaissance, mimesis remained the dominant approach to the arts throughout the sixteenth and seventeenth centuries. Rhetorical theories tended to focus on the pragmatic question of how to affect an audience, but they tacitly or expressly upheld the representational, imitative function of the arts, as is evident in the use of hypotyposis. Nevertheless, whereas imitation remained a central concept in discourses on poetry and was routinely used in composition, it seldom appeared as a theoretical term in seventeenth-century treatises on music and regained its centrality only in the eighteenth century where the so-called system of arts tightened its hold. This reappearance of the term *imitation* did not represent, however, a new aesthetics: since representation of the passions was already demanded by affect theory, the renewed centrality of imitation in music signified only a new context and mode of discourse.

I shall first sketch this new context in the works of Dubos and Batteux and then describe its implications for music. In the concluding sections of the chapter I will discuss the major shifts that occurred within musical mimesis itself.

Dubos

The *Réflexions critiques sur la poésie et la peinture* makes no reference to music in its title, though it devotes as much attention to it as to poetry and painting. Dubos believed that musical imitation has a subject of its own, namely, "all those sounds with which nature herself expresses her sentiments and her passions" (466–67). Accordingly, opera imitates "the tone, the accents, the sighs, and the sounds which are naturally fitted to the sentiments contained in words" (470), whereas instrumental music is at a fundamental disadvantage, because it is unsuited to the imitation of passionate sounds. In a passage that was to receive high praise in the *Encyclopédie* (art. "symphonie"), Dubos restricts symphonic overtures to the inferior task of imitating the sounds of nature—for instance, tempests and brooks. Pure instrumental music may also be used if words cannot excite the passions (473) or if inaudible sounds are to be imitated, but such mimesis can only be probable (481–82). Nonimitative music is merely pleasant and therefore inferior:

> As there are people who are moved more by the colors of a tableau than by the expression of passions, there are also people who are sensitive only to the charm of melody or the wealth of harmony in music and do not care much if the song well imitates the noise which it ought to imitate or if it suits the meaning of the words to which it is set. . . . They are satisfied if these songs are varied, gracious, or even bizarre. . . . [But] the

richness and the variety of chords, the sweetness and novelty of the melody in music should serve only to produce and to embellish the imitation of the language that belongs to nature and the passions. The so-called science of composition is a servant. [484–86]

Painting words is no more desirable than merely combining sounds, for "the expression of a word cannot move us as much as the expression of a sentiment, unless the word itself should contain a sentiment. If the musician gives some expression to a word which is only a part of a phrase, this must be done in such a way that we do not lose the general sense of the phrase he sets to music" (485).

Batteux

Emulating scientific rationalism, Batteux turns from the arousal to the representation of passion, for he believes that this way he can reduce the empirical variety of the arts to an underlying common imitative principle.

Man must imitate because he cannot create ex nihilo: "The human spirit can only create improperly, all its productions carry the imprint of a model" (10). Art is re-creation, because "to invent in the arts is not to give existence to an object, but to re-cognize where and how it is. . . . [Even geniuses] discover only what already existed before, they are creators in that they have observed" (11). The creative process demands that we select an object worthy of imitation and transform it by means of "polishing and intensifying it." Artistic reproductions should not be naturalistic, they must aim at a "possible truth, beautiful truth represented as if it truly existed and with all the perfections it is capable of attaining" (27–28); "the material of the arts is not the true (*vrai*), but the probable (*vrai-semblable*)" (14). Hence art is neither a figment of the imagination, a kind of Leibnizian possible world, nor nature itself, but "beautiful nature," which for Batteux means that it is pieced together from fractional perfections once observed. The artist "assembles the separate features of several existing beauties, he forms in his soul an artificial idea which results from all these features reunited" (25). By adding, subtracting, and transposing (30), the artist creates a possible world that nature is unlikely to produce, because it seldom unites so many scattered partial perfections. Hence art is an "exquisite whole more perfect than nature itself" (8), an unreal object where everything is "imagined, feigned, copied, artificial" (22).

Whereas poetry and painting imitate actions, ideas, or images (270–71), music, like dance, is an "artificial portrait" of the passions, in which the sounds associated with the raw emotions are regulated, intensified, and polished by means of consonance, dissonance, and taste (41). Music relies on the natural emotions, but in the *belle nature* it creates, "Nothing is true, everything is artifice" (277–78). Batteux is no rhetorician of music, and he allows a much broader role for pure instrumental music than Dubos does. Whereas the latter restricts instrumental imitations to the nonhuman sphere, Batteux believes that instruments can well imitate the passions: "Music without words is still music. It expresses complaints and joys independent of words; these assist . . . but neither add nor detract from it anything that would change its nature and essence. Sound is the essential expression of music, as color is of painting and movement of the body of dance" (40–41). Anticipating Rousseau, Batteux distinguishes language, the organ of reason, from music and gesture, the languages of the heart that provide us with an elemental and universal "dictionary of simple nature" known from birth (263–64). However, this very universality makes music so vague that the imitated emotion is often unclear. One cannot translate music into language: "It suffices to feel what the object of imitation is; one need not name it. The heart has its intelligence independent of words, and if this is touched it understands everything" (285–86).

If, in this manner, Batteux goes a long way toward emancipating music from language, he resolutely rejects the idea of an abstract harmonic order. What is one to say of a painter, he remarks, "who would be content throwing daring strokes and most lively colors on the canvas without any resemblance to any known object? The same holds for music" (280). To calculate the relation between sounds is inconsequential (279). Though musicians may pride themselves on conjoining disparate sounds into a chord, these characterless "measured noises" are like empty oratorial gestures or artificial verses: "No sound in art is without a model in nature" (281–82). Instrumental symphonic music "has only a partial life, only half of its essence" (284); though music need not imitate language, it is "half-way performed in words" (272), and in the best musical passages the continuity of expressive sounds constitutes a "species of discourse" (285), a "clear sense, without obscurity, without ambiguity" (281).

Thus Batteux defines music as an independent idiom of the emotions and subsequently rejects organizational principles immanent in it; finally, he regards it as an expressive and communicative medium comparable to language. The real weakness of his ideas about music is not that he could not conceive of music as a pure construct; rather, it is his narrow view that the mimetic transformation of nature into a *belle nature* is nothing but a refining of expression, an intensification of music's power by an infusion of grace (294). The "austere rules" of art do not constitute a harmonic syntax; they do not transform the natural material but merely filter it. "Possible" and "beautiful" truths result from a process of refinement, not from an imposition of form.

If Batteux was an "apostle of the half-true gospel of imitating nature," as Goethe thought (*BA* 21:668), one wonders why the apostle failed when so many believed the gospel. The truth is that Batteux's treatise incorporated several clashing views, all the while aiming at a rational system. Most critics responded therefore by criticizing Batteux's faults while silently adopting his concept of mimesis.[1]

THE PRIMACY OF VOICE AND MELODY

Dubos and Batteux confirmed two commonplaces of musical imitation that issued from rhetorical and monodic music, namely, that melody and voice were superior to harmony and instruments respectively. The origins of instrumental music were in no small degree responsible for its low esteem. Early instrumental music consisted of dances, rhapsodic (improvisational) forms, and fugal forms. The dances enjoyed great popularity but were regarded just for this reason as pure entertainment. Eggebrecht (*Term.* 907–17) and others have shown that rhapsodic forms probably had a tuning or intonational function originally, but gradually assumed under various names the role of a prelude. Brossard's dictionary (1703) still ascribes an introductory function to the fantasia, the capriccio, the ricercata, the symphony, the toccata, the sonata, and the canzone, and Mattheson (*Capellm.* 232 and 477) classifies most of them under "fantasia style" as prologues or postludes. Obviously, the very function of such pieces condemned them to secondary status. Fugal forms found disfavor in the early eighteenth century because of their baroque intellectuality, while the popular concerti were dismissed by the learned as mere opportunities to display technical brilliance. The first public concerts in England, Holland, and France popularized instrumental

music and stimulated instrumental composition, but critical acceptance was slow in coming.

The list of those who considered pure instrumental music inferior
is long, even if we temporarily disregard the philosophes. According
to Rousseau's *Dictionnaire*, Fontenelle had already asked, "Sonata,
what do you want of me?" (*Sonate, que me veux tu?*) (art. "Sonate").
Around 1700 Lecerf remarked that songs were made for the heart
while symphonies merely for the ear (2:165). This preference for the
voice as "the most perfect instrument" (Mattheson *Capellm*. 96) runs
through most of the century. Scheibe (206) and Hiller (528), Abbé
Pluche (7:115) and Bemetzrieder, restate the Platonic and Galilean
view that only vocal music can be morally and intellectually meaningful, and "even the most perfect instrumental music is but an inarticulate imitation of animal cries" (Bemetzrieder 235). As late as 1784,
William Jones of Nayland ruefully remarks: "Ever since Instrumental
Music has been made independent of Vocal, we have been in danger
of falling under the dominion of sound without sense: and I think
it an unanswerable objection against the modern Style, which must
have its weight with all lovers of Harmony, that if you try its effect
upon an Organ, you discover its emptiness and insignificance" (IV).
A residue of this prejudice survives even in Herder (4:118) and Reichardt (117), who claim a historical priority, though no superiority, for
vocal music.

Several arguments for the primacy of the voice existed. If songs are
"nature itself" (Blainville *L'Esprit* 117–18) or "primal sound" (Schubart 340), one can reasonably conclude that instruments must imitate
the voice (Mattheson *Capellm*. 8, 204; Brown 27–28). Taking this literally, Sulzer, Beattie (141), Burney (*Hist.* 1:22), and others asserted
that the instruments closest to the human voice were the best. Thus
Sulzer opted for the oboe (art. "Instrumentalmusik"). Hiller (541)
and others contended that instruments enlarged the vocal range, but
since sounds beyond the scope of the voice had little significance, the
argument did not boost the prestige of instrumental music.

More moderate versions of this doctrine demanded that instruments speak or sing without imitating language. If, as Mattheson
said, instruments spoke a "tone language or sonorous speech" (*Ton-
Sprache oder Klang-Rede*; *Capellm*. 82), they could arouse specific affects in the listener (Quantz 294). Krause repeatedly recommended
the use of a speaking voice (*ton parlans*; *Verm.* 5:5, 34, 286). For

d'Alembert, metaphors of language serve as a critique of instrumental forms: sonatas are dictionaries "whose aggregation constitutes no sense," while symphonies are "like a German discourse spoken to somebody who understands only French" (*Oe. inéd.* 155). The standard of articulate language highlights for d'Alembert the fragmentation, vagueness, and incomprehensibility of instrumental music.

The theoretical justification of instrumental music was slow in coming, and even composers working in the medium admitted its inferiority, as the example of C. P. E. Bach shows. His manual taught how to play "in a singing manner" (26); his keyboard sonatas often rehearsed conversations between voices; and his best-known "passionate tone-conversation," a trio describing a dialogue between a *sanguinicus* and a *cholericus* (Wotquenne catalogue no. 161.1), was singled out by Sulzer as a model of instrumental music. The poet Gerstenberg found Bach's music so expressive that he wrote a Hamlet monologue to the C minor fantasia in the sixth sonata attached to Bach's *Versuch* (Helm 279 and Werner 56, 62). But Bach, who in a sense legitimated instruments by making them sing, was still doubtful about their potential. When Gerstenberg asked him whether the piano could arouse emphatic feelings (*markierte Empfindung*) and suggested the composition of narrative sonatas with accompanying texts, Bach politely declined:

> I, as a keyboard player, make so bold as to assert that in fact one can say a great deal on our instrument with a good performance. I do not include here a mere tickling of the ears, and I insist that the heart must be moved. Such a keyboard player, especially when he has a highly inventive spirit, can do very much. Meanwhile, words remain always words, and the human voice remains pre-eminent [bleibt uns immer voraus]. [Helm 291]

The letter shows Bach's dilemma. His new sensibility asked for the painting and arousal of individualized passions, but since music was considered too vague to achieve this by itself, he reluctantly acknowledged the superiority of language.

Others were equally hesitant. Sulzer thought of music as a wordless language of emotions but trivialized the idea by limiting it to dances, festive music, and military marches (art. "Instrumentalmusik"). Beyond these social occasions, he allowed instrumental music in symphonies ("instrumental choruses," according to the article "Symphonie") and sonatas ("instrumental cantatas"). The remaining concertos and instrumental pieces were pure entertainment and "pleasant noise," occasion for musical "somersaults and rope-dancing" (art. "Musik").

The privileged position of singing supported the second mimetic principle, the preference for melody over harmony, which, to be sure, was vigorously contested by a number of musicians, foremost among them Rameau and mathematicians of music. But the harmonists were outnumbered by the melodists, whose credo was already stated in Mattheson's *Das forschende Orchestre*: "Supple melody is music's true wonder," while "harmony is not [yet] music" (341, 363). Melody moved the passions and was primal harmony and the source of imitation.

Mattheson's views were widely shared in Germany. Apart from the mathematicians of music, only Nichelmann dissented by arguing in an unfortunately opaque style that the "polyodic" mode of composition (voices of equal weight) was preferable to "monody" (a dominating voice accompanied by simple harmonies) (15–17). Though Nichelmann continued to uphold musical mimesis (he thought that the polyodic style was actually a better, more supple means of imitating the passions), he was ostracized for his opposition to the Berlin court style. As Burney remarked, "Whoever dares to profess any other tenet than those of Graun and Quantz, is sure to be persecuted" (*Germ.* 2:234).

The common view, well expressed by d'Alembert, was that harmony became the fashionable preference over melody when composers succumbed to sensation seeking. French composers, for instance, sought the favor of the audience by furiously stacking voice upon voice and creating sheer noise. But this penchant toward harmony smothered the voice and gave priority to sounds formerly restricted to the accompaniment (*Oe.* 1:541). Rousseau tried to reestablish the dominance of melody by proposing in the *Encyclopédie* the "thinning out" of full chords (art. "accompagnement").

The complaints of d'Alembert and Rousseau might be taken as signs that the harmonists were predominating. Yet, apart from a small group around Rameau, the theoretical preference for melody was virtually universal in mid-century France. In Germany the situation was not significantly different. From Scheibe (45) to Sulzer (art. "Melodie") theorists were concerned with the encroachment of harmony on melody, and Burney noted that the "venerable" J. S. Bach,

"though unequalled in learning and contrivance, thought it so necessary to crowd into both hands all the harmony he could grasp, that
he must inevitably have sacrificed melody and expression" (*Germ.*
2:263). According to Sir William Jones, "Our boasted harmony . . .
paints nothing, expresses nothing, says nothing to the heart, and
consequently can only give more or less pleasure to one of our
senses." Melody, the "musick of the passions," was therefore infinitely preferable to harmony, "the musick of mere sounds" (556).
Such preferences for melody were further reinforced by anti-intellectual and populist sentiments. Schubart, for instance, belittled harmony, modulation, and counterpoint as mere scholarly exercises
which could not match the beauty of melodic invention (11).

Others were more moderate. Scheibe advocated a fusion of melody and harmony (45), whereas Telemann allowed for experiments
with harmonic innovations if melodic invention dried up (284–85).
Sulzer responded to Rousseau polemically that harmony had improved music and that the decline of counterpoint was regrettable
(art. "Musik"), although he subscribed to the commonplace that "the
aim and true product of music is song, and all the skills of harmony
have merely beautiful singing as their final goal" (art. "Melodie").
Robertson concluded that to most people melody was "almost the
whole of Music. Not that Harmony wants charms; for she has
charms, and still more powerful than those of Melody; but study and
pains are required to understand them. Harmony is the amusement
of the learned and of the few: Melody, that voice which nations hear
and obey" (133). Ironically, the use of harmony was also said to foster
dilettantism, because it allowed composition by rules. As Reichardt
remarked, somewhat against his democratic sentiments: if the rules
of harmony were to be "discovered via speculation and founded
upon convenience," every simpleton could crank out a composition
(107). Schumann was to remark later, with more justification, that
simple and pleasing "melody is the war cry of dilettantes," although
he added that there is no music without the kind of true melody that
one finds in Bach, Mozart, and Beethoven (95f.). In any case, the je
ne sais quoi of melody was a weapon against excessive insistence on
rules and rationalism in music. While the mathematicians of music
and Batteux deduced everything from central principles, Scheibe
sympathized with Mattheson's empiricism (653). Rules have no a
priori force; they crystallize out of history and the contact with po-

etry and rhetoric. Hence taste is not inborn but an acquired mental ability to judge our sense experience (278). As Rousseau states more elegantly in the *Encyclopédie*, taste offers eyeglasses to reason (art. "goût"). Generally accepted principles are not natural laws, and genius has therefore the right to violate them.

Good melodies are light, distinct, lovely, and flowing, stated Mattheson (*Capellm.* 140–42). Because of these qualities, melody better suited the dominant norms of simplicity, reason, nature, and clarity, though nature and simplicity allowed for considerable interpretative latitude. For Scheibe, *natural* meant intellectual quality; for Batteux, Rousseau, Sulzer, and others, a sweet and simple "natural language of the heart." The difference indicates a shift in taste, but the meanings actually overlap and do not allow for a neat chronological sequence: the "enlightened" criticism of Scheibe and Marpurg is contemporaneous with the last years of J. S. Bach, Rousseau's advocacy of melodic simplicity, and the new personal dynamism of C. P. E. Bach and the Mannheim school of orchestral music.

Scheibe sought musical wit (128, 774) to stimulate the understanding (90–91), though he decried intellectual as well as emotional excesses. A popular epigram leveled a similar accusation against Rameau in France:

> Oui, si le difficile est beau,
> C'est un grand homme que Rameau.
> Mais si le beau par avanture
> N'étoit que la simple nature,
> Dont l'art doit etre le tableau:
> Le petit homme que Rameau.

> Yes, if the difficult is beautiful, Rameau is a great man. But if by chance the beautiful is simple nature, of which art must be the image, Rameau is a minor figure.

Rousseau harbored similar sentiments. Fugues, he said in the *Dictionnaire*, display the composer's wit instead of pleasing the listeners (art. "fugue"). Genius is generally "not at all that bizarre taste which disseminates everywhere what is baroque and difficult. . . . It is that inner fire which incessantly inspires new and always pleasant melodies, and lively and natural expressions which go to the heart" (art. "compositeur"). He scorned emotional excesses equally and warned not to take "the baroque for the expressive, nor harshness for energy,

nor give a shocking presentation of the passions you wish to render"
(art. "expression"). In this he was anticipated by Mattheson and
Krause, who wanted to banish from music naturalistic shrieks and
expressions that represented or aroused violence, anger, or pain
(*Capellm.* 194; *Poesie* 74).

Simplicity and natural style were even compatible with embellishments. Scheibe recommended the moderate use of musical figures
and tropes (642–43, 684–85); Quantz, who asked for "clean and distinct" performances (104) that were comprehensible even to the musically uneducated (103), gave detailed instructions for the decoration
of a piece; and C. P. E. Bach devoted an entire chapter to the same
topic. Kirnberger reconciled the conflicting demands by stipulating
that every aria, when stripped of embellishments, should reduce to a
simple chorale (224).

This rococo taste for elaboration and decoration blended with the
preference for a "middle" style and the "round and complete," "light
and flowing" performance advocated by Quantz (105–06). Scheibe
thought it ridiculous "to avoid all embellishment in a pure and moving style" (645), whereas Burney enjoined composers to avoid degrees of simplicity in music "which border upon dryness, rusticity,
and vulgarity" (*Germ.* 2:159). Such artifices were still thought to allow for the "noble simplicity" that Mattheson (*Capellm.* 138),
Quantz (82), and Krause (*Poesie* 178–79) advocated well before it became Winckelmann's ideal. In sum, the norm of nature did not exclude stylization and artifice, only naturalism.

CATEGORIES OF MUSICAL IMITATION

Having considered the juncture between affect theory and imitation,
we may now survey five categories of eighteenth-century musical imitation: (1) purely musical imitations, (2) imitations of the ancients
and of other models, (3) imitations of verbal intonation, (4) imitations of affects, and (5) imitations of sounds, movements, and physical objects.[2]

Purely musical imitations in canons, fugues, and variations need
not concern us here, for they are basic structures of nonrepresentative music. The second type of imitation was attempted by the
Camerata and was debated in the protracted *querelle des anciens et des*

modernes, but ironically the resultant music was expressive rather than imitative in the narrow sense. The imitation of model composers, mentioned already in the previous chapter, became unfashionable with the cult of genius in the 1770s, although Sulzer, limping behind the times, still recommends it.[3]

Having already discussed imitations of intonation and affects, I can now concentrate on the most common form of mimesis, the imitation of sounds, movements, and physical objects. In the literal sense music can only imitate noises, since it has only sounds at its disposal. Silent movements can be indicated only by tempo; immobile, silent objects must be represented via associations shared by the composer and the audience. The musical representation of words referring to objects and events in the external world can thus be achieved in two different ways: by directly representing natural sounds or by relying on associations established by convention.

Baroque music frequently imitated sound, directly or by means of associations: Vivaldi's *Four Seasons* depicted storms; Rameau's *Les Indes galantes* evoked earthquakes; Kuhnau's first biblical sonata portrayed the fight between David and Goliath; J. S. Bach's *Capriccio* allowed the coach-horns of his departing brother to fade into the distance.[4] Yet sound or word painting never constituted the heart of baroque music, and its defense was never vigorous, for subsequent generations took as a guideline Galilei's precept that word painting must not detract from the portrayal of affect or correct intonation. Dubos preferred the "natural language of human passions" to the music of "finches and canaries" (491), whereas Gottsched ridiculed Heinichen's attempt to illustrate fluttering birds with tremulous voices that obscured the text (725). In the preface to his biblical sonatas Kuhnau defended nonnaturalistic representations, albeit with the caveat that analogical representations needed commentaries to explain the figure. Furthermore, since listeners could not tell whether the musical laughter belonged to Goliath or somebody else, for example, or that an unexpected modulation (a "deception of the ear which the Italians call *inganno*") represented Laban's deceit, Kuhnau had to relate the highlights of his stories below the score. Mattheson praised similar imitations by Froberger and Buxtehude, though he regarded excessive tone painting as mere "monkey play" (*Capellm.* 202). When he later objected that rising notes could not represent *Weltuntergang* (the fall of the world, that is, the Last Judgment),

Marpurg emphatically replied that one ought to paint "emotions and expressions," not "mere words." An oratorial rise in pitch gave more weight to *Untergang* than a chromatic descent (*Briefe* 1:77, 377). By 1770 Burney had condescendingly noted that "this good man," Mattheson, "had more pedantry and nonsense about him, than true genius. In one of his vocal compositions for the church, in which the word *rainbow* occurred, he gave himself infinite trouble to make the notes of his score form an *arch*. This may serve as a specimen of his taste and judgment, with respect to the propriety of musical expression and imitation" (*Germ.* 2:276).

From 1750 onward the word painting of Handel's and J. S. Bach's generation came under increasing attack. In Quantz's opinion, earlier German composers were more eager "to express the mere words rather than their sense or the related affect. Many thought they did what was needed if, for instance, they expressed the words heaven and hell by means of extremely high and low notes, whereby much foolishness often crept into their compositions" (325). "German instrumental music of bygone times looked pretty colorful and dangerous on paper. . . . [The composers] were more eager to reproduce the sounds of . . . the cuckoo, the nightingale, and the quail . . . than to imitate the human voice" (327). In England this became a standard criticism of Handel. His biographer, Mainwaring, noted that composers often miss the meaning of a sentence by paying too close attention to particular words. "Handel himself, from his imperfect acquaintance with the English language, has sometimes fallen into these mistakes. A Composer ought never to pay this attention to single words, excepting they have an uncommon energy, and contain some passion or sentiment" (185). Handel, says Goldsmith, "has been obliged, in order to express passion, to imitate words by sounds, which tho' it gives the pleasure which imitation always produces, yet it fails of exciting those lasting affections, which it is in the power of sounds to produce" (93). Webb accepted that "Handel seldom fails to ascend with the word *rise*," but his patience ran out with Purcell's practice of accompanying "every idea of *roundness* with an endless *rotation* of notes" (143).[5]

Such strictures on musical imitations of sounds, movements, and objects actually reaffirmed the principles of affect theory. Lockman thought that music was fit to imitate words of "passionate sentiment" but not descriptive nature poetry (XVIII–XIX). Similarly,

Batteux distinguished imitations of "nonpassionate sounds and noises," a kind of "landscape painting," from expressions of "animated sounds," which he called "portraits" (283). Although he permitted both types of musical representation, word paintings had to be integrated into the expression of the affect: "Our musicians frequently sacrifice the general tone, that expression of the soul which must be spread over the whole musical piece, to an idea which is accessory and almost indifferent to the principal subject. They linger on to paint a brook, a breeze, or another word which makes for a musical image" (288–89).

The preference for so-called portraiture over musical landscapes became even more explicit in Batteux's German commentators: Ruetz accused Batteux of allowing only imitations of language (301), while Hiller objected to imitations of bird twitter. Music's source and model ought to be man (520), and hence natural sounds are to be imitated only sparingly and only if they appeal to the imagination (rather than to the senses) (532–36). According to Krause, storms and murmuring brooks are "musical only inasmuch as they contribute to the arousal of an affect or a special feeling of pleasure." "Listening to a musical piece, we do not care whether it imitates a motion in the corporeal world, only whether it is beautiful, whether it pleases and affects us" (*Poesie* 54). The success of musical landscapes depends therefore on the composer's ability to charge them with emotional power, and not on the fidelity of the imitation.

Diderot distinguished simple from figured imitative style but preferred both types to mere modulations and tonal combinations. According to his third *Entretien sur le fils naturel*, simple style follows the modulation of the emotions in the text, while figured style illustrates thunders and lightnings. The first follows the accents of passion and captures nature's inarticulate and violent cries, whereas the second paints. But the tableau diminishes the impact of pathos and appeals to the ear instead of penetrating the soul. Persons of taste will therefore scorn poets who merely offer composers catchwords to paint, and they will hold in low esteem painterly musicians who pass over the dominant passion of a situation (*Oe. esth.* 168–70). Sulzer dismisses all descriptive music, including witty baroque figures and direct imitations, as childish artifices (art. "Gemählde"). Inanimate nature is to be imitated only if the music accompanies a text that conjures up images in the mind (art. "Mahlerey").

THE INTERNALIZATION OF IMITATION

Word painting and direct representation of natural sounds had few defenders. Blainville recommended the musical painting of landscapes, though he admitted the higher value of portraying the passions (*L'Esprit* 13, 78–79); Potter retorted to Addison that music was just as capable of evoking scenes and events as painting (33–34); Hayes, professor of music at Oxford, vociferously countered Avison that the emotional power of Handel's setting of Milton's "L'Allegro" and "Il Penseroso" matched the colors of Claude Lorrain and Poussin (67).

The most effective defenders of descriptive music advocated some form of indirect representation. As we shall see, d'Alembert proposed that music ought to produce an impact that equals the impact of the imitated external objects and events. Although this usually led to a favoring of figurative representation, interest in it occasionally served as a defense of instrumental music. Sir William Jones thought that instruments were less expressive and less powerful than the voice but that they were capable of indirect representation, "by a kind of *substitution*, that is, by raising in our minds, affections, or sentiments, analogous to those, which arise in us, when the respective objects in nature are presented to our senses" (559). Adam Smith agreed: instrumental music produces "upon the mind, in consequence of other powers, the same sort of effect which the most exact imitation of nature . . . could produce" (170). One may take this psychologizing of representation a major step further by representing not the external world but the impressions it produces on us. This genuine internalization of imitation was first formulated by Engel in an undeservedly neglected little essay entitled *"On Musical Painting"* (*Über die musikalische Malerei*) of 1780.

Engel established three categories of musical imitation. The composer may simply reproduce physical sounds—for instance, battle noises; or, if the subject is inaudible, he may rely on "transcendental similarities" (302), which are analogies between sound and other sensory impressions (allegro may suggest speed)—this is the indirect imitation suggested by d'Alembert; finally, the composer may choose to represent not the object but "the impression which the object usually makes upon the soul" (307). This last category, in which "musical imitation acquires its broadest domain" (307–08), internalizes imitation, since it portrays psychic events rather than the external world.

As Beethoven allegedly remarked, his *Pastoral* Symphony was "more an expression of sentiment than painting" (*mehr Ausdruck der Empfindung als Mahlerey*) (Thayer 3:99).

When Engel finally lists nine different means of portraying emotional reactions—namely, mode, key, melody, movement, rhythm, harmony, pitch, instrument, and intensity (308–13)—it becomes clear that this mediated imitation of the external world reduces to a representation of affects, based on an association between sound and emotion, musical features and affects. This internalization of mimesis thus revitalized affect theory because it attempted to individualize the emotions and achieve greater mimetic fidelity. The development of new and more expressive instruments and the use of a greater range of sound were both in the service of this refinement of imitation. Engel's "first rule" reveals that imitation theory is but a variant of affect theory: "The musician should always paint the impressions (*Empfindungen*) rather than the objects of the impressions, always the state of mind (and thus of the body) which the contemplation of certain objects and events produces rather than the objects and events themselves" (319–20).[6] Engel, and Heydenreich (154–56) after him, permitted the representation of objects as long as it did not clash with the representation of the relationship between objects and subjects (325–27). Forkel (*Gesch.* 55) and Herder (23:567) took a stricter line and wished to banish completely the representation of objects and external sounds.

To summarize, the internalization of imitation toward the end of the century reinforced rather than weakened the mimetic principle inherent in affect theory: as the assault on external imitations intensified, music became "in the actual sense of the word a painting of feelings and passions" (Heydenreich 203). The growing conviction that objects and events in the external world should be represented only by the emotional impact they have on us refined psychological mimesis. With few exceptions,[7] writers continued to believe that a sympathy and an analogy existed between the forms and signs of music and the affects themselves.

Imitation theory evolved differently in music than in the other arts, but its life was neither shorter nor less significant. On the contrary: the internalization of imitation allowed the renewal of seventeenth-century affect theories and their extension well into the nineteenth century. The metamorphosis of mimesis delayed more revolutionary upheavals.

5 RAMEAU

Mattheson's attacks between 1713 and 1721 destroyed the Pythagorean metaphysics of music with arguments based on Locke's empiricism. But the mathematical tradition survived, for Rameau's *Traité de l'harmonie* (*Treatise on Harmony*; 1722) assumed the Cartesian heritage by rejecting obedience to tradition and authority and affirming the primacy of reason over experience:

> Greater authority almost always outweighs reason and experience. . . . Neither reason nor experience has guided those who have given us the rules of music. [119]

> However much progress music may have made until our time, it appears that the more sensitive the ear has become to the marvelous effects of this art, the less inquisitive the mind has been about its true principles. One might say that reason has lost its rights, while experience has acquired a certain authority. . . . Even if experience can enlighten us concerning the different properties of music, it alone cannot lead us to discover the principle behind these properties with the precision appropriate to reason. . . . If through the exposition of an evident principle, from which we then draw just and certain conclusions, we can show that our music had attained the last degree of perfection and that the Ancients were far from this perfection . . . we shall know where we stand. . . . The light of reason, dispelling the doubts into which experience can plunge us at any moment, will be the most certain guarantee of success that we can expect in this art. . . . Music is a science which should have definite rules; these rules should be drawn from an evident principle; and this principle cannot really be known to us without the aid of mathematics. . . . Only with the aid of mathematics did my ideas become clear and did light replace a certain obscurity of which I was unaware before. [XXXII–XXXV]

> Let us be ruled then by reason alone whenever possible, and let us call experience to aid only when we desire further confirmation of its proofs. [139–40]

Rameau often reaffirmed this Cartesian credo of his first theoretical work, sometimes with special reference to Descartes.[1] But, unlike

Descartes, he wrote in such a ponderous and obscure style that his reputation grew only slowly. Nevertheless, during the 1730s and 40s he gradually established himself, both as a theorist and as a composer of operas, and by 1750 his star was at its apogee. Having finally triumphed over the Lullists in opera and conquered the academy with his "Mémoire," Rameau was now an artist-scholar, considered by some the Newton of music theory.[2] But the hard-fought and sweet victory was short-lived. In the *querelle des bouffons* (1752–53) the attacks on the French *tragédie lyrique* damaged his reputation as a composer, and the subsequent bitter debates about his theory continued until the end of his life in 1764.

While Rameau's reputation as a composer is firmly established today, his contributions to music theory remain controversial and, due to their technical nature, mostly accessible only to specialists. Girdlestone's inspired book on Rameau loses its élan, for instance, when it reluctantly broaches the subject of the composer's theory, claiming that it did not survive the test of time. Yet Rameau himself believed that it was not enough "to feel the effects of an art or a science, one must conceptualize these effects in a manner to render them more intelligible" (*Treatise* XXXV). Even if he failed in this enterprise, we must understand what this postulated unity between sentiment and reflection meant for him, for this is what linked his special talents to the larger concerns of his age.

Rameau's debates with the philosophes are often recounted in a merely anecdotal way. Yet, as I shall show in the following three chapters, his theory can only be appreciated by grasping the intellectual issues of these debates. Rameau may have been occasionally wrong, often narrow-minded, and almost always obscure, but these very qualities turned him into a kind of irritant for the philosophes so that they were eventually forced to develop their own antidote. Rousseau, d'Alembert, and Diderot all started as disciples of Rameau, and when they turned away from him, they developed a critique that was instrumental in forming their aesthetics, and even their general philosophical principles. Furthermore, if instrumental and harmonic music achieved a revolutionary breakthrough in Germany during the next decades, and if France remained entranced by the pleasant and melodic but conventional music of Grétry, an admirer of Diderot and Rousseau, we must blame in part the terms and the outcome of the battle between Rameau and his opponents, which defined the dominant French musical taste for decades to come.

One belittles Rameau by labeling him a belated Cartesian and a latter-day representative of French classicism.[3] Seen in this light, he becomes a somewhat pathetic and quixotic figure who hopelessly battled the rising tide of empiricism, Newtonianism, and melodrama. While this image agrees with Rameau's self-presentation as a rationalist and a methodological Cartesian, it does not fully account for his philosophical orientation; he also believed that his theory was superior to earlier ones because it was experimentally verifiable. Indeed, a fundamental tension exists between the mathematical and the physical, the logical and the experimental bases of his theory. The dominance of mathematics in the *Traité* and the early works gives way to a concern with the physics and metaphysics of the overtones in the later ones; the resonating body (*corps sonore*) becomes "the unique principle, generator, and organizer of all music . . . and immediate cause of all its effects" (*Wr.* 3:76). Of the many logically possible chords Rameau permits only a few, in part because he believes that they alone are rooted in nature, in part because of traditional musical practice, and in part because he judges some to be unpleasant to the ear. None of these principles of exclusion are compatible with Cartesianism. In fact, Rameau's war with the philosophes was unleashed by his insistence that music is natural rather than constructed; as we shall see, in Rameau's debate with d'Alembert on the introduction of new chords, its was Rameau that insisted on the importance of musical practice.[4]

PRINCIPLES OF HARMONY

Two complementary methodological principles shaped Rameau's concept of harmony, allowing him to forge a new system out of materials inherited from Zarlino, Mersenne, and Descartes: a generative-deductive principle and a permutational one. The deductive principle is central to Rameau's rationalist credo, though, as Shirlaw, Chailley, and others have demonstrated, his premises as well as his deductions often beg the question. The real significance of the deductive principle is to establish a hierarchy among musical materials.

Intervals are generated from a fundamental sound, according to the principle that the higher notes are in some way contained in the

lower ones. They are ordered according to two, occasionally clashing, principles. Like Descartes and others, Rameau ranks consonances according to the simplicity of their mathematical ratios: "The
order of origin and perfection of these consonances is determined by
the order of the numbers. Thus, the octave between 1 and 2, which is
generated first, is more perfect than the fifth between 2 and 3" (*Treatise* 6). However, this ranking is modified by the permutational principle of inversion. The inversion of an interval—obtained by raising
its lower note by an octave—is always a derivative of, and hence subordinate to, the primary interval which alone contains the "natural
order" (*Treatise* XLVI).[5]

The *Treatise* actually states that there are only two types of chords,
the perfect and the seventh (52-53, 70, 392-94), and within these types
Rameau establishes the perfect major chord (c-e-g in the key of C
major) as fundamental to the generation of all consonances, and
what we now call the dominant seventh (g-b-d-f in the key of C
major) as fundamental to all dissonances. But since all dissonances
are generated by piling up consonant thirds and fifths (*Treatise* 35,
110), the dominant seventh (and therefore all dissonances) is itself
derivative.[6]

All consonances are inversions of the perfect major and minor triads and may be put together from thirds contained in the perfect
chords. Rameau regarded this deductive hierarchy as an advance over
Zarlino and others who had already conceived of inversions but had
given no priority to chords in the root position: since "the first
sound and the first chord revealed to them was given no sort of pre-
rogative, everything was considered to be equal" (*Treatise* 119). The
perfect chord was assigned this privileged position already in the
Treatise but found a "natural" explanation only later, after Rameau
had become familiar with the overtones. To adapt the overtones to
his theory, Rameau added the claim that the different octaves were
"so to speak" identical (*Treatise* 6), for this allowed him to invert intervals and chords: "telescoping" the first overtones within the compass of a single octave, he obtained the notes of the major triad (Ex.
8).

Thus the major triad now appeared to have been generated "naturally" out of a fundamental sound by means of its overtones. Rameau
was so impressed by the role of overtones in harmony that he even
claimed—erroneously—that only musical sounds had overtones,

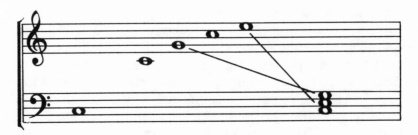

Example 8.
The first overtones of the generating tone c are c′, g′, c″, and e″. The "telescoping" of
these overtones into the octave immediately above the generating tone results in the
perfect major chord.

sheer noise having none (*Wr.* 3:29, 172). Consideration of the overtones also allowed him to conclude that the major chord with the
generating sound in the bass had priority over its inversions, the so-
called sixth and six-four chords (Ex. 9).

While the major chord could this way be assembled from the lowest overtones, the minor chord could not be found at all, and this
presented a serious problem when Rameau cast about for a "natural"
explanation of it. He first utilized the so-called co-vibration of the
"undertones," erroneously believing that strings tuned to the twelfth
and the seventeenth below a generating sound resonated to it. But
no such vibration was observable, and in any case, it would have destroyed Rameau's principle that the generating sound had to be the
bottom note in the uninverted chord.

In the *Démonstration* Rameau finally established the correct explanation, that strings tuned a twelfth and a seventeenth below a vibrating string will indeed co-vibrate, but not at their fundamental fre-
quencies: a string a twelfth below divides into three segments and

Example 9.
In the root position the root note is in the bass. In the first inversion (sixth chord) the
third is in the bass (the root being raised by an octave). In the second inversion (six-
four chord) the fifth is in the bass (both the root and the third being raised by an
octave).

emits the octave below the generating note, while a string a seventeenth below divides into five segments and emits the generating
sound itself. Rameau pounced on this observation as proving the
natural origin of the minor chord, though he had to admit that the
minor third was still less natural than the major and even derivative
from it. He took recourse in the biblical account of gender differences: "The major mode, nature's first shoot, has a force, a brilliance,
and, if I may say, a virility, which raise it above the minor and com-
pel us to acknowledge it as the master of harmony. Existing less
through simple and unique nature, the minor, in contrast, receives
from art, which partly shapes it, a weakness" (*Wr.* 3:207). Like Eve,
the minor is thus an indirect product of nature, being merely "indicated" by it (*Wr.* 3:199).

The seventh, ninth, eleventh, and all other dissonant chords are
generated from consonant chords by adding one or more thirds. In
the *Nouveau système* Rameau states that any third may be placed
above any other (*Wr.* 2:16–17), but he actually excludes most combinations on the basis of musical practice. Dissonances therefore are
certain permissible combinations of major and minor thirds.

In the Pythagorean sense, dissonances make "the perfection of
consonant chords more wonderful" (*Treatise* 42), but Rameau also
uses them for modulation and for establishing the key (*Wr.*
3:66–67). Since the sequence of two perfect chords leaves the key
ambiguous, a dissonance-consonance progression, or cadence, must
be used to establish the key. A "perfect cadence" resolves the dominant chord to a perfect chord by moving the so-called leading note of
the dissonance to the fundamental note of the key (Ex. 10).

This dominant-tonic progression is in Rameau's scheme the elementary and archetypal musical structure, of which all other disso-

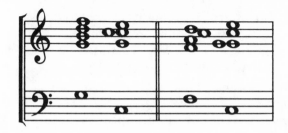

Example 10.
The perfect cadence (from dominant to tonic) and what Rameau calls the "irregular"
cadence (from sub-dominant to tonic).

nance-consonance progressions are weaker variations. "The progressions of harmony are nothing but a chain of tonic notes and dominants" (*Treatise* 288), or, to put it differently, music is a chain of cadential moves between dissonance and consonance. "The perfect cadence alone is . . . the origin of the principal varieties introduced into harmony. One inverts this cadence, interrupts it, imitates it, avoids it—this is what variety consists of" (*Wr.* 4:117). Thus Rameau generates music by performing variations on an archetypal pattern of cadence. The disorienting dissonances are soon followed by chords that reassert the key, so that one constantly senses an underlying reassuring tonal center. The dynamics of music consists not so much of a steady flow as of a series of pendulum swings toward dissonance each followed by a cadential reassertion of the tonic chord, which marks the gravitational center and the ultimate resting point of all motion.[7] It is from this classical order of cadence and tonality that subsequent generations dared ever longer and more esoteric excursions into the infinite sea of dissonance.

The famous *basse fondamentale*, "the unique compass for our ears" (*Wr.* 3:9), represents a second organizational center in Rameau's system. In the traditional *basso continuo* the bass was the line of reference. Rameau retains several features of this bass (for instance, its slow motion), but he no longer uses it as a reference. The new reference line is the "fundamental bass," which contains the generating notes of the chords. Because of inversions, this line crosses freely from one voice to another; it indicates the harmony and its progression, but it does not constitute a voice beneath the others (*Wr.* 3:109). The old polyphonic style consisted of a number of voices moving along the horizontal axis of time, the vertical harmonies being formed by them accidentally, as it were. Rameau's harmonic system destroyed this horizontal thinking, not only by highlighting the chords but also by replacing the basso continuo with a generating line moving both vertically and horizontally.[8]

Rameau continued to uphold affect theory, and he rejected purely "constructive" music; but, in contrast to the monodists, he held that the affective meaning of music is encoded principally in harmony, from which melody is derived (*Wr.* 3:317). The resultant theory of musical meaning is affective rather than rhetorical. Rameau assigns traditional affective meanings to intervals, chords, and keys (*Treatise* 154–56, 163–64) and regards the "expression of thought, feeling, and passion" as the "true purpose of music" (*Wr.* 4:194). Considering his involvement with opera, he attaches a surprisingly low value to the meaning of words and to their rhetorical inflection: "We must let ourselves be carried away by the sentiment that music inspires, without reflecting on it, without thinking of words at all, and then this sentiment becomes the organ of our judgment" (*Wr.* 3:297). This disregard for verbal meaning and the concomitant search for a semantics of musical materials indicate that Rameau was perhaps not a born composer of opera. Indeed, in his *Observations sur notre instinct pour la musique (Observations on our Instinct for Music*; 1754) Rameau argued that since music is natural to us, we can instinctively (i.e., nonverbally) respond to it: the harmonies of a resounding body resonate in our soul. Such Pythagorean notions of harmony gradually became more prominent toward the end of Rameau's life, though he accused the ancient philosopher of having deviated from nature.

Mattheson was among Rameau's first and most persistent opponents, and he used him as a kind of whipping boy among harmonists, without any deep knowledge of his work. In words of typical Matthesonian verve: "One finds in the works of the Clermont organist some hundred tons of tireless work and prominent nitpicking, five hundred stone of tiresome oddities and eccentricities (*Grillen und Sonderlings-Fratzen*), about three pounds of personal experience (not counting hearsay), two ounces of healthy judgment, and hardly an ounce of good taste" (Rameau *Wr.* 3:XV).

Serious resistance to Rameau's theory developed only in the 1750s, when d'Alembert popularized it and Rameau subsequently clashed with the philosophes, as I shall describe in the next three chapters. For now, we may conclude by restating the two principles in Rameau's approach to music: one is a combinatorial and permutational principle, which allows the generative construction of chords and their cadential progression within the framework of the major-minor tonal system. Seen from this angle, Rameau's system is an order constructed out of arbitrarily chosen generative principles. However, Rameau himself saw his system in terms of a second principle that also operates in it, the deductive principle. Starting from the notions of "sonorous bodies" and overtones he sought to derive everything and demonstrate that music has indubitable natural laws. Unfortunately, Rameau was so successful in posing his theory as a system of natural laws for music that his contemporaries as well as

later generations tended to overlook the combinatorial and constructivist dimension in it. Pierre Boulez, for instance, has allegedly said
that Rameau's era has come to an end, meaning thereby that musical
structures are no longer founded on preexistent, organic entities
(Pousseur 172). This remark, like most of the literature on Rameau,
seems to overlook to what extent Rameau was a father not only of
the era attributed to him but also of the kind of thinking that underlies serial music.

6 ROUSSEAU

Rameau's reputation started to decline when he embroiled himself ever more deeply in controversies with the philosophes. A discussion of these controversies must start with Rousseau, both because he was Rameau's most formidable opponent and because his quarrel with Rameau essentially shaped his intellectual development. Just how pivotal a role music and music theory played in Rousseau's thought will become evident if we bring it to bear on a contemporary debate on Rousseau between Derrida and de Man. The aim of this chapter is thus somewhat more complex than that of the previous ones, inasmuch as I shall place the historical issues in the context of contemporary critical debates, and this new focus will necessitate a departure from a straightforward historical narrative. I shall first state the terms of the debate between Derrida and de Man and then proceed to show how the quarrel between Rousseau and Rameau may bear on their differences.[1]

MUSIC AESTHETICS AND THE DECONSTRUCTION OF ROUSSEAU

Derrida's now classic book *De la Grammatologie* (1967) focuses on Rousseau and his *Essai sur l'origine des langues*. In brief, Derrida questions the metaphysical tradition of logocentrism that prefers speech for its immediacy and presence. Logocentrism depreciates writing, for the letter mediates over space and time, merely supplementing living presence in a state of absence. Rousseau, according to Derrida, assumes an ambiguous position with respect to logocentrism. On the one hand, he prefers speech to writing, accentual to articulate language, and hieroglyphics to phonemic notation: "The *Essay on the Origin of Languages* opposes speech to writing as presence to absence and liberty to servitude. . . . Writing takes the status of a tragic fatality come to prey upon natural innocence, interrupting the golden age of the present and full speech" (168). But Derrida goes beyond this traditional view of Rousseau, which found its most recent exponent in Lévy-Strauss, by showing that Rousseau's language constantly undermines his thesis:

> Rousseau is suspicious also of the illusion of full and present speech, of the illusion of presence within a speech believed to be transparent and innocent. It is toward a praise of silence that the myth of full presence . . . is then carried. [202]

> On the side of experience, a recourse to literature as reappropriation of presence, that is to say . . . of Nature. On the side of theory, an indictment of the negativity of the letter, in which we must read the degeneracy of culture and the disruption of the community. [207]

De Man's major response to *Of Grammatology* suggests that the familiar message attributed to Rousseau emerges from a superficial reading that ignores the countervoice that Rousseau deliberately sustained. If, as Derrida has established, Rousseau's valorization of the origin is infinitely regressive, why does he hold that Rousseau actually believed in a metaphysics of presence (119, 122)? Derrida's deconstruction applies not to Rousseau himself but only to those critics who nailed him down on one side of a set of binary opposites, such as presence and absence, north and south, articulation and accent, speech and writing.

Mimesis and music are central to this debate. According to Derrida, "Rousseau is sure that the essence of art is mimesis. Imitation redoubles presence, adds itself to it by supplementing it. . . . In the living arts, and preeminently in song, the outside imitates the inside. It is expressive. It 'paints' passions. The metaphor which makes the song a painting is only possible . . . under the common authority of the concept of imitation" (289). Although Derrida's subsequent reading of passages from the *Essai* and *Emile* acknowledges that Rousseau, like Plato, had moral and didactic objections to imitation, de Man wants to show that the *Essai* departed from mimesis even in narrower, aesthetic terms. His evidence is a remarkable passage in chapter 16:

> For us, all sounds are relative and distinguished only in comparisons. No sound possesses by itself absolute properties that would allow us to iden-

tify it; only with respect to another sound is it high or low, loud or soft. By itself it has none of these properties. In a harmonic system, a sound is nothing on a natural basis. It is neither tonic, nor dominant, harmonic or fundamental. All these properties exist as relationships only, and since the entire system can be shifted from bass to treble, each sound changes according to its rank and place as the system changes in degree. [*Essai* 173]

In this passage, musical sounds are viewed as empty characters, meaningless arbitrary signs that acquire significance only within a structure that man imposes on the infinite continuum of sounds.[2] But does it constitute, as de Man sees it, a remarkable vision of "music as a pure system of relations that at no point depends on the substantive assertions of a presence?" One questions, above all, the conclusion that for Rousseau "music is a mere play of relationships" (128).

Now Rousseau, like Diderot and d'Alembert, actually belittled instrumental music for containing merely playful relations. As chapter 16 of the *Essai* argues with great vigor, individual sounds or mere harmonic relations are, like colors in painting, intrinsically meaningless and must be turned by means of melody into "signs and images" of ideas and feelings: "As painting is not the art of combining colors to please the eye, music is not the art of combining sounds to please the ear. If that were all, the former and the latter would be natural sciences and not fine arts. Imitation alone raises them to that rank. For what makes painting an art of imitation? Design. What makes music another? Melody" (*Essai* 153).

De Man, cognizant of Rousseau's dislike of pure, nonreferential music, notes that the philosopher "seems eager to safeguard the importance of subject matter" and is unwilling "to dissociate the sign from the sensation or to state its autonomy. The sign never ceases to function as a signifier and remains entirely oriented toward a meaning. . . . [Rousseau wants to show] that the sensory element that is necessarily a part of the pictorial or musical sign plays no part in the aesthetic experience" (127).

But how can music be a "mere play of relationships" if its signs always point beyond the signifier? According to de Man, Rousseau upheld musical mimesis even though he believed that the world had been drained of meaning; the signifier continues to point beyond itself but only toward a void: "The sign is devoid of substance . . . because the meaning itself is empty; the sign should not offer its own sensory richness as a substitute for the void that it signifies" (127).

Music is "hollow at the core" because meaning and presence have disappeared (128).

De Man supports this reading with a passage in which Rousseau extols the ability of music to represent silence, sleep, and even death:

> Painting is closer to nature and . . . music is a more human art. . . . The musician has the great advantage of knowing how to paint things one cannot hear; the greatest wonder of this art which can only be effective through motion is its ability to shape images of rest. Dream, calmness of night solitude and even silence enter into the tableaux of music. . . . Let all nature sleep, those who contemplate it are awake, and the art of the musician is to substitute for the intangible images of the object those movements which its presence excites in the heart of the contemplating person. . . . [The musician] does not represent things directly, but he excites in the soul the same sentiments one feels in seeing them. [*Essai* 175–77]

This poignant passage, which Rousseau rephrases in the *Dictionnaire* (art. "opera"), is based on the operatic practice of letting characters sing in their sleep—such scenes of *sommeil* had already been praised by Diderot (*Oe.* 5:465) and d'Alembert (*Oe. inéd.* 188–89)—and it can be read as a prophetic anticipation of art as play only if we disengage it from its historical and creative context. But de Man aims at a historically accurate reading, for he wants to display the richness of Rousseau's text against both its reductive interpretations and Derrida's reading. De Man urges us not to let "Derrida's version replace Rousseau's own story of his involvement with language. The two stories are not quite alike, and their differences are worth recording" (119). As a result, de Man's reading of the *Essai* conjoins two antagonistic intentions: on the one hand he wants to show, in the manner of deconstructive criticism, the fundamental ambiguity of Rousseau's text; on the other he aims at the reconstruction of an authentic historical meaning against a series of misunderstandings. But misunderstandings can be measured only against an unequivocal historical intentionality, the existence of which de Man himself denies. My purpose is to show that Rousseau's ideas on music were not fundamentally indeterminate if viewed in terms of his intellectual development and the historical context. The interpretative weakness of de Man's essay is to attempt to decide a historical issue with an antihistorical attitude and an ahistorical method.

To begin with, de Man ignores counterevidence that appears in the very midst of his textual choices, a passage that ascribes the silence and peace of music to a uniquely human space rather than to absent meaning:

> Painting is frequently dead and inanimate; it can transport us into the heart of a desert. But as soon as the vocal signs strike our ears they announce a kindred soul. They are, so to speak, the organs of the soul, and even if they paint for us solitude, they intimate that we are not alone. Birds whistle, man alone sings, and we cannot listen to songs or symphonies without telling ourselves instantly: another sensible being is present. [*Essai* 175]

Musical meaning, then, is neither absent nor given by nature, but the human message that "another sensible being" is present. De Man disarmingly protects himself with the caveat that textual support is inevitably selective, but this does not excuse his dismissal of such a patently relevant passage. The pointed juxtaposition of a human musical space and a natural realm of deserts and bird whistles is incompatible with both the commonplace view that Rousseau was a champion of primitivism and de Man's suggestion that he considered the world empty of meaning. The cited contrast between nature and man becomes comprehensible only if we observe how Rousseau's ideas on music developed in opposition to the naturalistic tendency in Rameau's thought. As Derrida rightly remarks, the issues of chapters 13 and 14 of the *Essai* are hard to understand outside their immediate context, the polemic with Rameau (210). We should follow, then, the polemic that de Man ignores.

RAMEAU AND ROUSSEAU

Rousseau, like Nietzsche, was a musician manqué, for he admits in the *Confessions*: "I must have been born for that art, for I started to love it in my childhood, and it alone I have loved persistently throughout the years" (*Oe. Compl.* 1:181).

Rameau is largely to be blamed if that love of music also occasioned much pain. As an instructor of music in Chambéry (1733–37), Rousseau had already valiantly struggled to understand Rameau's *Traité* and had owned a manuscript entitled *Leçons de musique*, which summarizes the composer's teaching (Tiersot 58). Upon arrival in

Paris in 1742, he proposed to the academy a new system of musical notation, which he published the following year as his first work under the title *Dissertation sur la musique moderne*. The revolutionary notation did not catch on, and by an irony of fate Rousseau often had to support himself by copying traditional sheet music (more than 12,000 pages in the 1770s!), but he remained fascinated by the project in spite of its acknowledged faults, and gave it exposure in the *Encyclopédie* (art. "notes")[1] as well as in the *Dictionnaire de musique*. At the end of his life, he started to copy his own opera in the new notation, and he commended it to Burney's attention. Such persistent adherence to a project that was both mathematical and indebted to Rameau is puzzling.

The Project on Musical Notation

Rousseau's project conceives of tonal space within the coordinates of pitch and time. No point in this continuous and homogeneous space is privileged, for "no sound in nature possesses a special and known property by which one could distinguish it every time one hears it" (*Ecrits* 47). Thus musical structures hover in tonal space, and their purely conventional reference point is "as arbitrary as one or the other meridian" (*Ecrits* 52). To compose is to select from within this infinite natural tonal space reference points for pitch and time and to structure a work around them. The size of the temporal units, the measures, is completely arbitrary, but pitch is more complex: Rousseau still follows Rameau in believing that the scales are naturally determined by the overtones of the chosen basic note. Now traditional notation does not exploit the fact that the pattern of a scale repeats itself every octave. Rousseau proposes a notation that would make use of this periodicity by replacing notes with numbers that represent the distance of the sound from the basic note of the key. In C major, for instance, $c = 1$, $d = 2$, $e = 3$, and so on, but the same tones would be represented by different numbers in the keys of D major or E major. Thus Rousseau's notation is based on the pivotal role of tonality in Rameau. Transposition of whole pieces to other keys would become very simple, since the distances (and hence numbers) between tones remain invariant from key to key; however, the numbers would have to be recalculated after every modulation, to represent the distance to the new basic note. The notation clearly becomes cumbersome in music with frequent modulations and is useless in atonal music.[3]

Measures, Rousseau argued, arbitrarily chop up the flow of time, but note lengths are treated as if they had independent temporal values. A quarter note, for instance, can designate not only a longer or a shorter time, depending on the tempo, but also varying proportions of a measure, depending on the meter. Once more, Rousseau wanted to reveal the relative character of music, by defining the length of a note in relation to the beat in the chosen measure: if there are two notes, each will last half a beat; if there are four, each will last a quarter of a beat, and so on. Thus the length of a note would now depend on the chosen units of measures and beats (*Ecrits* 121).

This ingenious, if impractical, system illuminates Rousseau's early music aesthetics. He apparently accepted that scales were natural, but he had already "de-materialized" music by shifting his attention from physical sounds to their interspacing, their relation to each other and the tonal space: "We are not touched, properly speaking, by the sounds, but by the relations (*rapports*) between them" (*Ecrits* 99). He chose an arithmetic sign system, because "numbers merely mark relations, and the expression of sounds is also only the relation they have among themselves." The theory has a distinctly Pythagorean flavor, though Rousseau stresses the constructed quality rather than the naturalness of his system.

In sum, Rousseau's first publication describes an abstract, rational system of musical *écriture* that designates an arbitrary origin and builds a system around it. The proposed signs and their system are arbitrary and nonmimetic, because they bear no resemblance to what they represent; according to Rousseau, there is no more reason to indicate pitch by the height of the note on a staff than to mark the rank of a number by size or thickness (*Ecrits* 38).[4] The mathematical notation is meant to display the mathematical structure of music: "Since music depends on numbers, it should have their arithmetic expression" (*Ecrits* 40). Furthermore, the mathematical notation imposes economy and abstract order, in accordance with the intent of representing all the sounds in the twenty-four keys with a minimum of characters (*Ecrits* 41).

This eminently mathematical theory seems incompatible with Rousseau's later approach to music, yet his attitude remained consistent and only his perception of particulars changed. For the aesthetic and semiotic notions of the project had been fed by two disparate sources: Rameau's theory of harmony, which, especially in its later versions, traced sound to the physical corps sonore, and Rousseau's own preference for de-materialized Pythagorean tonal relations. Rousseau remained so faithful to the antimaterialist impulse that he later turned against not only Rameau's corps sonore but, paradoxically, his glorification of harmony, which now seemed to him to favor physical sound over the spiritual qualities in melody. Thus Rousseau's own later preference for melody was actually fed by the same desire for simplicity and economy that was already at work in the notation project. His changing view of harmony and his turn against Rameau should not blind us to the consistency of his basic perspective.

The Encyclopédie *and the* Dictionnaire de musique

Rousseau must have been distressed that Rameau did not warm to a project inspired by his theory, but apparently the rejection did not hurt his pride. Rameau's next criticism hit where he was most vulnerable, however, at his ambition to become a composer. As book 7 of the *Confessions* and Rameau's *Erreurs* (*Wr.* 5:41–42) record the incident, from opposing angles but in essential agreement about the facts, Mme. Pouplinière had excerpts of Rousseau's *Les muses galantes* performed in the hope of gaining Rameau's support for it, but Rameau tore it to shreds. The criticism embittered Rousseau, and the stage was set for lifelong hostility between the two men.

Rousseau's articles on music theory in the *Encyclopédie* represent somewhat of an enigma in this conflict.[5] In the preface of his *Dictionnaire* Rousseau recalls that he dutifully delivered the articles within the deadline of three months and never saw them again prior to publication.[6] He says in a letter of January 27, 1749, that he intends to use the articles to get even with some of his enemies, which has led some critics to believe that the generally favorable account of Rameau's theory in the articles was largely due to d'Alembert's intervention. But Rousseau graciously accepted d'Alembert's revisions on June 26, 1751, and he would surely have deviated more from the *Encyclopédie* in his later *Dictionnaire* had his acceptance not been genuine. D'Alembert's role was probably restricted to smoothing Rousseau's tone and to signed addenda, which actually became more polemical in the later volumes. Rousseau relied more on Brossard's dictionary perhaps but gave fair attention to Rameau's theory,[7] and he even saw him as a kindred genius and maverick, whose new system (like Rousseau's notation) was a victim of professional jealousy. Rameau's anonymously published *Erreurs* had to acknowledge that the *Encyclopédie* had rendered his theory justice—thought it added nastily that this had happened in spite of M. Rousseau's "confusing" commentaries (*Wr.* 5:70–71).

Rousseau's *Dictionnaire de musique* mostly expands rather than deletes, sharpens, or revises the *Encyclopédie* articles,[8] though it repeatedly chastises Rameau for not having demonstrated the natural roots of the minor mode. Rameau's ingenious system, like Tartini's and Blainville's, "is founded only on analogies and conventions which an inventive person can replace tomorrow by other, more natural ones" (art. "harmonie"). All musical systems now appear as mere hypotheses (art. "système") and accidental products of history. While the *Encyclopédie* still speaks of *the* principles of harmony, the *Dictionnaire* regards the foundation of the keys in *our* harmony no more secure than the affective foundations of the ancient modes. Still, attacks on Rameau alternate with passages of praise and even outright acknowledgments of indebtedness to him (e.g., art. "harmonie"), which indicates that Rousseau, unable to develop his own system of music, had decided to expand his battle with Rameau. For an understanding of Rousseau's philosophical response to Rameau, we have to turn from the *Dictionnaire* to his other writings, in which music aesthetics is developed in conjunction with his social, historical, and psychological views.

Letters to Grimm

Ironically, Rousseau had succeeded as a composer and music theorist by the time he surrendered his dream of becoming a professional musician. His opera, *Le devin du village*, triumphed at Fontainebleau on October 18, 1752, just seven weeks after Pergolesi's *La serva padrona* set off the battle about French and Italian opera, though it was apparently not intended as a contribution to it. Soon afterward, however, Rousseau's views became the very center of the debates.

In a seldom cited letter to Grimm of 1750, Rousseau belittled Italian opera on three grounds. First, it was no national achievement but a universal art that was merely developed first by the Italians. Second, Italian music was merely pleasing and was therefore inferior to emotive French music: "The trills, the passage work, the tracts, the roulades of the Italians highlight the voice and charm the ear, but the seductive sounds of the French go straight to the heart. If music is made only to please, let us give the laurel to the Italians, but if she is to move as well, let us hold it for ours" (Jansen 461). Finally, Rousseau still preferred the variety found in Rameau's operas to the monotonous alternation of arias and recitatives in Italian operas.

Rousseau's perception of Italian and French opera had reversed itself so radically by 1752 that one questions the authenticity of this letter. In any case, the shift in national sympathy was not due to any fundamental change in Rousseau's notions about music: he still favored pathos, humanity, and simplicity but found them now in Italian rather than French melodies. The change of heart was probably triggered by Grimm's devastating review of Destouches's *Omphale* in February 1752, which held up the "sublime" Rameau against those other French composers who could not match "the beautiful and happy simplicity" of Italian music (16:305). Grimm reserved a special place for Rameau in his heart's "temple for privileged mortals," because the composer was a "Proteus, always new, always original, always seizing upon the true and the sublime of each character" (16:307).

The point of Rousseau's anonymous reply was that Rameau, far from being an exception, epitomized French failure in opera. He drowned the voice with a "confused" accompaniment consisting of dense, unrelenting harmony, and while he was unequaled in capturing details and providing contrast, his operas lacked unity. They were merely "deformed monsters, monuments of bad taste that should be relegated to the cloister as their last asylum" (*Ecrits* 448–49). A long and carefully constructed key sentence manages to balance every faint praise with yet another damning judgment:

> One must recognize in Rameau a very great talent, much fire, a striking head, great knowledge of inversions, harmonics, and all kinds of effects; much art to appropriate, alter, decorate, and embellish the ideas of others and to refashion his own; very little facility to invent new things; more skill than fecundity, more knowledge than genius, or at least a genius smothered by too much knowledge; but there is always force and elegance, and very often beautiful melody. [*Ecrits* 447]

Rousseau applies here Rameau's own principles of simplicity and economy against the excesses of his operas, just as later he turns the same principles against Rameau's "overburdened" and "opaque" theory, as we shall see in the chapter on Goethe.

The Letter on French Music

Rousseau's belated entry into the querelle des bouffons, the *Lettre sur la musique française* (November 1753), contained a deeper though less personal attack on Rameau. While still acknowledging that melody is a product of harmony, Rousseau now also claims that verbal rhythm shapes melody and "the unique character of a national music" (*Ecrits* 261, 264). This central thought of Rousseau's later music theory serves here as a principle to rank national styles. The musicality of Italian makes for the glory of its music, whereas the monologue from Lully's *Armide*, hesitating between recitative and aria, illustrates what disastrous consequences the a-musicality of French has for French music: "There is neither measure nor melody in French music because the language is not susceptible to them." Further, the French have no music, "they cannot have any, and if they should ever have one it will be so much the worse for them" (*Ecrits* 322). Ironically, Rameau, the champion of supranational harmony, is thus handicapped by writing operas in a congenitally crippled national language.

We shall pass over the howl of protest that this calculated concluding insult predictably unleashed. We shall rather be concerned with the concept of *unité de mélodie* (music with a single melodic line), which Rousseau introduced in this letter and later developed into a counterpart to Rameau's notion of harmony. Rameau would probably not have attacked Rousseau's theoretically innocuous *Encyclopédie* articles had the *Lettre* not raised more fundamental objections meanwhile. By this time, Rousseau held that the roots of harmony in nature allowed only the growth of some stunted musical plants or weeds, whose cultivation indicated the absence of the fertile linguistic soil necessary for the growth of more "genuine" music. Harmonic, polyphonic, and instrumental music emerged, he thought, from a congenitally weak language that had many "mixed sounds, mute, deaf, or nasal syllables, few sonorous vowels, many consonances and articulations," and inexact prosody (*Ecrits* 261, 265). A language without euphony may have a grammar, but it cannot serve as a soil for good music; people with the sharpest logic will develop the best grammar, but the best music will be written in a country where the language is the most appropriate for it (*Ecrits* 269–70). Italian melody thrives on the "sweetness of language," the "extreme precision in beat," and the "daring of their modulations" (*Ecrits* 279–80), whereas in a "hypothetical" country with an a-musical language, composers have to supplant the missing verbal music by "cold, graceless, and expressionless" modulations, or artificial trills and cadences:

> The impossibility of inventing pleasant songs would force the composers to direct all their attention to harmony, and in the absence of true beauties they would introduce beauties of convention which have hardly any merit other than having conquered difficulty. Instead of good music they would imagine a learned music; to replace the song they would thicken the accompaniment; it would cost them less to pile many bad voices on top of each other than to make one good one out of them. In order to avoid insipidity they would augment confusion; they would believe they made music, though they only made noise. [*Ecrits* 263]

In sum, Rousseau inverts Rameau's priorities by turning his origin into a supplement: harmony becomes a crude substitute for music rooted in language, and instrumental music turns into a "bad supplement" that drowns its melodic source. In an a-musical country the voice is reduced to an "accompaniment of the accompaniment" (*Ecrits* 267, 282).

Rameau responded in his *Observations sur notre instinct pour la musique* (1754) and in his anonymous attack on the *Encyclopédie* articles, maintaining that thoughts on music ought to "consult nature, not our own opinion" (*Wr.* 5:21). The natural source of music was the corps sonore, which grew roots, engendered proportions, progressions, and relations as soon as it was made to resonate (*Wr.* 5:118). Only harmony, "the mother of melody" (*Wr.* 5:46), could engender affects, because melodies were emotionally indeterminate (5:51–52), and only harmony could encode emotions in music scientifically. It was his task, Rameau thought, to make explicit the scientific rules that had always, though "instinctively," guided composition and listening, and he illustrated what he meant by giving a line-by-line analysis of the monologue of Lully's *Armide*, to reveal what Lully had done instinctively and Rousseau had overlooked, namely, the representation of emotions by means of chord progressions and modulations. He even completed passages in Lully's ciphered bass, arguing that he merely carried out Lully's unconscious intentions.

The Making of the Essay on the Origin of Languages

Rousseau intended to respond to Rameau by examining his principles of harmony and corps sonore, but the sketch for this counterattack, the *Examen de deux principes avancés par M. Rameau*, gradually grew in scope until it finally merged with Rousseau's other philosophical concerns. Indeed, as recent research has shown, the broadening of the polemic with Rameau played a formative role in the complex genesis of the *Essay on the Origin of Languages*.

Older research, including Derrida's careful reconsideration of it, held that the *Essay* had received its initial impulse from Rousseau's second discourse on inequality and had become an independent work only in 1761. However, the renewed interest that Derrida's book stimulated in the *Essay*, led to the discovery of a fragment entitled "L'origine de la mélodie," which originally constituted a long digression in the *Examen* and later became, in part, the core material for chapters 18 and 19 of the *Essay*. The fragment thus constitutes a link between the polemic with Rameau and the broad philosophical argument of the *Essay*, which no longer refers to the composer personally. The *Essay* emerges therefore in large part from concerns about music and may be considered "as an indirect philosophical response to Rameau" (Duchez 48).

"L'origine de la mélodie" confronts Rameau's theory of natural harmony with a history that "relies on facts and yields . . . conclusions directly contrary to Rameau's system" (Duchez 75). It sets out to show that music and language are tragically separated twins, that harmony is an artificial modern invention, and that to understand music one has to seek the origin of melody (Duchez 61). For melody, as Rousseau reaffirms in the dictionary article on it, is a "pure work of nature," but only in the sense that it is natural for man.

Musical pitch and rhythm, Rousseau suggests, corresponded originally to verbal stress and rhythm. Greek speech rhythm was constitutive of melody, and melody was just the emphatic expression of grammatical and rhetorical accent.[9] This original link between verbal and musical rhythm delayed the development of pure instrumental music (*Ecrits* 353), but when discourse gradually assumed the form of logical argumentation, the affective power of language became weaker (*Essai* 189), melody was gradually cast off from discourse and was forced to assume an independent but enfeebled existence, and calculated intervals were substituted for subtle inflections (*Essai* 189, 195). This process of separation, which Rousseau describes in Condillac's terms, continued and accelerated precipitously during the barbaric invasions that destroyed the vestiges of harmonious language: the dominance of people raised in the northern climate with crude and musically insensitive ears deprived melody of rhythm, so that it now became shrill and insistent noise without moral pleasure (Duchez 75, *Ecrits* 355).

This account of the verbal origin of melody and music assumes that music is an imitative art, and Rousseau must now, therefore, explicitly reject the principle underlying his project for a musical notation, namely, that "everything in the universe is mere relationship" (*Essai* 151). If imitation makes music into an art, music must be more than just "the art of combining sounds in a manner agreeable to the ear" (153).

Such a rejection of musical formalism does not square with de Man's claim that the value system of the *Essai* "is structural rather than substantial" (127), for Rousseau moved from structure to substance rather than in the reverse direction. If earlier he had considered music as an art of "mere relations," he now held that "sensations often do not affect us as mere sensations but as signs or images, and . . . their moral effects also have moral causes. As our sentiments are not aroused by the colors in a painting, so the sovereignty of music over our souls is not the product of sounds" (*Essai* 147). Hence the musical signifiers must denote: chords must offer something that is neither sound nor chord (*Essai* 167), melodies are "not much as simple objects of the senses," only as "signs of our affections and sentiments" (*Essai* 163).

These are but commonplaces of eighteenth-century musical mimesis, which are of interest to us primarily in relation to Rousseau's earlier project on musical notation. In one sense we see Rousseau trading in constructivist and formalist ideas for a fairly traditional notion of mimesis. But in another sense we find a deep continuity between the two views. Earlier, the art of "mere relations" was prized because it de-materialized sound, whereas now the disappearance of referential content in a merely relational art is suspected of foregrounding the material character of the signifier. Rousseau now perceives in formalism a species of materialism, because, contrary to Pythagorean conceptions, form would not point toward spiritual meaning. The shift is no doubt related not only to Rousseau's changing relationship with Rameau but to internal ambiguities in Rameau's harmonic theory. As the *Encyclopédie* entry on "music" shows, Rameau's theory had originally appealed to Rousseau because it ascribed the power of music to the abstract relations between actual sounds. It did not escape Rousseau's attention that Rameau gave increasingly more attention to the natural and physical foundations of his theory at the cost of the mathematical relations, as evidenced by the new prominence of the corps sonore. This new natural foundation appeared to Rousseau as a form of materialism, for it seemed a preposterous idea to him that the mere vibration of physical bodies could generate musical meaning. His metaphysical and moral aversion to this idea was reinforced by his doubts about its scientific soundness. If the beauties of harmony, especially the minor mode and dissonances, could be appreciated only by educated taste, they had to have originated with man rather than with nature (*Essai* 155–57, 193). Compositional rules had to be cultural conventions.

The defense of melody and imitations that accompanied this two-pronged attack on harmony rested on Rousseau's new perception of music as a historical, temporal, and human phenomenon. Melodic imitations, like outlines in drawing, were de-materialized and therefore superior to the sensuous operatic extravaganzas of color, pageantry, and counterfeit thunders (*Essai* 140, 153). Musical imitations had to transform the sounds and objects of the external world: "The objects must speak in order to make themselves understood; a species of discourse must always supplement the voice of nature in every imitation. Musicians who want to render noise by noise are mistaken. . . . Teach them that noise must be rendered by song, that if frogs are to croak one must make them sing" (*Essai* 161).

The passage illustrates Derrida's suggestion that Rousseau had repeatedly and inadvertently undermined the negative meaning he usually attached to supplements. Though they indicate absence and distance from the origin, they are nevertheless inevitable in the human condition. Musical imitations may be supplements, inadequate replacements of real objects, but their deficiencies cannot be remedied by reverting to an original and "natural" voice—of frogs, for example.

Furthermore, in Rousseau's conception, music is not just a supplement to speech, like writing.[10] If mankind spoke originally "as much by means of sound and rhythm as by means of articulation and voice" (*Essai* 141), then music, a constituent of musiké, originally extended the range of linguistic expression by voicing what is ineffable in words:

> By imitating the inflexions of the voice, melody expresses the complaints, the cries of pain or joy, the menaces and the groans; all the vocal signs of passion are at its disposal. It imitates the accents in languages and the linguistic turns that certain movements of the soul create in every idiom; it speaks instead of merely imitating, and its inarticulate but quick, ardent, and impassioned language has a hundred times more energy than the word itself. [*Essai* 159]

As Derrida says, such states are for Rousseau always already in the process of disintegration and decline. When language moved from accent to articulation, from emotion to thought, from speech rhythm to syntax, and from eloquence to logic, it lost its musicality and became impoverished: "A language that has only articulation and speech possesses only half its wealth; it renders ideas, to be sure, but to represent sentiments and images it also needs rhythm and sounds, i.e., melody; here, then, is what the Greek language possessed and ours is lacking" (*Essai* 141–43).

Since this linguistic decline is irresistible, the destruction of music, accelerated by the "Gothic invention" of harmony, continues in the present and extends into the future: "Abandoning oral accent and attaching itself exclusively to harmonic arrangements, music becomes noisier to the ear and less sweet to the heart. It has already ceased to speak; soon it will no longer sing, and then, for all its chords and harmony, it will no longer have any effect upon us" (*Essai* 179). The malaise of the French language, as described in the *Lettre sur la musique française*, will become universal. In a sense, though hardly to the taste of French linguistic chauvinists, eventually all languages will become French!

The resolution of Rameau's "eternal musical laws" into historically and socially determined rules engenders a heightened awareness of the temporality of music in melody and rhythm. Whereas painting is spatial, music is the art of time (*Essai* 171) and therefore best suited to the mimesis of the inner life: "The emotions aroused by successive impressions of a discourse are very different from those generated by the presence of the object, which allows for a total instantaneous overview. . . . Visible signs render the imagination more exact, but our interest is better excited by sounds" (*Essai* 35). As an art of absence, music mobilizes memory and imagination, both because it evokes for us a cultural tradition and because attention to repetition enhances musical pleasure (*Essai* 155 and 165).

Rousseau in Perspective

De-materializing sound, equating melody with outline, focusing on the representation of time rather than space, preferring vocal to instrumental music, postulating a primeval unity between language and music, insisting that music imitate the passions—all these indicate Rousseau's turn from the world to inwardness, in an almost Rilkean sense that "nowhere is world but within us." But Rousseau's particular choices among these polar opposites seem often to have been arbitrary, and his fundamental antinaturalist disposition could easily have found reasons to choose the alternatives. His de-materialization of sound, for instance, led ultimately to a preference for melody, but it could have become a Pythagorean preference for harmony, as the project for notation indicates.

But if he turned away from nature rather than back to it in the popular sense, this cannot be read in de Man's manner as a "negation of the substantiality of meaning" or a "negation of all presence."[11] By turning a partial loss—that of the physical world—into a "negation of all presence," de Man disregards the gain in the personal voice, the expressive-imitative doubling of the self in music. To be sure, the singing voice resounds in a world that is emptied of metaphysical presence. The power of music for Rousseau is precisely to create presence in the condition of absence, not by replacing or reminding us of the divine but, in the words of his *Essai*, by creating a human space: "As soon as the vocal signs strike our ears, they announce a kindred soul. They announce a being similar to us; they are, so to speak, the organs of the soul, and even if they paint for us solitude, they intimate that we are not alone" (*Essai* 175).

The German Romantics, equally aware of their metaphysical separation, followed Rousseau in exploring inwardness rather than in uniting with nature in the conventional sense. But this general affinity only highlights their different concepts of music. For Rousseau, music was so deeply and directly lodged in the individual voice that he could not appreciate polyphonic, harmonic, or instrumental music. His demand that music be simple, melodic, and vocal issues from a radical subjectivity rather than a regressive primitivism. Ironically, Rousseau's authority is in part to blame if French composers until Berlioz contented themselves with pleasant, simple music that was harmless compared to the radical subjectivity of a Beethoven. By insisting on a direct encoding of sentiments in music, Rousseau failed to see that musical forms without voice or imitation could have meaning. Wackenroder, Novalis, and E. T. A. Hoffmann, on the other hand, came to the new insight that classical-romantic instrumental music can speak where words fail. Rousseau anticipated the mood, temperament, and predicament of the coming generations, but he championed the wrong musical means for their expression.

Rousseau's attempt to find in history an answer to Rameau also provides a final comment on the contemporary critical issues discussed above. De Man misreads the *Essai* because he disregards its genetic impetus. Derrida arrives at a historically more plausible interpretation, in spite of his intention of illustrating the general proposition "that reading should free itself, at least in its axis, from the classical categories of history" (7). Such denigration of history is salutary as an antidote to both mere description and mechanical studies of influence, but it cannot render genetic approaches superfluous altogether. Indeed, one of the admirable achievements of Derrida's book is to explore persistently, cogently, painstakingly, and lucidly the pervasive ambiguities in Rousseau's work—by means of historical evidence. Is he not, just in this sense, an heir to Rousseau battling the latter-day Rameaus?

7 D'ALEMBERT

D'Alembert's serious interest in music theory seems to have been aroused when Rameau presented his *Mémoire* to the academy in 1751. D'Alembert actually presided over the committee that enthusiastically endorsed Rameau's work on December 10, 1749, and concluded:

> The fundamental bass, found by the author and anchored in nature itself, is the principle of harmony and melody; . . . nobody before him has reduced [the facts of music] to such a tight and broad system. . . . Harmony, which is usually subjected to arbitrary rules or suggested by blind experience, has become through M. Rameau's work a more geometric science. . . . This is why M. Rameau, after having acquired a great reputation with his work in practical music, merits also . . . the philosophers' approbation and praise. [Rameau *Wr.* 3:244–46]

To similar words in the *Discours préliminaire* of the *Encyclopédie*, d'Alembert added: "I hasten to seize the occasion to celebrate this artist-philosopher in a discourse dedicated principally to the praise of great men. His merit, which he compelled our century to acknowledge, will only be well known once time will have silenced envy; and his name, dear to the most enlightened part of our nation, nobody shall be able to tarnish" (*Oe.* 1:80–81).

But mere praise was not enough; d'Alembert actually produced an *haute vulgarisation* of Rameau's theory under the title *Elémens de musique, théorique et pratique, suivant les principes de M. Rameau* (1752). The popularization demanded simplification, but quite possibly d'Alembert deliberately imposed limitations on his presentation to deflate Rameau's grandiose ambitions. In any case, the *Elémens* relegates all mathematics to the footnotes and omits references to the physical resonance in the corps sonore as well as to the metaphysics of harmony: "The sole purpose is to show how one can deduce from a single principle of experience the laws of harmony, which artists have found, so to speak, by groping" (*Eléms.* V–VI). As Condillac elegantly remarked when censoring the book, "M. Rameau should be flattered to see at the reach of all intelligent readers a system of which he discovered the principles, and which, as I see it, needs only to be known in order to be approved"—an admiration that Condillac seconded in his *Essay on the Origin of Human Knowledge* (2.1.5). Indeed, when d'Alembert sent Rameau a copy of "my or rather your work," the latter publicly expressed his gratitude to that "savant of simple manners and elevated sentiments" for presenting him with "the most glorious testimony to which an author could ever aspire" (Rameau *Wr.* 6:233, 238). He even admitted that his ideas had never before been expressed so clearly.

But the honeymoon was short. Though d'Alembert's treatise was generally well received, Estève immediately disputed the identity of octaves and the distinction between sound and noise; more important, he claimed that Rameau presented hypotheses rather than demonstrations. Eventually, d'Alembert accepted all these objections. The same year the querelle des bouffons broke out. Though d'Alembert may have disagreed privately with the pro-Italian sentiments of his friends,[1] his public stance must have given Rameau the impression that he was a critic of French opera. Rameau, apparently eager to maintain good relations, tried to restrict his criticism of the *Encyclopédie* to Rousseau's contributions, but at the end of his *Erreurs* he could no longer refrain from enlightening the editors to the effect that "in music one merely interprets nature, and opinions are misplaced" (*Wr.* 5:128).

The editors resented the schoolmasterly admonition and declared their unequivocal support of Rousseau in a prefatory note to the sixth volume of the *Encyclopédie* (1756). They also expressed their feigned incredulity that Rameau should have been the author of such intemperate attacks and ridiculed the pamphlet's alleged claim that geometry was founded on music. Rameau, probably still unaware of this note, continued his attack on the music articles in the *Encyclopédie* the same year, and even the next year he attempted to mend his fences by claiming to quarrel only with Rousseau. It was too late. D'Alembert's articles "fondamental" and "gamme" in the seventh volume (1757) outlined his substantial objections to Rameau's theory, and he summarized his final position in the introduction to the revised, 1762 edition of the *Elémens*.

As the article "fondamental" restates, d'Alembert's central objec-

tion to Rameau was that the overtones of a fundamental sound generated only the notes of the major chord; the minor third was not
among the overtones. Concerning fundamental chords, to Rameau's
dismay, d'Alembert identified ten rather than two basic types. Even
worse, though d'Alembert refused to treat chords algebraically or ge-
ometrically, he thought of them as combinatorial possibilities rather
than realities offered by nature. Whereas Rameau believed that nature allowed only a small number of chords, d'Alembert remembered
that Rameau had also thought of chords as composites of major, minor, diminished, or augmented thirds: "I fear that most musicians,
some blinded by routine, others by the systems, have not drawn
from harmony all the knowledge they could have, and they excluded
an infinity of chords which could produce good effects on many occasions." If, for instance, c-e-g-b is a bona fide chord, why should
c-e-g♯-c, c-e-g♯-b, c-eb-g-b, c-eb-gb-c, or c-eb-gb-b not be equally permissible? Does reason, cultural tradition, or nature decide on such
matters? D'Alembert did not go as far as to suggest that the ear may
get accustomed to newly invented tonal combinations, and he cautiously admitted that the ear and experience must decide; but, by
confronting actuality with logical possibilities, he encouraged experi-
mentation that might accustom the ear to new chords. In remarks
added to Rousseau's article on genre, he actually indicated that history and culture condition the ear.

D'Alembert's albeit hesitant suggestions for a new chord vocabulary indicate that for him musical laws were broader and more flexible than they were for Rameau. As stated in the *Réflexions sur la
musique* (1777), he considered these laws not as mere descriptions or
codifications of nature but as means of reshaping it and opening up
new possibilities: "Once we find the theory of music, it will not be,
as one may first think, an object of pure speculation that explains
poorly or well the pleasure awakened in us by melody and harmony.
Discovering the true sources of that pleasure, we could also find
there the means to provide new pleasures in that art. Music could
then leap forward like the construction of lenses did after finding the
true laws of light refraction" (*Oe. inéd.* 142).

If music belonged to the realm of the possible and the potential,
then the fundamental bass could hardly be a product of the physical
laws of sonorous bodies as Rameau had claimed. Nature's "first"
product, the perfect major chord, was lacking even the first natural

overtone, the octave. "All other chords, be they consonances or dissonances, are absolutely products of art, and the more they are dissonant, the more artificial they are. . . . We ought to reject therefore
the principle that the accompaniment represents the corps sonore
and we ought at least to doubt the rules that were established solely
on that fundament." Hence d'Alembert agreed with Rousseau that
most of Rameau's rules were not natural laws but merely "products
of reflection," and that harmony was accompaniment which should
never overpower melody: since "harmony serves to nourish a beautiful song . . . let us recognize melody as being usually the principal
object that pleases the ear."

The concluding section of the article "fondamental" must have disturbed Rameau the most, for it questioned the validity and appropri-
ateness of mathematical approaches to music, undermining thereby
Rameau's claim to be a savant worthy of the academy:

> The consideration of proportions and progressions was a totally false ex-
> planation for the pleasure offered by consonances. . . . The geometricians
> who wanted to introduce calculation into that science were quite wrong
> to look for the cause of musical pleasure in a source quite alien to it. . . .
> How strongly do we have to disapprove then of some musicians who
> amass numbers in their writings, believing that all such machinery is nec-
> essary for the art. . . . Physical explanations and arguments are not more,
> but rather actually less, useful to the theory of musical art than geometric
> calculations.

Specifically, d'Alembert found the physical explanation of music in
the first chapter of Rameau's *Génération harmonique* purely conjec-
tural and inadequate.[2]

The revised edition of the *Elémens* praised Rameau for tackling the
chaos in music theory but reaffirmed that progressions and proportions were of little use: "One should not look here for the striking
evidence which is proper only to works in geometry and is found so
rarely when physics is involved. The theory of musical phenomena is
always penetrated by a sort of metaphysics . . . which contributes its
own natural obscurity. One should not expect in this matter what
one calls a demonstration" (Rameau *Wr.* 6:466).[3]

In sum, d'Alembert had two fundamental objections to Rameau's
rationalist principles: the mathematics of chords was irrelevant to the
aesthetic pleasure of music, and the attempt to turn music into a de-

ductive system was a mistaken application of the *esprit de système*. Music will progress only "if those who cultivate it will refuse to commit themselves to all systems and not be captivated by any routine" (Rameau *Wr.* 6:226). Thus d'Alembert seems to have been as skeptical about mathematics in music theory as Buffon, Diderot, and Condillac were about its application to natural science. But his objection to deduction and systematization went hand in hand with his suggestion of broadening the imaginative scope and vocabulary of music. Acquaintance with the purely invented and therefore limitless vocabulary of mathematics allowed him to conceive of a musical organization that had little debt to nature. His pioneering, though seldom appreciated, contribution to music theory was the idea that all possible combinations of thirds within a given key are potential musical materials, not only the ones considered to be rooted in nature. Indeed, his desire to enrich the vocabulary of music complements his argument that no systems be imposed upon music until we have broadened our experience of sounds. The primary function of systems is not to discard what is unfit but to foster new discoveries by means of errors (*Oe. inéd.* 140–41).

It must be noted, however, that the proposed combinatorial expansion of the chord vocabulary was for d'Alembert a means to refine musical mimesis. The premise of the *Discours préliminaire* is that "music which does not paint anything is just noise" (*Oe.* 1:39), and d'Alembert actually proposed broadening mimesis by writing compositions whose impact on us would resemble the impact of specific external objects and events. A frightening object, for instance, could be represented by a similarly frightening noise (*Oe.* 1:39). This was a first step toward the internalization of imitation, toward using psychic rather than physical analogies, which must account for Rousseau's enthusiastic acknowledgment of the *Discours* on June 26, 1751:[4] "I find your idea about musical imitation very appropriate and new. The musician's art is not at all to render direct paintings of objects; rather, he puts the soul into a disposition which resembles the disposition produced by the presence of the objects themselves" (*Corr.* 2:160).

Unfortunately, d'Alembert equivocated on what he meant, and in a clarification to his *Elémens de philosophie* he reduced indirect representation to a traditional notion of figure: sunrise, for instance, could be represented by slowly rising and swelling notes. When music undertakes to paint or recall silent objects, it ought to substitute notes for what we ought to perceive (*Oe.* 2:259). The association is produced here not by induced fear or joy but by means of a rather complex intellectual process that necessitates wit and excludes, as d'Alembert acknowledged already in the *Discours* (1:39), the uneducated part of the audience. The same intellectual penchant made him favor Arnaud's proposal for a musical rhetoric that would have utilized intellectual figures heavily (*Oe. inéd.* 157–58).

The conventionality of d'Alembert's notion of synaesthetic imitation struck no less a reader than Frederick the Great. Upon d'Alembert's repeated request for an opinion, he finally responded by taking issue with the proposed broadening of mimesis: "Music can properly articulate only the emotions of the soul, and everything that can be the domain of the other senses does not belong therefore to the hearing." Musicians may well express the sweet and quiet joy felt at sunrise, "but to climb from the lowest string to the highest and descend again according to the wishes of a geometrician can never establish the least analogy between the spectacle of a beautiful morning and articulated sounds. Let us limit music therefore to the expression of the emotions in the soul, and let us refrain from rendering the frog's croaking, the raven's crowing, and a hundred other things whose musical images are as pernicious as those of poetry" (Friedrihk II, *Oe.* 24:466). Frederick had the right attitude, but he too conflated naturalistic sound reproductions with figurative representations of a sunrise, and so d'Alembert could reply that he never allowed music to paint everything, he merely suggested that music can sometimes "put us into states of mind which resemble those produced by certain objects of sight" (*Oe.* 5:270). Frederick's objections to figurative imitation were thereby left unanswered.

D'Alembert intended to broaden mimesis in part because he thought that music was imperfect, inherently vague, and too indeterminate to represent the emotions well. In order to refine it, one had to translate or interpret it, either by pinning down its emotional content with words or by using figures of wit. Instrumental music represented the affects poorly and was simply bad music (*Oe. inéd.* 135, 182).

8 DIDEROT

The contrast between the intellectual clarity and the dark recesses of Diderot's mind and heart is preeminently evident in his reflections on music. Though less extensive than his writings on the fine arts, Diderot's preoccupation with music highlights more clearly his reservations about mimesis. He spontaneously loved instrumental music, and he developed in his youth a theory with strong mathematical and formalist leanings. Though he abandoned the premises of this theory later, he remained uneasy with Batteux's aesthetics, and as I shall show, his commitment to mimesis remained hesitant.[1]

THE AESTHETICS OF *RAPPORTS*

The young Diderot apparently favored Rameau's operas as well as his theory of music. Chapter 13 of *Les Bijoux indiscrets* (1748) takes a satiric view of opera, but Rameau (Uremifasolasiututut) is decidedly preferred to the followers of Lully (Umiutsol). The good man may be "occasionally asleep," but for the most part he is "unique, brilliant, sophisticated, learned, occasionally all too learned." This discoverer of the sources of harmony gave the public "soaring ariettas, sensuous arias, and expressive tone-paintings," and "captured the fine nuances that separate the tender from the lustful, the lustful from the passionate, and the passionate from the lascivious" (*Oe.* 4:174–76).

The same year, 1748, Diderot also published a collection entitled *Mémoires sur différents sujets de mathématiques*, which contained several pieces on music, among them a study on the *Principes d'acoustique* that was heavily indebted to Sauveur, Euler, and Rameau. Music was chosen here as the touchstone of all the arts because it was amenable to scientific treatment and seemed to be rooted in nature. If, as Euler and Rameau had claimed, consonances had physical foundations and gave pleasure to everybody, music may develop "invariable principles and a unified theory" (*Oe.* 4:85).

The *Principes* states that beauty is to be defined and measured by the quantity and complexity of relations (*rapports*) within the object. The principle derives from two different sources: the mathematics of harmony and the doctrine held by St. Augustine (*Musik*), Crousaz, André, Hutcheson, and others, that beauty is the synthesis of a manifold. Elements common to these two traditions form the core of the aesthetics in Diderot's *Principes*, the *Lettre sur les sourds et muets* ("Letter on the Deaf and Dumb," 1751) and the *Encyclopédie* article "beau" (1752).

Following Euler, Diderot seeks the "eternal and immutable" norms of beauty (*Oe. esth.* 391). Actually, as Crocker has shown, Diderot's criteria for beauty include not only such objective standards as the simplicity or complexity of relations in the artwork but also subjective ones: the *perception* of tonal relations gives pleasure (*Oe.* 4:84); paintings, poems, and music please us "by means of relations we perceive in them" (*Oe.* 1:406).

It remains uncertain, however, to what extent the perception distorts the actual relations in the object. In the *Lettre* and the article "beau," the actual and perceived relations are labeled respectively "external beauty" and "beauty in relation to the subject" (*Oe. esth.* 418), but, in effect, unmodified "beauty" usually means relational beauty: "The *perception* of relations is therefore the fundament of the beautiful" (*Oe. esth.* 428; my italics). Yet, while Diderot makes beauty dependent on perception and its psychological determinants, he is critical of Wolff and Crousaz for adopting a subjective notion of beauty (*Oe. esth.* 395). The *Principes* shows that the hesitation between objectivism and psychologism is, in part, produced by a conflict between Diderot's intellectual elitism and his democratic sympathies. Since an aesthetic object contains complex relations, only an elite with specially trained and refined organs will appreciate it; unsophisticated people can enjoy only simple melodies (*Oe.* 4:85). The intellectual bias is weakened by conceding that listening is not intellectual (Belaval 74–75) and that the relations may be perceived unconsciously. This actually amounts to the Leibnizian formula that music is unconscious counting:

Does the soul know [these laws] without comprehending them, somewhat in the manner we judge the size and distance of objects without the least notion of geometry? . . . We do not decide anything about this; suffice it to observe that the most perfect chords are those which entail the simplest interrelations, that these relations can affect our soul in two ways, via sentiments or apperception, and that perhaps they affect most people in the first manner. [*Oe.* 4:106]

I do not require . . . that somebody attending a concert should know . . . that a sound has the ratio of 2:4 or 4:5 to another. It is enough to perceive and feel . . . that the sounds of this musical piece have relations, either among themselves or with other objects. [*Oe. esth.* 419]

The article "beau" distinguishes between two kinds of relations under "external beauty," those within the aesthetic object and those relating it to other entities, such as the imitated object. Characteristically revising Hutcheson's terminology, Diderot calls the first "real beauty" (*beau réel*) and the second "relative beauty" (*beau relatif*) (*Oe. esth.* 422). Hence real beauty is to be found in pure, nonimitative music.

The self-contained beauty of the *beau réel* joins the neoclassical tradition with the mathematics of harmony. Whether defined in strictly mathematical terms or by general principles of symmetry, regularity, and order, real beauty is based on the formal and structural properties of the object, without reference to mimetic, moral, or other external criteria. Diderot anticipates thereby the notion of autonomous art and its judgment in terms of organization and complexity, though he is not ready to accept a formalism without objective criteria: the mathematics of harmonic relations should eventually make scientific aesthetics possible. However, such an aesthetics seems implausible to him, because we perceive only a fraction of the actual relations, and this varies in size and composition from listener to listener. Short of constructing a full-fledged theory of perception, there can be no reliable science of perceived beauty. Hence Diderot is dissatisfied with purely formal notions of real beauty and concentrates on the rapports that relate the art object to the world and that ground aesthetic judgments in extrinsic criteria.

Yet mimetic art is equally subjective, because the relations "out there" must also pass through the distorting filter of perception. A science of mimesis faces the additional obstacle that there exists an inevitable discrepancy between the object and the medium of representation, as the central section of the rambling but stimulating *Lettre* inadvertently shows while treating the difficulties of representing psychic life. Perfect imitations are impossible, because "the state of our soul is one thing, the account we render of it to ourselves or others is a different matter. . . . Our soul is a moving tableau which we incessantly paint; we spend much time on rendering it faithfully, but it is a totality which exists all at once: the mind does not march step-wise, measured out by expression" (*Oe.* 1:369).

We shall encounter a similar concern with the mimetic weakness of sound in the writing of British critics, but Diderot's concept is less rigidly mimetic because it includes play and allusion. For him, the limitations of representation result not from the poverty of the medium but from its very wealth, its suggestive multiplicity: art often flourishes at the expense of precision, as Diderot knew so well from observing his own imagination and wit. This subordination of referentiality to density and wealth of texture is indicated in the *Lettre* by the daring concepts of hieroglyph and emblem. "We have to distinguish in all discourses between thought and expression. . . . Poetic discourse does not merely interlink powerful terms to expose thought with force and elegance. . . . It is furthermore a tissue of amassed hieroglyphs which paint that thought. In this sense one could say that all poetry is emblematic" (*Oe.* 1:374). The passage seems to plead for the Horatian "ut pictura poesis," but the striking image of amassed hieroglyphs suggests that more is to be rendered than a plausible copy of thought and emotion: as the complex image inevitably assumes a life of its own, the represented content fades into the background.

Diderot's interlocutor justly asks why music must, then, represent at all if its "tissue of hieroglyphs" is more indistinct, general, and suggestive than that of language. Certain compositions delight everybody, though they neither conjure up images nor constitute hieroglyphic paintings. But Diderot, without fully repudiating nonrepresentational music, disapproves of such an extension of his ideas on two grounds. Music without reference is like a rainbow, which gives only the pleasure of "pure and simple sensations"; if the pleasure is to be of a higher order, the "truth of imitation" must accompany harmony (*Oe.* 1:407–08). This suggests that matching the copy against the original gives intellectual pleasure. Indeed, according to Diderot, listeners seduced by the visceral pleasures of sheer sound cannot judge the quality of the imitation: "They almost always exceed that gentle emotion in which the sentiment does not detract from the comparison" (*Oe.* 1:408).

Harmony seems to appeal, then, to volatile sensibilities incapable of the mental effort required by imitation. But Diderot does not seriously believe in this traditional defense of imitation, for he almost immediately reaffirms the primacy of pleasure in sheer sound: the "light and fugitive" musical hieroglyphs are easily lost or misinterpreted; the "most beautiful symphony would produce no great effect if the infallible and immediate pleasure of pure and simple sensations did not infinitely surpass the frequently equivocal expression. Painting shows the object itself, poetry describes it, music scarcely excites an idea of it; intervals and duration of sound are its only resources" (*Oe.* 1:408). Indeed, the closing series of rhetorical questions further loosens the tie between art and its represented objects by suggesting that musical signs need not have intrinsic kinship with the objects or events imitated:

> What analogy is there between such sketches [of intervals and duration] on the one hand and spring, darkness, solitude . . . and most objects on the other? How is it then that among the three imitative arts the one whose expression is the most arbitrary and the least precise should speak most forcefully to our soul? Is it that in showing less of the objects it leaves more to our imagination? [*Oe.* 1:408–09]

If Diderot embraces "the doctrine of musical imitation of nature" (Lang. *Did.* 103), the affair is but a brief flirtation. The coquetry is evident in the article "beau." Planned as an answer to Batteux, this article pays much more attention to internal beauty than to the relative beauty of representation, whose treatment by Hutcheson Diderot finds utterly conventional and uninteresting (*Oe. esth.* 405). His fascination is with André's *Essai sur le beau* (1741), in which beauty is said to be essential, natural, or artificial, depending on the degree to which it is based on eternal, historico-social, or merely arbitrary rules respectively (*Oe. esth.* 407). Imitation does not seem to be a source of beauty. Diderot's own distinction between real and relative beauty, an adaptation of André's categories, also dismisses imitative beauty; relative beauty depends only on the environmental context, the resemblance of the object to others, and the relation of the object to our temperament and affects. A phrase that is beautiful in one dramatic situation may be ridiculous in another; moreover, a tulip is beautiful only in relation to other tulips, flowers, or plants (*Oe. esth.* 421–23). The relations of a phrase or of painted tulips to entities in the world do not seem to interest Diderot. In his writings on music he is more intrigued by relations of context and contiguity than by the relation between signifier and signified.

In short, the young Diderot hesitates between an aesthetics of internal (mathematical and harmonic) relations and a mimesis relating the artwork to its model. In subsequent years he opted for mimesis, not because he had resolved for himself its problems but rather because he had become disenchanted with the mathematics of music and, as *De l'interprétation de la nature* (1753) indicates, with mathematics in general. The shift was surely related also to Diderot's acquaintance with Rousseau, who criticized Diderot's rapports in the *Encyclopédie* (art. "consonance") as pure hypothesis. The critique was seconded in d'Alembert's article "fondamental." As a result, the rapports and the concomitant idea of autonomous artworks disappeared from Diderot's aesthetics; but, as I shall show, his acceptance of mimesis remained tentative.

RAMEAU'S NEPHEW

The composer's name in the title points toward the debates between the philosophes and Rameau, but *Rameau's Nephew* is so rich and complex that this is easily overlooked. Yet, it was surely part of Diderot's strategy to settle accounts with the uncle by means of the nephew, a historically insignificant figure who wasted away his life as a buffoon and a sycophant at the tables of the Parisian aristocracy, to achieve, finally, a dubious immortality courtesy of Diderot, and, via Diderot and Goethe, as the representative of modern alienated consciousness in Hegel's *Phenomenology*. We should remember, however, that the literary fame attaches to Diderot's fictional figure and not to the historical Jean-François Rameau. As in the case of *D'Alembert's Dream*, Diderot uses a real person in fiction to efface the speaker.

The partners in the dialogue, Moi and Lui, agree that the composer was a hard, brutal, inhuman, and miserly man, "a bad father, bad husband, and bad uncle" (*Oe.* 5:395); as Lui complains, this man "of stone . . . could see my tongue hanging out a foot long and not give me a glass of water" (*Oe.* 5:460). Such inhumanity could be overlooked in a Racine, but Moi wonders whether the Italians will not bury the "disconnected ideas," the "clatter," the "insipid mythology," and the "triumphal marches" of Rameau, just as Rameau had buried Lully (*Oe.* 5:390, 395, 462).

Lui's rhetorical theory of musical mimesis (5:458–68) is in any case deliberately set against the "many incomprehensible visions and apocalyptic truths" of Rameau's mathematical system (5:390). Melody imitates "declamation if the model is . . . a thinking being . . . and physical noise if the model is inanimate" (5:459). The song "twists itself" around its prototype, declamation (5:459); recitatives and arias should therefore easily convert into one another. Instrumental symphonies are imitations of an imitation, for they are to songs as songs are to declamation (5:461). Moreover, declamation is emotional rather than intellectual: "Passion rules over prosody almost at will." The melodic line ought to be dictated by "the animal cry of the passions," not by unnaturally witty and epigrammatic librettos that read like La Rochefoucauld's maxims or Pascal's *Pensées*: "Each phrase must be short, its meaning broken off for suspense, so that the musician can make use equally of the whole or of a part, omit a word or repeat it, add a new one he needs, turn the phrase inside out like a jellyfish without destroying the sense" (5:466). Any passion will suffice, "provided it is energetic enough to supply the musician with a pattern."

This stretches the rhetorical concept of music to its limits, where words abdicate their governing role and become arbitrary instruments of the passions. Indeed, the whole dialogue climaxes in Lui's subsequent musical performance, where language falls back into a subservient role:

He jumbled together thirty different airs, French, Italian, comic, tragic—in every style. Now he sank to the pit in baritone, then straining in falsetto he tore to shreds the upper notes of some air, imitating the while the stance, walk and gestures of the several characters; being in succession furious, mollified, lordly, sneering. First a damsel weeps, and he reproduces her kittenish ways; next he is a priest, a king, a tyrant; he threatens, commands, rages. Now he is a slave, he obeys, calms down, is heartbroken, complains, laughs; never overstepping the proper tone, speech, or manner called for by the part . . . he was kept in the grip of mental possession, an enthusiasm so close to madness that it seemed doubtful whether he would recover. He might have to be put into a cab and be taken to a padded cell. . . . His art was complete—delicacy of voice, expressive strength, true sorrow. . . . . Did I admire? Yes, I did admire. Was I moved to pity? I was moved. But a streak of derision was interwoven with these feelings and denatured them.

Yes, you too would have burst laughing at the way in which he aped the different instruments. With swollen cheeks and a somber throaty sound, he would give us the horns and bassoons. For the oboes he assumed a shrill yet nasal voice, then speeded up the emission of sound to an incredible degree for the strings, for whose tones he found close analogues. He whistled piccolos and warbled traverse flutes, singing, shouting, waving about like a madman, being himself dancer and ballerina, singer and prima donna, all of them together and the whole orchestra, the whole theater; then redividing himself into twenty separate roles, running, stopping, glowing at the eyes like one possessed, frothing at the mouth.

The heat was stifling and the sweat, which, mixed with the powder in his hair, ran down the creases of his face, was dripping and marking the upper part of his coat. What did he not attempt to show me? He wept, laughed, sighed, looked placid or melting or enraged. He was a woman in a spasm of grief, a wretched man sunk in despair, a temple being erected, birds growing silent at sunset, waters murmuring through cool and solitary places or else cascading from a mountaintop, a storm, a hurricane, the anguish of those about to die, mingled with the whistling of the wind and the noise of thunder. He was night and its gloom, shade and silence—for silence itself is depictable in sound. He had completely lost his senses. [5:463–65]

Spitzer rightly remarks that Lui departs from his own mimetic theory in that his gestures "come more and more to constitute a reality in themselves" (*Diderot* 153), though it is doubtful that Diderot let Lui be seduced by his rapacious imagination as a warning against the volatility of his own mind.[2] This would ascribe to the text a coherent authorial self and intentionality. As Hegel had already indicated and as Trilling has more recently reaffirmed, the portrayal of Lui's alienated consciousness depreciates the notion of an integral self. Both Hegel and Trilling minimize, however, the general implications of this: Hegel by contrasting Lui's "base" self with Moi's intact one, Trilling by believing that Lui is more conventional than Hegel paints him (46). I intend to show by means of the incongruity between the music theory and the performance that the text radically diffuses the self.

Trilling notes that Lui's culminating performance propounds the idea that Nietzsche was to articulate a century later, namely, that man's true metaphysical destiny expresses itself not in morality but in art (33). But the Nietzschean shadow cast over Lui's performance and Diderot's text belongs to the mature Nietzsche, who ruthlessly destroys all metaphysical illusions, not to the author of *The Birth of Tragedy*, who replaces the metaphysics of knowledge and morality with a metaphysics of music. The aesthetics of *The Birth of Tragedy* still upholds the Apollonian principle of individuation, no matter how fragile this self ultimately is in facing cosmic chaos. According to Nietzsche, the primal creative urge in the self, one of the two indispensable forces in all great art, breaks forth by means of preverbal sounds.

These shouts and cries are the origin of music for Lui as well, but only in theory. While his mimesis proclaims that the singing voice is the highest instrument for revealing the impalpable self, Lui has no such self to express, and he does not know what he is at bottom (5:439). He surely has no moral self to embody through voice as his theory would demand, and, though he may have "understood good music far better than good morals" (5:457), his aesthetic identity is no less diffuse. Approaching him in Trilling's sense, from an aesthetic rather than a moral perspective, we note that he creates no genuine music and his performance often sinks to the level of pantomime. Standing in the shadow of his uncle, he is essentially impotent, and his performance is symptomatically just an imitation of music. His mimicry and general cynicism are incompatible with the "moralistic mimesis" he adopts from his age. His kings, priests, and weeping damsels may be genuine selves, but their impersonation covers up his own missing identity. His performance divides Moi as well, for Moi, far from being carried away by emotion, is torn between pitying the impersonated characters and deriding Lui. The derision "denatures" the compassion.

The alienation deepens as the performance progresses and Lui turns to the imitation of instruments, natural objects, and sounds, for to "ape" the instruments with the voice was to violate the hierarchy of sounds, which involved a degrading dehumanization of the voice. As Lui himself states earlier, violins merely ape singers; should singers ever ape violins, "acrobatics will have replaced beauty" (5:461).

The sheer technical virtuosity of the mimicry reveals its supplemental character, its inferiority to language and music. Diderot's brilliant verbal description of it highlights Lui's inarticulateness.

It may be argued that this verbal brilliance of Diderot's text provides a principle of integration. But the unity of the text is a priori undermined by the diffused identity of Moi, a self to be sure but not the author's. To speak of a "Diderot-Moi," a "philosophe with his archaic love of simple truth and morality, with his clearly defined self and his commitment to sincerity" (Trilling 44) is to overlook the possibility that Moi may have been introduced to efface the authorial self. Trilling himself admits that Moi's "divided judgment of Lui's performance weakens his identity" (45), whereas others have noted that Moi comes off remarkably pale with respect to Lui.

Some critics believe that the moral and intellectual unity of the text is balanced by an aesthetic unity identifiable by means of the metaphor of musical structure. But the dialogue explodes logical chains and organic forms with equal vigor. The texture of the dialogue may be compared to the interweaving of themes in a symphony, but this does not impute to it a personal expressive form in the sense of Nietzsche's *Birth of Tragedy*. The aesthetic metaphysics in the latter assumes the creative, shaping force of a strong self, a concept with which Nietzsche struggled to the end of his life. Diderot's text, in any case, diffuses the self into several weaker selves that obliterate rather than balance each other.

The diffusion of the self is marked by the weakened role of the signifiers in the text. To read it as Diderot's mimetic credo (e.g., as Levaillant does in Duchet and Launay 207) is naive, and not only because Lui's theory is contradicted by his performances and by Moi. Indeed, the very presentation and structure of the dialogue dislocate and weaken the traditional linkage between signifier and signified. For the familiar superiority of language over music is replaced here by a circular interrelation between the various arts, each of which now functions alternately as signifier and signified, model and mirror, for an other. Lui's performance imitates imaginary operas by means of sounds and gestures, and we witness this by means of the verbal mediation of the text: Lui's representation of music is duplicated by Diderot's representation of the pantomime. Yet language both theoretically and practically informs the music of those operas that Lui "performs" mimetically. The reader is referred from lan-

guage to music to pantomime and back to language, each imitating
and constituting a meaning that never finds support in some objective, preexistent reality. In this circular constructedness, embodied in
the text but not enunciated in discursive language, Diderot decisively
departs from traditional mimesis and surrenders the demand for presence which is still so powerful in Rousseau. Indeed, it is here that
self and sign are subjected to a most radical metaphysical deflation.

Diderot never articulated this explicitly, and he never decisively
surrendered the principle of mimesis: "Beautiful chords . . . please
my ear; [they are] abstractions made from all sentiments in my soul,
all ideas in my mind. However, to tell the truth, I would not listen
long to a music which had only this merit." But in his late writings
the representative function of the signs continues to be weakened by
the emphasis placed on their generative power. The passage just
quoted continues: "I never listened to a good symphony, above all to
an adagio or andante, that I did not interpret—at times so happily
that I hit exactly upon the painting proposed by the musician" (*Oe.*
8:508). While imitation is still the guiding principle here, Diderot no
longer insists that music convey the "accents of the animal cry," and
he interprets listening, in part, as an intellectual guesswork aimed at
the composer's intention. This approach to the understanding of music is carried a step further in Bemetzrieder's work.[3] When the philosopher figure (Diderot) suggests to his daughter that the composer's ideas will be interpreted "differently by each of your listeners,"
the teacher responds that the composer's meanings are indefinite:
"Sounds are like abstract words, whose definitions ultimately dissolve
into infinitely many examples touching at a common point. It is the
privilege and fecundity of the indeterminate and vague expression
in our art that each person makes use of our songs according to the
momentary state of his soul, and in this manner the same cause becomes the source of infinite pleasures and diverse sufferings" (*Oe.*
12:490–91).

In Diderot's early writings mimesis is not yet firmly entrenched,
but the road toward autonomous music is blocked by his desire for
objective meaning. In the late writings music remains representational, but the listener is allowed to endow music with a personal meaning. The movement is not, as Blume (83) and Hugo
Goldschmidt (105) think, from rational mimesis to expression but toward an eventual liberation of musical signs. By no longer seeking a

unique meaning encoded either in the internal relations or in the objects and events depicted, Diderot takes a decisive step toward a new appreciation of music. The composition now appears as a generator of meanings constructed by the listener. Diderot thereby anticipates Kant, who defined aesthetic ideas by their ability to conjure up an infinity of thought, none of which is adequate to the generating aesthetic idea.

9 GOETHE, DIDEROT, AND RAMEAU

THE ANNOTATIONS TO *RAMEAU'S NEPHEW*

Diderot left *Rameau's Nephew* unpublished. After his death, a copy of it was transferred, with all of his library to the imperial archives in Moscow, and from there came into Goethe's hands in 1804 through the mediation of Schiller and the Sturm und Drang poet Klinger, who became a Russian officer. Goethe found the satire "more impudent and better formulated, more witty and daring, more immoral-moral" than just about anything he had ever encountered (*BA* 21:882), and he set out to prepare an annotated translation of it.[1]

Goethe had already published a translation-commentary of Diderot's *Essais sur la peinture* in Schiller's *Horen* (1799), and on this occasion he had exchanged critical opinions with Schiller on Diderot's notion of mimesis. In a letter of August 7, 1797 Schiller stated that Diderot's art was not artistic enough:

> His gaze in aesthetic works is still too intently fixed on alien and moral purposes; he does not search enough for these in the object and its representation. For him, the beautiful work of art must always serve something else. And since the truly beautiful and perfect in art necessarily improves man, he seeks this effect of art in its content and in a determinate result for intellect or moral feeling. I believe it is one of the advantages of our newer philosophy that we have a pure formula to express the subjective effect of the aesthetic without destroying its character.

Although Goethe was less enthusiastic than Schiller about Kant's "newer philosophy," he shared Schiller's aversion to moralizing in art: "Music is just as incapable of swaying the moral sense as any other art, and to expect such results from the arts is always wrong. Only philosophy and religion can do this." Accordingly, he replied to Schiller on August 12 that Diderot, for all his "elevated genius, deep feeling, and clear mind, could not reach the point to see that culture must take its own path in art, that it cannot be subordinated to anything else."

In his commentary on the *Essai*, Goethe also detected a penchant for naturalism in Diderot's demand that ugly people be portrayed faithfully. Goethe, whose notion of imitation was closer to Batteux's belle nature, found that Diderot's "theoretical statements tend to confound nature and art, to amalgamate nature and art completely." In his own view, "artists should strive to produce a perfect artwork, not a work of nature" (*BA* 21:735 and 775).

Since the cited passages suggest in various ways that art is autonomous, one would expect Goethe to be receptive to the notion of pure instrumental music. However, a longer annotation on music in the translation of *Rameau's Nephew*—possibly adopted from the article "composition" in Rousseau's dictionary—reveals that Goethe was as skeptical of "emancipated" music as the philosophes:

> All newer music is treated in two different ways. Either one regards it as an independent art, develops it for its own sake, practices it, and enjoys it through one's refined external senses as the Italians usually do, or one relates it to one's understanding, emotion, or passion, and cultivates it so that it can appeal to several intellectual and spiritual forces in man—as is and will remain the manner of the French, the Germans, and all northerners. [*BA* 21:680–81]

Goethe agreed, then, with Rousseau, Diderot, and d'Alembert that independent music appealed only to the ("refined") senses and remained inferior to the music of "intellect, sensibility, and passion." The definition of this second type of music all too easily conflates intellectual and emotional music, but it indicates that Goethe expected meaningful music to reach beyond the senses. This traditional view, which grants intellectual respectability to instrumental music only if it accompanies the voice and paints concrete meanings, is reconfirmed by Goethe's fictional Wilhelm Meister: "The instrument should merely accompany the voice; for melodies, runs, and progressions without words and sense seem to resemble caterpillars or beautiful colorful birds that hover before our eyes and we wish only to capture and acquire; in contrast, singing rises towards heaven like a genius, and spurs the better self in us to accompany it" (*BA* 10:132).

The case would seem clear, had Goethe not complicated matters by taking Italian opera, the most voice-centered music, as the para-

digm of autonomous art, evidently because he thought that Italian
operas displayed sensuous vocal brilliance without paying attention
to the text:

> The Italians will aim at the sweetest harmony and the most pleasing mel-
> ody. They will delight in consonance and movement as such; they will
> consult the vocal chords of the singer and will most happily highlight
> what these can offer in sustained or rapidly succeeding notes, to delight
> thereby the cultivated ears of their countrymen. But they will not escape
> the reproach not to have done any justice to the text—for, after all, a
> song must have a text. [BA 21:681]

The pure music of Italian opera is surprisingly related therefore to
German instrumental music: "The Germans treated instrumental music like the Italians singing. For a while, they regarded it also as a
special, autonomous art, they perfected its technique, and practiced it
with passion, almost without any further relation to the inner powers" (BA 21:682). Whether Goethe refers here to the new, classical instrumental music or to baroque counterpoint remains unclear,
though his use of the past tense suggests the latter.

But how could Diderot have preferred "pure" Italian opera if, as
Goethe claims, he did not respect the autonomy of art? Indeed,
Goethe thinks that within the proposed scheme of music history Diderot's position is not easily understood (BA 21:682), for he, "who so
intently demands meaning," should actually have preferred Lully's
and Rameau's "meaningful" operas. He must have opted for the simple Italian form out of protest against the baroque mannerisms and
conventions of the French tradition (BA 21:683).

Yet Diderot's inconsistencies pale in comparison with Goethe's if
we consider that Goethe criticized Diderot for not granting enough
autonomy to art while at the same time he himself expected of music
intellectual, emotional, and moral concerns. His approach to Diderot
remains curious. The critique of Diderot's Essai does not apply to
Rameau's Nephew, a work that undermines rather than advocates naturalism and didacticism in art, and Goethe was aware of this, for he
repeatedly noted how iconoclastic and capricious Rameau's Nephew
was. But the author of Werther, who waged a hopeless battle against
the confusion of author and protagonist, seems guilty of the same
sin, for he ascribed all the irreverence in Diderot's satire to Lui and
identified the author with the staid and morally conventional Moi.

Rameau's Nephew seems to have hit the blindspot in his critical faculty, which failed him consistently when faced with manifestations of the irrational, grotesque, and demonic. In the case of a Kleist or a Hölderlin, this led to summary rejections, whereas in Diderot's case the demonic and misshapen elements were both ascribed to the fictional Lui, thereby saving but also sanitizing Diderot himself. Goethe was inclined to ascribe Diderot's irrationalism to an excess of wit rather than to fundamentally centrifugal and destructive forces in his personality.

Indeed, Goethe's own theory of musical imitation was probably more deeply moored to conceptual language than was Diderot's, for even as late as November 9, 1829, he understood quartets as conversations: "One hears four intelligent people conversing, imagines to gain something from their discourses and to become acquainted with the character of the instruments." In this sense, he wanted composers to serve poets, and he disliked through-composed songs because they abandoned the strophic structure of poems.

As to imitations of physical objects and events, Goethe preferred a d'Alembertian indirection to naturalism. On March 6, 1810, he praised Zelter's setting of his poem "Johanna Sebus" as "a kind of symbolism for the ear, whereby the object, insofar as it is in motion or at rest, is neither imitated nor painted but produced in the imagination in a completely unique and incomprehensible manner, because the signified and the signifier seem to have scarcely any relation to each other."

The passage evidently echoes the notion of symbolic representation that Goethe derived from his visual experience and advocated for literature, but a moment's reflection will indicate how much further he went in music beyond the principles of concretion and imitation. In Goethe's visual symbol the idea is "infinitely effective and elusive," but the signifier remains a concrete representation. In music, signifiers have almost no natural tie to the objects signified; they function semi-independently, as if emancipated from nature, merely triggering the imagination. Passages in letters reinforce this point:

To your question, what a musician may paint, I venture to respond with a paradox: nothing and everything. He may imitate nothing as received by his senses; but he may represent everything he feels when receiving such external physical impressions. To imitate thunder in music is no art, but I should highly esteem the musician who makes me feel as if I heard thundering. Thus we have for utter peace, silence, and even negation contrasting definite musical expressions, of which I possess perfect examples. To repeat, the great and noble privilege of music is to tune inwardness to a mood without using ordinary external means. [To Schöpke, February 16, 1818]

The purest and highest painting in music is the one you [Zelter] practice. The aim is to attune the listener to the mood suggested by the poem; the imagination will form images then without knowing how it arrives at it. [To Zelter, May 2, 1820]

Zelter modestly responded on May 16 that in this sense all good artists, especially Bach, Handel, Haydn, and Beethoven, were imitators, but he failed to notice that Goethe was actually concerned with the creation of Stimmung and barely asked whether the engendered mood corresponded to the represented object.

RAMEAU AND THE MAJOR-MINOR POLARITY

Mimesis relates music to nature by insisting that musical sounds represent. But music may also be linked to nature in the manner of Rameau, if we trace its structural properties to the natural order. How much did Goethe know about Rameau? Curiously, just at the time when Lui carved out a stone image of the composer for Moi, a portraiture of purple appeared in Lavater's *Physiognomische Fragmente*:

See this pure intellect! . . . See this pure, correct, and tender sense, which *is* without effort, without strenuous search; and see meanwhile this heavenly rectitude!

The most perfect and loving harmony has shaped this figure. Nothing is sharp, nothing is angular in this whole contour, everything undulates, everything hovers without swaying, without being indeterminate. This presence affects the soul like a piece of brilliant music, our heart is in rapture and saturated by its amiability, and is at the same time transfixed and inwardly strengthened, not knowing why. The truth, the correctness, the eternal law of tuneful nature lies hidden under this pleasantness.

Look at this forehead! These temples! the purest tonal proportions dwell in them. Look at this eye! It does not gaze, it does not notice, it is all ear, all attention to inner feeling. This nose! How free! How solid! without being stiff—and, then, how the cheek is animated by a content self-satis-

faction, drawing the mouth toward itself! And how the friendliest deter-
mination rounds itself in the chin! [Goethe *WA* 1.37:340–41]

Goethe's letter to Reich of April 19, 1775, seems to confirm the
barely believable, namely, that he actually authored this embarrassing
piece of trash. How much he studied Rameau in preparation for this
"ode" on his nose and forehead we do not know, but the features
could not have impressed him deeply, because his annotation on the
composer in *Rameau's Nephew* is simply lifted from Rousseau's 1753
letter to Grimm:

> Rameau's theoretical works experienced the strange fate of having great
> success without being read. And now they will be read even less, since
> Mr. d'Alembert has taken the trouble of publishing this author's theory
> in excerpts. [Rousseau's French more correctly says "summary".] This
> will surely destroy the original, and we shall be compensated by not miss-
> ing them at all. These various works contain nothing new or useful save
> the principle of fundamental bass. But it is no small merit to have firmly
> established a basic, if arbitrary, principle in an art which hardly seemed
> amenable to it, and to have made the rules easier so that one can now
> complete the study of composition within a few months whereas for-
> merly twenty years were needed. [*BA* 21:695]

Goethe omits Rousseau's malicious conclusion that the praiseworthy simplicity of Rameau's theory is to blame for the wave of medio-
cre composers, but hardly because of his earlier admiration of
Rameau. After the contribution to Lavater's book, Goethe has nothing more to say about Rameau as a person, and this may well be the
reason why Rameau is among the last major figures of the eighteenth
century not yet honored with a study on his relation to Goethe. Yet
Rameau's theory of tonality became the subject of discussions between Goethe, Zelter, and Schlosser, and it forms the nucleus of
Goethe's ideas for a *Tonlehre*, a theory of sounds. While these ad hoc
writings cannot match the sustained effort of the *Farbenlehre*, Goethe
considered the topic important enough to post the outline of the
Tonlehre in his study.

When Goethe asked Zelter why composers preferred the minor tonality, Zelter replied on May 2, 1808, with a lengthy historical disqui-
sition that evaded the answer and merely asserted that the minor
third was not a gift of nature but a "work of recent art," derived by
contracting the major third. This disturbed Goethe, who was just

then deriving all colors from the duality of black and white, and in his letter of June 22 he gave a lengthy refutation of the theory that the minor was derived from the major: augmenting the minor was just as reasonable as contracting the major, and if the division of the vibrating string did not yield the minor third, this merely disqualified the experiment.

Like Rameau, Goethe attempted to put major and minor on an equal footing, but his superficial agreement with Rameau on the equality of the tonalities belies their fundamental differences on the status of theories in general, on the role of mathematics in science, and on the relationship between nature and art. Rameau thought that musical harmony had objective, "Newtonian" laws independent of the observer. If the historical practice of music showed a development that culminated, as he thought, in the parity of major and minor, these tonalities had to be rooted in the sound-producing bodies and not in man's accidentally formed auditory mechanism. Goethe also thought that compositional practice was based on rules. If composers treated the minor third as a consonance, even though it was not among the overtones of the vibrating string, it could not be a dissonance (*Zelter* 1:231). But similar convictions sent Rameau out into nature and referred Goethe back to man, as the famous concluding passage of his June 22 letter (later divided into several epigrams in *Wilhelm Meisters Wanderjahre*) indicates:

> Man himself, inasmuch as he makes use of his sound senses, is the greatest and most exact physical apparatus possible. And the greatest evil of modern physics is that the experiments have become so to speak "distanced" from man, and nature is recognized only in indications of artificial instruments, and this is even supposed to limit and prove what nature is capable of producing. The same holds for calculation. Much of what is true cannot be computed, just as there is much that cannot be subjected to a decisive experiment. But man ranks so high precisely because what is otherwise unrepresentable is represented in him. What, after all, is a string and all its mechanical divisions compared to the musician's ear? One may even ask what all the elementary phenomena of nature are compared to man, who must first control and modify them to be able to assimilate them to some degree.

Zelter's conciliatory response terminated the debate, but Goethe returned to it shortly before his death, on March 31, 1831, rekindling his still smouldering anger that the "theoretical cheap-jacks" would not recognize the minor third as a gift of nature: "Truly, a chord of wire or gut is not so precious that nature should solely entrust to it her harmonies. Man is worth more, and nature has given him the minor third so that he can express with innermost pleasure what is nameless and desired. Man belongs to nature, and he is the one to know how to appropriate, regulate, and modify the tenderest relations of all the elementary phenomena."

Diary entries, letters, and other biographical documents testify that the 1808 debate with Zelter continued to concern Goethe throughout the completion of the Farbenlehre, culminating in an 1810 sketch for a Tonlehre. This Goethean acoustics consists of three parts, each accommodating a dimension of sound: (1) the organic, subjective, or physiological one; (2) the mechanical or instrumental one; and (3) the mathematical or objective one. The first part asserts that the ear has reactive and shaping powers. The second concerns sound production and states that the voice expresses the whole person, whereas instruments are mechanical and mathematical, hence inferior, surrogates for it. The third part, finally, reaffirms the equality of the major and minor tonalities as poles of a fundamental duality between man and nature: "The minor sound [third] is not among the first series of harmonic tones generated. It is manifested in less evident numerical and measurable proportions; and yet, it is perfectly suited to human nature, even better suited than that first, more evident mode" (Zelter 2:427).

But what makes the minor tonality better suited to man than the major? The question came to haunt Goethe in 1816, when Schlosser proposed to him a link between his color theory and the subjectivity of the minor. Goethe responded enthusiastically to Schlosser's idea that a Tonmonade generated both the major and the minor thirds, for he perceived in this concept a kind of Urphänomen that was impervious to verbal or mathematical analyses: "Here we meet completely, inasmuch as you say that the foundation of the so-called minor lies within the tone-monad itself. This is said from my heart. . . . The expansion of the tone-monad generates the major, its contraction the minor" (WA 4.25:305). But Goethe was taken aback when Schlosser claimed that only the major tonality was natural and that the duality of major-minor could therefore not be fundamental (WA 4.25:303). To Schlosser's Romantic sensibility, music was the medium of inwardness and the best expression of a yearning for the infinite:

In a wider sense it is true that the minor sounds are better suited to human nature than the major ones. . . . It has metaphysical foundation,
namely as follows. As the world of light speaks to the eye, the sense for
the understanding, positing a serene relation with the outer world, so the
world of sound speaks to the ear, the sense for inwardness (to use a somber word), and destroys the relation with the outside. Therefore, music
moves our soul unlike any other art, including even poetry. Its power
makes our hankering for the infinite, the distant, the undivided swell over
the dams of today and yesterday, rising to heights and sinking to depths
where it cannot sojourn because it lacks the sense which alone can give
reality to it. . . . If, then, the minor mode is better suited to human nature than the major, this actually means that even man's happiest attachment to nature is forced, coerced; music, and within it the minor (furthest from nature and shaking its foundations), attunes us to a
melancholy which we all have to fight. All of us would like to conceal this
melancholy but cannot escape it, whether we admit it or not.

But just because it most decidedly turns our mind against nature or
away from it, it does not lie in nature, at least not in an original way. Its
appeal is to be sought in the moral sphere. [*WA* 4.25:308–09]

Goethe must have been disturbed by several remarks in this passage. Approaching music from the standpoint of the listener rather
than the creator, Schlosser believed that music aroused in the listener
a destructive spirit of defiance against nature. Goethe, of course, was
keenly aware of music's power to release violent, irrational, and potentially destructive forces. But in his mature years he shunned violent theatrical or musical catharses. His fear of the demonic prevented him from appreciating fully the talent of Beethoven, whose
music, according to Hoffmann, awakened an arch-Romantic yearning for the infinite. Goethe's *Novelle* shows that he preferred music
that neutralized, calmed, harmonized, and harnessed rather than agitated the passions. Because of this, the irrational powers latent in
music preoccupied him to the very end of his life, particularly while
finishing the second part of *Faust*. Thus, on March 2, 1831, he remarked to Eckermann that musicians had a stronger streak of the demonic than painters, and six days later, anticipating Thomas Mann's
Faustian musician, he added: "Music contains something demonic,
for it ranks so high that no understanding can reach it, and it exudes
a power that dominates everything and of which nobody can give
himself an account. Religious cult can therefore not dispense with it;
it is one of the best means to have a miraculous effect on man."

Schlosser's suggestion that music in a minor tonality disposed the listener against nature had little appeal to Goethe. Like Schiller, Schlosser perceived confrontation rather than harmony between man and nature; he saw in the minor an ethical will to overcome nature. Goethe could not share such an idealist and Romantic interpretation of music, but Schlosser's passionate words must have reminded him of Schiller's struggle, for he softened his polemical answer with the highly flattering proposal that the two of them engage in a cooperative venture that Goethe had once shared with Schiller, namely, "to steadily follow a common educational experience," even if they moved in diametrically opposed directions (*WA* 4.25:313). As a gesture, Goethe ingeniously reinterpreted Schlosser's notion of a Tonmonade to suit his own theory of polarities. The major tonality was an expansion of the monad and represented man's drive to reach out actively into the world of external objects. The minor represented a withdrawal of the subject that was not necessarily melancholic and self-destructive but an act of concentration, a mobilizing of positive forces. In a polonaise, for instance, the minor represented no suffering or bereavement; it suited rather a social "gathering," an entwining and embracing in the social self.

Here, as elsewhere, the instinct that led Goethe from naturalism toward abstraction is countered by an equally powerful aversion to pure subjectivity. The sweeping and pulsating passion of Romantic music was for him, contrary to appearances, akin to pure mathematics, for both of them were sheer inventions, human constructs without natural bases. His own image of art, as offered to Zelter in the June 22, 1808 letter, was quite different:

All the arts, inasmuch as they could improve only through exercise and thinking, practice and theory, seem to me like cities whose foundations and soil, the stuff they are built on, can no longer be deciphered. Rocks were blasted, the same stones hewn into shape and made into houses. The caves were found very convenient and converted into cellars. Where solid ground gave way, people dug and shored it up; perhaps a bottomless patch of swamp was found just next to the primal rock, where posts had to be driven in and a pile foundation be prepared. When all this is at last finished and habitable, what is to be called nature and what art? Where is the fundament and where the supplement? Where the matter and where the form? How difficult it is, then, to give reasons when we wish to assert that in earliest times, still with a ready overview of the

whole, all the installations could have been arranged more naturally, art-
fully, and purposefully. If one considers the piano or the organ, one
thinks one sees the city of my simile.

It may not be accidental that Goethe's image of music should be a
cityscape, whereas art and nature are represented as patterned and
embellished organic forms in his *Elective Affinities*, written just a few
years earlier. He knew that music was the art furthest removed from
nature and most highly structured according to abstract principles.
He was among the first to defend the autonomy of art, but he went
along with it only part of the way, stopping short of giving full recognition to the new, nonrepresentational art of instrumental music.
If Goethe's constructed city resembles neither Axel's symbolist castle
nor the elusive goal of Kafka's land surveyor—if, in other words,
Goethe felt uncomfortable with an art that was a totally human construct, a pure reification of thought or passion—this was not because
of a deficiency in his imaginative powers. Here, as in the Philemon
and Baucis scene of Faust, Part II, he voiced the paradoxical fear that
the more the world bears the stamp of the self the more dehuman-
ized it may become.

IO THE SISTER ARTS

Blest Pair of Sirens, Pledges of Heaven's Joy,
Sphere-Born harmonious Sisters, Voice and Verse,
Wed your divine Sounds, and mixt Power employ.
　　　　　　—Milton, "At a Solemn Musick"

The impulse that gradually extricated music from its scientific position within the quadrivium did not simply set music free, but, as I have indicated, gradually tied it up again, now in the newly emerging system of the arts. The conflict between emancipation and renewed integration within the context of the arts is the subject of this chapter. First we shall look at speculations on the common origin and envisioned reunification of the arts; second, we will deal with semiotic studies of the arts, which generally helped to establish sharper distinctions between them; and finally, we shall consider opera as both the most popular and the most controversial synthetic art.

THE SEARCH FOR ORIGINS

The assault on the Pythagorean eternal laws of harmony furthered historical and genetic approaches to music. These new, historical interpretations form part of an emergent general historicism, observable in the writings of Vico, Rousseau, and Herder. As we have seen in the case of Rousseau, such writers postulated a primitive, prerational, and poetic language that was musical and metaphoric rather than logical. The unity of music and language in the *Ursprache* was therefore a broad historical and philosophical issue for the eighteenth century, which insistently raised the question as to whether that primeval unity had been lost irretrievably. Even those who nostalgically yearned for the past, like Robertson, often had to admit that ancient music was "perfectly heterogeneous to everything modern" and therefore incompatible with the modern political and cultural climate (446).

The leading British advocate of the reunion of the arts, John Brown, shared Plato's and Rousseau's opposition to autonomous music:

[When the counterpoint was invented] instrumental Music, having assumed a new and more inviting Form, and being ennobled by the principles of a complex and varied Harmony, was introduced as being of itself a compleat Species, independent of Poetry or Song. This gave it an artificial and laboured Turn; while the Composer went in Quest of curious Harmonies, Discords, Resolutions, Fugues, and Canons; and prided himself (like the Poet) in a pompous Display of Art, to the Neglect of Expression and true Pathos. And thus modern Music, on its first Rise, was in a Manner divorced from Poetry, Legislation, and Morals.[198]

Though the separation of poetry and music, bard and legislator, had led to a general decline of morals and politics, a general reunification is not possible (222), and one can, at best, hope for rulers who support bards and occasionally make music themselves. The reunification of poetry and music is unattainable, except for genres like the ode, the hymn, or the simple, "pathetic" song (225–26). Brown, a moralist rather than a man of artistic sensibility, suggested that the cultivation of such genres "may possibly by Degrees be made a Part of Education, and applied to the Culture of the youthful Mind, in Subjects religious, political, and moral" (228).

Many theories of the origin of music did not lend themselves to such an agenda. At one extreme, music was derived from physical nature in the sense of Lucretius (*De rerum natura* 5.11:1378ff.), who suggested that music was originally an imitation of bird whistles. This mimetic theory, which was the companion to the onomatopoeic theory of the origin of language, persisted tenaciously, even though Burney, Robertson, and others rightly responded that music was a human artifice that did not exist in nature. At the other extreme were the mythical accounts of Orpheus, the sirens, David, Arion, Amphibion, Jubal, and Timotheus, which embodied primitive beliefs that the magic of music was a divine gift.

Between these natural and supernatural explanations, both of which sustained mimesis, there existed, however, a third vision of music as a human instrument, a more elemental, universal, and richer language than words. Speculations about the Ursprache were deeply motivated by dissatisfaction with the expressive power of language, and they reached down into prerational psychic and historic depths in order to unearth buried modes of expression. Seminal issues remained obscure, according to Brown, "for Want of beginning our Inquiries at this early and neglected Period [of man's savage and uncultivated state]" (26). Such excavations searched not for a rhetorical, logical, or semantic unity between music and language but for a primitive medium of rhythm and accent, in which music dominated language. Burnett (Lord Monboddo) considered that primitive music was man's sole mode of communication in the natural state (6:136–37), though he would not call it as yet a language; for Jacob, music alone suited the mystery and serenity of ritual, because it was a universal language that "must have been born at the same Time with this rude Kind of Lyric Poetry [of feasts and sacrifices], and proceeded at first from a certain Fulness of Heart, from a Kind of Exultation, and overflowing of Joy, and Mirth on these Occasions" (11).

Music is in such conceptions "the first and immediate daughter of nature" (Bayly 2), the passionate expression of feeling via sounds (Forkel *Gesch.* 2), not because it imitates natural sounds but rather because it is man's original and natural mode of expression. If seized by vehement passions, "we no longer think of words but are penetrated by the matter itself" (Heinse 5:243), and in such states music "expresses what is inexpressible in language." The assignment of this new value to music led to the "musicalization" of poetry in Romanticism and Symbolism and to the inversion of the relation between music and words. In Nietzsche's view, folksongs strain language to its utmost that it may imitate music, and "melody generates the poem out of itself." The search for the common origin of music and language seemingly retards the emancipation of music but actually prepares its position of dominance.

MUSICAL SEMIOTICS

Dubos was probably the first to hold that sounds are "the signs of passion instituted by nature" whereas "articulated words are just arbitrary signs" (467). In this view, musical signs are natural because "the combination of the signifier [sound] with the signified is grounded in the property of the signified" (Mendelssohn 182). To put it in less abstract, Cartesian terms, sounds are natural signs because they are universally understood, immediate expressions of agitations in the soul, whereas the meaning of words is defined by convention—in other words, cries need no dictionary.

The doctrine of natural signs in music is therefore a dimension of affect theory. Today we tend to consider music the most arbitrary artistic sign language, because we no longer believe that music originated in passionate cries. In the eighteenth century, however, musical signs were widely believed to be natural, and this feature was used as a means of distinguishing between the imitative modes of poetry and music.[1]

We find in Mendelssohn's *Hauptgrundsätze der schönen Wissenschaften und Künste* (*Main principles of the beautiful arts and sciences*) of 1757 a representative example of the eighteenth-century separation of the arts on semiotic grounds. All languages have a natural component, writes Mendelssohn, but music is fully natural, and composers should therefore avoid in it "concepts that have no natural relation to sound" (186).

Composite media, among them vocal music, have multiple effects: "As long as music is used merely to give greater emphasis to the arbitrary signs of poetry," it must be subservient and occasionally break its own rules (190). The text serves music only in the sense that it makes indeterminate sounds concrete:

> One feels imbued with a certain sentiment, but this is dark, general, and not limited to any particular object. This shortcoming can be helped by the addition of clearer, arbitrary signs. They can determine the object from every side and turn the sentiment into an individualized one, and this can burst forth more easily. Now, if this sharper definition of the musical sentiment occurs by means of poetry and painting, or stage decor, the modern opera results. [192]

Thus language must clarify music even when the latter dominates their union, though Mendelssohn does not explain why conventional linguistic signs should be more distinct than the natural sounds of music. Since music expresses the emotions naturally, the fault cannot lie in the relation between signifier and signified. Rather, Mendelssohn finds the sentiments themselves inherently vague and needful of the mediating and clarifying assistance of language.

Mendelssohn's reflections on musical signs played an essentially negative role in the making of Lessing's *Laokoon*, one of the most important essays in eighteenth-century aesthetics.[2] Lessing's attention shifted from natural and arbitrary signs to temporal and spatial ones, and for this reason the essay concerns itself with the difference between poetry and art, leaving music beyond its scope. But the notes for a planned second part indicate that Lessing considered the possibility of nonnatural signs in music: "The use of arbitrary signs in music. Attempt to explain the miraculous and the value of old music from it. About the power that the lawgiver acquired by means of it" (6:605–06). The point seems to be that the Greek emancipation of music from verbal rhythm, which so disturbed Plato, actually enlarged the power of the lawgiver, since arbitrary signs are easier to manipulate than natural ones. More important, Lessing associated the legendary and miraculous power of music with arbitrary signs, for only these would free the imagination from the natural order.[3]

British critics seldom asked whether musical sounds were natural, but they insisted that they resemble the signified object (a condition frequently called isomorphism today). Since most natural signs do not resemble their referent (smoke, for instance, is a natural sign of fire but does not resemble it), this demand seriously limited compositional freedom and actually reduced imitation to naturalistic copying. The later eighteenth century gradually repudiated both the dogma of natural signs in music and the demand that they resemble the imitated object. Webb, for instance, admitted that we have no clear idea "of any natural relation between sound and sentiment" (1–2), while Morellet and others concluded that music was actually more conventional than language and restricted to less perfect resemblances (121). Diderot, as we saw, hinted that music, the most arbitrary and least precise art, spoke to us most forcefully, for "showing less of the objects it leaves more room for the imagination" (Oe. 1:409). Forkel found it ridiculous to represent the loss of a child with musical imitations of the mother's whimpers, cries, and moans (Gesch. 59). Twining differentiated such literal imitations (44–45) from indirect ones, which aim, in d'Alembert's sense, to produce an effect similar to the effect created by the imitated object or event (48). Adam Smith, finally, spoke out most resolutely against the requirement of isomorphism. Taking his example from a yew tree clipped in the shape of a pyramid, Smith argued that just "the disparity between the imitating and the imitated object is the foundation of the beauty of imitation. It is because the one object does not naturally resemble the other, that we are so much pleased with it, when by art it is made to do so" (144).

OPERA: EMANCIPATION OR ENSLAVEMENT OF MUSIC?

Eighteenth-century music theory was not, perhaps, first and foremost an aesthetics of opera, as Dahlhaus claims (*Mus. poet.* 117), but in terms of sheer volume and vitality the debates on music were undoubtedly dominated by opera. Here was an issue that appealed to highbrow as well as popular taste, to theorists and practicing musicians alike, because the abstract arguments were larded with gossip, jealousy, intrigue, politics, and chauvinism. Most of the untold number of pamphlets on opera sound like an entertaining but lightweight opera buffa, but the important story of how this Johnny-come-lately among the arts battled to gain a rightful place on the stage is yet to be told. Flaherty's recent book on German opera criticism is an important contribution to the writing of that story.

Opera was the offspring of a theoretical and imaginative reconstruction of ancient musical drama. Yet, after having reached early maturity with Monteverdi, it denied its intellectual origins and slowly descended to the lowlands of popular taste, so that this offspring of intellect became a problem child. Although serious observers condemned it on Aristotelian grounds and called it stillborn, opera triumphantly conquered Europe, ignoring their high-minded carping.

The debates on opera revolved around three major issues: (1) whether it conformed to traditional aesthetic norms; (2) whether it merely entertained or could also morally edify; and (3) whether Italy, by virtue of its language, vocal talent, and climate, had unrivaled dominion in opera. I shall pass over this last and perhaps most volatile issue because it has the least theoretical significance.[4] Debates around the first two issues were largely responsible, however, for gradual changes both in opera and its aesthetics. In the end, opera cleansed itself of its worst excesses, and, more important, the development of a new rationale for it gave important impulses for the rethinking of aesthetics in general.

Representative condemnations of opera indicate its problems:

The contemporary opera, regarded as dramatic poems, as tragedies, are a monstrosity and a conglomeration of a thousand improbabilities. [Muratori 197]

[The opera] is a bizarre undertaking of poetry and music, where the poet and the composer, equally bothered by each other, go to plenty of trouble to create a wretched work. [Saint-Evremond 154]

The opera is the most absurd work that human reason has ever invented.
[Gottsched 739]

By the sober and judicious part of mankind it [the opera] has ever been
considered as the mere offspring of luxury; and those who have examined
it with a critical eye, scruple not to pronounce that it is of all entertainments the most unnatural and absurd. [Hawkins XXXVIII–XXXIX]

To a large measure, opera suffered from being judged against tragedy, its progenitor. Not only did the comparison usually work in favor of tragedy, it also fanned fears that the craze for opera would
ruin tragedy, "the most beautiful thing we have, the most proper to
lift the soul and the most capable of shaping the mind" (Saint-Evremond 154). More specifically, Dennis (382) and other English and
French critics feared that the Italian cultural invasion would wipe out
indigenous tragedy. In France, opera came to be distinguished from
tragedy by the new name *poème lyrique* ("lyrical poem"), yet d'Alembert still considered it a spoken and uncontestably inferior sort of
tragedy, fatally flawed by being "mere spectacle" (*Oe.* 1:524, 526).
Even Chabanon, who was in favor of operas, insisted that they obey
the rules of tragedy (*De la mus.* 283). Yet, judged by the classical
unities of space and time, opera violated "laws of nature that are immutable" (Hawkins XL). As Saint-Evremond said, people with
"good taste for the probable and the marvelous" must find opera
"quite extravagant" (163).[5]

If opera was a variant of tragedy, music was a nuisance that obscured the text. As Corneille explained in the preface to his libretto
Andromède, he made sure "that nothing is sung that is necessary for
the comprehension of the play, because usually the words that are
sung are only poorly understood" (Weisstein 26). Indeed, librettos
seemed to shackle poets. Boileau recounts how Racine reluctantly
embarked on a libretto upon the express wishes of Louis XIV but
happily abandoned it when the jealous Quinault started to intrigue
against him. Boileau's sketch for an allegorical Prologue shows how
the separation of Music and Poetry is prevented only by a *deus ex
machina* descent of "divine harmony," sustained by the authority of
His Majesty the King (229–37).

Repetitions of syllables, words, or phrases absurdly disfigured
good verses, and the text was lost completely when Italian operas
were performed for foreigners. As Addison noted in the March 6,
1711, issue of the *Spectator*, the finest Italian writers "express them-

selves in such a florid form of Words, and such tedious Circumlocu-
tions, as are used by none but Pedants in our own Country"; he
added on March 11 that it will be difficult to explain to posterity
"why their Forefathers used to sit together like an Audience of Foreigners in their own Country, and to hear whole Plays acted before
them in a Tongue which they did not understand" (79). There was
little hope of remedy, for the intonation of recitatives could not be
translated, and most singers were monolingual. Countless satires
show how librettos became truncated, mutilated, and manipulated
according to commercial demands, the vanity of the singers, or the
caprice of directors.

Operas violated not only the unities but the general Aristotelian
principle that dramas ought to imitate human action. Saint-Evremond, Muratori, Gottsched, and Brown all complained that operas
departed from verisimilitude: they were stacked with "a confused as-
semblage of gods, shepherds, heroes, enchanters, phantoms, furies,
and demons" (Saint-Evremond 163); the actors persisted in singing in
the most trivial and sublime moments; and the action was improba-
ble and full of miracles. Preoccupation with love made operas soft
and effeminate, yet the passions were presented so unconvincingly
that no catharsis ensued (Muratori 163, 181, Dennis 384, Saint-
Evremond 150, Gottsched 738–42). Opera spoke neither to reason
nor to the emotions, and its success could therefore be explained
only by its appeal to the lustful senses (Muratori 171, Gottsched 741,
Porée 35). In the March 6, 1711, issue of the *Spectator*, Addison recounts having met a man who collected sparrows "to act the part of
Singing Birds" in an opera. But the sparrows served merely as a visual distraction, for the music was performed by "a Consort of
Flagellets and Bird-calls which was planted behind the Scenes."
Many agreed therefore with Dennis that music could only become
"profitable as well as delightful, if it is subordinate to some nobler
Art, and subservient to Reason" (385).

The responses to these objections were initially quite timid and
narrow. Batteux tried to find a niche for the anomaly in the taxonomy of genres by distinguishing imitations of heroic human behavior
(tragedy) from the "lyrical spectacle" of opera, which was supposed
to display divine actions and human passions:

> The divine actions make the spectacle marvelous, strike the eyes, and oc-
> cupy the imagination; the expression of the passions produces the emo-

tion in the heart, fueling and troubling it. To unite these two parts in a
work of art one must therefore select first the actors who are to be gods,
demigods, or at least men who have something supernatural. Then one
places these actors in situations where they experience lively passions.
This is the foundation of the lyrical spectacle. [274]

This was a poor recipe and an ill-timed attempt to accommodate
the new genre amidst the crumbling Aristotelian edifice. To be sure,
Rousseau temporarily accepted it because he considered opera inherently incredible and fit to enchant us by means of the fabulous, the
spectacular, and the mythical (Jansen 456), but he later concluded in
the *Dictionnaire* that the marvelous could not induce Aristotelian ter-
ror and pity, and that opera could not be defined in terms of content
(art. "opera").

Aristotelian defenders of opera argued that it was perfectly plausible to repeat words or phrases, for in the heat of passion the
mind fastened onto verbal fragments and was naturally inclined to
burst into song (Smith 155, *Encyclopédie* art. "poème lyrique").
Others noted that opera was no more artificial than rhymed poetry,
animals speaking in fables, bodies of clay or stone, and landscapes on
canvas.[6]

But the more interesting defenses of opera challenged the Aristotelian norms, especially their claim to eternal validity. J. A. Schlegel
compared the taxonomy of the arts to the pre-Renaissance globe
with its undiscovered continents and remarked that Batteux put opera on the map of genres but failed to notice that genres, unlike continents, change: Batteux's definition of opera as the genre of the marvelous was based on a historical and accidental manifestation of it,
namely, Quinault's librettos (307–11).

Such arguments not only forced a reconsideration of established
norms but often questioned the very possibility of normative aesthetics. According to Feind, there could be no law for an artistic form,
for "the features vary with the customs of the times and with each
nation; for our plays, specially the musical ones, are vastly different
from the ancient tragedies and comedies. . . . The French, in turn,
differ in many respects from the Italian and German ones" (*La Costanza Sforzata*). If, as Uffenbach wrote, "times change customs," and
customs determine artistic rules (406), classical norms could not be
binding, and one should not disdain opera just "because Aristotle

knew nothing of it and gave no rules for it" (Hiller 530–31). Such arguments eventually convinced even the rationalists, who would have preferred eternal laws in aesthetics but became suspicious of them once they were advocated merely on ancient authority.

Some interpreters even went beyond rationalist aesthetics by proclaiming that opera was an art of illusion in which the rules of reason no longer applied. For Feind, the theater was a "shadow play," a kind of make-belief that had to be taken on its own terms, for no rational argument could make it plausible.[7] In such an artificial world, Hudemann suggested, the intellect overlooked license with time as long as unity of character was preserved (147).

During the last decades of the century such cautious defenses were superseded by radical assaults on the demand for verisimilitude. According to Justus Möser:

> The opera is a representation taken from a possible world that the poet can create according to his own designs if he can make the spectator believe in it. The one and only nature in our real world is too narrow for the poet's imagination, and everything the opera composer needlessly borrows from it indicates his weakness. The stage of the opera is the realm of chimeras. . . . The highest praise one can give an opera or an epic poem . . . may therefore be that both are completely unnatural in comparison to our world. [72]

Opera now turns into "the most perfect and exalted entertainment" and "the height of Embellishment," because its beauty "does not own Nature to be its standard" (Robertson 354–55). Chabanon expects opera to be a "magic lantern," for the theater is "a magic domain where time and space contract" into a fraction of their normal extension (*De la mus.* 282, 266–67).

The magic and enchantment that reappear on the Romantic stage differ from Batteux's "marvelous" because they are no longer attributes of a mythological world but indices of the power of the imagination to overcome the spatiotemporal world of nature. The pastoral, the divine, the miraculous, or the fairy tale in opera need not be made plausible, for they are understood as manifestations of an inner experience that knows no time and space: "Are we not similarly in a magic world in real dream?—And how true dreams are for us! May there be no art, then, which delights us with most beautiful dreams even when awake? Once set in a world where everything sings and

dances, the world around us should also correspond to this disposition; it should enchant us" (Herder 23:333–34).

What had been an anomaly in neoclassicism thus became the exemplar in the aesthetics of German Classicism and Romanticism.
Goethe could have used opera as evidence against Diderot's aesthetics, for he thought it proved that "the truth of art and the truth of
nature are completely different" (*WA* 1.47:261–62). His own *Märchen* was, according to Novalis, a "narrated opera" (2:535), because it
was a perfect artifice. The idealist foundations of this new opera aesthetics are perhaps most evident in Schiller's letter to Goethe of December 29, 1797, in which the poet expresses the hope that

> a nobler form of tragedy would spin off from the opera, as was the case
> with the chorus of the old feasts of Bacchus. In opera one truly abandons
> the servile imitation of nature, and, although only under the name of in-
> dulgence, the Ideal could this way steal its way unto the stage. Through
> the power of music and a freer harmonious stimulation of the senses, op-
> era attunes the mind to a finer aesthetic sensibility. Even pathos is more
> of a free play here, because it is accompanied by music, and the miracu-
> lous, which, for once, is tolerated here, should by necessity make us more
> indifferent to the content.

Opera helped unburden the stage of didacticism and moralizing as
well as strict imitation, by defending it as pure entertainment.
D'Alembert still pejoratively assigned comedy to the mind, tragedy
to the soul, and opera to the senses (*Oe.* 1:523). But Krause would already consider opera "not only the most beautiful, splendorous, and
magnificent theater but also the one that can please and move us
most" (*Poesie* 447), because all theater was for him first and foremost
entertainment: "People read poets and visit the theater not in order
to learn something, but to pleasantly shorten time and to be entertained" (380). Möser went even further: "We do not listen to merry
music because Graun and Pergolesi want to convert our hearts; no,
we seek only to soothe, calm, and invigorate ourselves, and to prepare our tired spirits for more serious duties" (74). Thus entertainment is a recuperative medicine, though it does not cure anything in
particular.

Such an account of the theoretical debate may suggest that opera
was a monolithic entity that appeared in changing perspectives. In
reality, the revaluations of opera paralleled its transformations,

though its trajectory from Peri and Caccini to Gluck constitutes a spiral rather than a straight line, leading from the initial rhetorical form by way of the melody-dominated Venetian and Neapolitan styles back to the word-dominated art of Gluck. It may therefore be asked if Gluck's revival of the rhetorical style did not retard the emancipation of music from language. My answer will constitute the remainder of this chapter.

Gluck

The rhetorical style evolved by the Camerata and its successors culminated in Monteverdi, but in the Venetian opera of the next generation it had already become restricted to recitative, the vehicle of the plot. Melody came to dominate the second component, the aria, which offered occasions for reflection, expressions of mood, and the "overflow of the emotions" (Sulzer, art. "Arie"). But the da capo (ABA) structure of the new aria was too rigid to fit specific plots and moods; its contrasting sections made psychological verisimilitude difficult; and its purely musical principles allowed a display of vocal brilliance without serving the affective and imitative needs of the text. This is why Goethe regarded it as pure music and Brown as a striking absurdity (205).

A similar tension between pure form and representation existed in the overtures. The French and Italian overtures of the seventeenth century seldom tied in with the plot or the musical material of the opera. Several eighteenth-century proposals suggested means for endowing overtures with a mimetic quality. Scheibe recommended that overtures and musical interludes be thematically and affectively linked to the characters and actions (603–18), and Lessing enthusiastically endorsed this idea in the twenty-sixth piece of his *Hamburgische Dramaturgie* (4:348ff.). D'Alembert, who had only contempt for the conventional fast-slow-fast pattern, asked for overtures that "started in a dream from which the veil was lifted with the first measure." But while he believed that overtures could set the mood, he opposed "analytic" overtures with dramatic confrontations between themes, because he doubted that pure instrumental music could enact a drama (*Oe.* 1:544–45). His view was later shared by Engel (323).

The French operatic tradition was perhaps less formulaic than the Italian, and it gave more attention to librettos, especially at the outset, when Quinault wrote for Lully. But Rameau had less success with his librettists, and the increased role he gave to the orchestra further reduced the significance of his texts. As d'Alembert remarked, the notes in French arias were usually squandered on words empty of sense (*Oe.* 1:538). In the wake of the querelle the French tradition, with its outdated mythology and elaborate machinery, had to yield the stage to Italian opera, but this was a mixed blessing, since the Neapolitan opera seria had its own problems with librettos. Nevertheless, Italian opera underwent important changes at the time, partly in response to critics like Algarotti, who postulated that "the poet should resume the reins of power, which have been so unjustly wrested from his hands" (11). Zeno and Metastasio tightened their plots and shifted the subject from mythology to ancient history or legend, while the composers Jomelli and Traetta slowly started to dismantle the rigid boundaries between event and affect, recitative and aria.

The foregoing sketch of developments in opera may illuminate the historical role of Gluck. Presenting himself as a reformer, Gluck (or, more likely, his librettist Calzabigi) announced in the preface to his *Alceste* (1769) that he had eliminated all the abuses "which have so long disfigured Italian opera and made the most splendid and beautiful of spectacles the most ridiculous and wearisome." Gluck considered himself a reviver of musical drama because he wished to restrict music "to its true office of serving poetry by means of expression, and by following the situations of the story, without interrupting the action or stifling it with a useless superfluity of ornaments."[8] Specifically, he intended to avoid the artificialities of the da capo aria, "to apprise the spectators of the nature of the action" by means of the overture, to introduce the instruments "in proportion to the interest and the intensity of the words, to leave no sharp contrast between the aria and the recitative in the dialogue," and to devote himself to the search for a beautiful simplicity without a display of technical brilliance. His new dramatic scheme intended to substitute "for florid descriptions, unnatural paragons and sententious, cold morality, heartfelt language, strong passions, interesting situations, and an endlessly varied spectacle" (Einstein 113–14).

Ingenuity was needed to make this palatable to the French public, and Gluck's librettist for *Iphigénie*, du Roullet, made the tactical error of announcing the new opera as an answer to Rousseau's charge that the deficiencies of French precluded great French operas. Gluck immediately wrote a letter of his own, ignoring this divisive issue and emphasizing instead that his rhetorical style reinstituted language in music in the spirit of Rousseau: "Inasmuch as it is within my power, I direct my music, which is always simple and natural, only to the greatest expression and to the reinforcement of the declamation of the poetry." Furthermore, Gluck announced that he was planning to consult the great Rousseau so that "we might perhaps succeed together by searching for a noble, affective, and natural melody, with an exact declamation suited to the prosody of each language and the character of each people," and he even proposed cooperating with Rousseau to find a "music suitable for all the nations" in order to abolish "the ridiculous distinctions of national music." The letter closed with highest praise for Rousseau, especially his analysis of the monologue in Lully's *Armide* (Einstein 182–84).

Such a disarming ending probably tempered the objections that Rousseau must have entertained concerning supranational operas and Gluck's own style. Did Gluck manoeuvre to preempt expected Rousseauist attacks on his music, or did he really believe that his style conformed to the principles advocated by the writer? The question is difficult to answer. Rousseau's ideal was the Greek musiké, yet he was too fond of melody to advocate a rhetorical submission of music to language. But then, Gluck arrived in Paris with Italian credentials, and this could have endeared him to Rousseau. It seems likely that Gluck submitted his *Alceste* for Rousseau's critical comments in the hope that the courtesy would tilt the judgment in his favor. In any case, he soon withdrew the score; Rousseau intended to include his incomplete remarks in a letter to Burney (1774); however, this was only accomplished by his editor, posthumously.

These comments reveal, for the first time, that Rousseau was aware of the conflict between rhetorical accentuation and melody, and that he decisively favored the latter: "The pleasure of the ear ought to outweigh the truth of expression; for music can reach the heart only by means of the charm in melody; and if only the accents of passions would matter, the art of declamation alone would suffice" (*Ecrits* 389–90). A fusion of verbal and musical rhythm was possible in antiquity, but musical rhythm was quite different from poetic rhythm now, and no modern nation could "make language sing and music speak." Thus the rhetorical accentuation of modern languages must be restricted to a-musical declamation, which fits tragedies but has no place in operas. As soon as music joins language, "it must arm itself with all its charms to subjugate the heart by means of the ear" (*Ecrits* 393). At moments of highest emotional intensity the voice must therefore become silent and leave expression to a purely instrumental (symphonic) ritornello: "The silence of the actor speaks then more than his words" (*Ecrits* 397). We see how the praise of musical representations of silence in the *Essai* gently slips into an acceptance of instrumental music here.

Indeed, Gluck's salutary impact on French theories of opera was to foment reflection on the tension between the affective and aesthetic qualities in music, and he may actually have moved several important critics toward a greater sympathy for pure music. Marmontel, for instance, was as hesitant as Rousseau about Gluck, but whereas Rousseau feared a lessening of the emotional impact, Marmontel was more worried about the destruction of melodic beauty. He preferred the charm of Italian melodies to Gluck's expressive style (18). Since the object of music was not just to move the soul but also to give pleasure, strong shouts and cries had to be moderated, embellished, and thereby made palatable. Composers must endow musical expression with "a charm that the cries, complaints, the somber or painful accents of the natural passions do not have." To banish melody from opera would be as strange as to prohibit beautiful verse in tragedy (25).

Though Gluck had no intention of destroying melody, his music challenged French theorists to come to a defense of it. Marmontel preferred melody to the tensions of the expressive style, because he found sheer delight in graceful order; and his disposition was fostered by the French hedonism of the day, as we shall see in the essays of Boyé and Chabanon. The fundamental impact of this new appreciation of melody and form was to diminish the role of didacticism and remove the passions from the center of aesthetic experience. Less well-intentioned and philosophically minded proponents of sheer melodic music sponsored Piccini to oppose Gluck, but the French resistance to Gluck was not merely petty intrigue against a man of genius. It was also an aesthetically important intermediate stage in the movement toward the emancipation of music from language, intellectual truths, and moral messages.

The confrontation between melodic and expressive styles was similar in Germany. Heinse reluctantly acknowledged Gluck's genius but regretted his persistent search for expression and thought that the Italians were better at creating a beautiful voice (5:302–03). The question was whether poetry or music should dominate in opera: "Seduced by his system, Titan-Gluck wanted to drain all the beautiful seas on which the [singing] Farinellis and Faustinas swam and sailed around in inexpressible happiness." Luckily, Gluck recognized how meager his arias were and compensated for them with rich choruses, rhythmic dances, and strong instrumentation (5:317).[9]

Herder's position was similarly ambiguous. Recommending to Gluck his libretto, on November 5, 1774, he emphasized that the words were only meant to pin down the musical affects; they were "to be what a subscript is to a painting or a column: an explanation, a guide to the stream of music by means of words strewn into it." Now, this was a curious recommendation to send to a composer whose program was to restore music "to its true office of serving poetry by means of expression." Herder obviously did not think that expressive music had to affirm language; he respected the composer for not "rounding off everything" into smooth and slick melodic lines, but he wanted music to have its own voice: "Words ought just to enliven the moving body of music, and the latter ought to speak, act, and move." To be sure, in the later *Adrastea* Herder scorned operatic "pure music" (23:335), and he pitied Mozart for having wasted his music on miserable librettos. He even envisioned a man in the coming century who, contemptuous of this "odd lot (*Trödelkram*) of wordless sounds," would recognize "the necessity of intimately connecting pure human sentiment with plot by means of sounds" (22:336). The prophetic reference to Wagner pleads for a dramatic unity of action, expression, and music, but no longer in terms of eighteenth-century musical rhetoric.

Gluck's brilliant attempt to reunite poetry and music by means of a rhetorical style did not become a model for the next generations. As Einstein writes, in the "eternal and for ever undecided fundamental conflict between opera and drama," Gluck shifted the balance toward the latter, as the Venetian musicians after Monteverdi had moved it the other way (*Gluck* 119). Gluck had only minor successors like Spontini, while the more decisive innovations soon came from comic opera, which spawned *Die Zauberflöte* and *Don Giovanni*. For Nietzsche, the emergence of the *stilo rappresentativo*, the style which Gluck reconstituted, was a result of an "extra-artistic tendency," which stood in the shadow of "the vaulted structure of Palestrina's harmonies." The rhetorical opera, so Nietzsche thought, used the language of "the theoretical man."

11 MUSICAL EXPRESSION?

As if emotion had ever been able to create anything artistic.
—Nietzsche, *The Birth of Tragedy*, section 19

All critical terms are problematic, but few have been questioned as vigorously as *expression*. Hanslick mounted a campaign against it in the middle of the nineteenth century; Stravinsky remarked that "music is, by its very nature, powerless to express anything at all" (83); Popper, a leading contemporary philosopher, declared that "the expressionist theory of art is empty" (48); and a recent article by Leahy is entitled "The Vacuity of Musical Expression."

Scruton's article on expression in the *New Grove* joins these critics in declaring that the traditional meaning of the concept is useless, although it undertakes a rather curious rescue attempt by postulating that the term can also be used intransitively: a face or a piece of music may have expression without expressing anything in particular. Though Scruton cites Wittgenstein as his authority, the evidence for such use of the term seems thin. As Scruton himself remarks, "The popular view remains essentially that of Rousseau and Diderot: music evokes emotion because it expresses emotion. Music is the middle term in an act of emotional communication" (329). In his review of the *New Grove*, Rosen rightly notes that the history of the term has no bearing on Scruton's philosophical treatment of it.

Kivy's philosophical and historical "reflections on musical expression" (his subtitle) is burdened with a similar confusion, for it takes Mattheson and Hiller, two rather traditional theorists of the affects, labels them as eighteenth-century theorists of expression, and then constructs a modern theory of expression that nobody in the eighteenth century actually held. Kivy, relying on Tormey, argues that expression has nothing to do with authorial intention (it does not mean that Beethoven was sad when he wrote the second movement of the *Eroica* Symphony, or even that he wanted to write sad music);

nor, Kivy says, does expression mean that music can arouse certain affects in the listener (23). Thus, instead of saying "this music expresses sadness," we ought to say that it is "expressive of sadness," which saddles the listener with attributing expression to music. Fair enough, but this analytically developed concept of expression has little to do with its eighteenth-century meaning, and it certainly has no connection with the ideas of Mattheson and Hiller, which were firmly rooted in the traditional presupposition that music represents, and arouses, the affects.

Another recent impetus for the revival of interest in expression comes from the work of Goodman, especially his *Languages of Art*, which argues that expression is a special form of reference, in which emotional content is assigned to art by metaphorical transference. Essays by Howard and Newcomb fruitfully apply this approach to music, and the result is a theory of expression that has neither the denotational fixities of eighteenth-century theories nor the claim to intersubjectivity that Kivy still upholds.

These contemporary reconsiderations of expression directly relate to my topic, though in a negative way. As I shall show in this chapter, eighteenth-century theories of expression were denotative (in that they advocated the depiction of passions), and they conventionally held that the purpose of music was to arouse passions in the listener. The popular notion that Scruton somewhat unjustly assigns to Rousseau and Diderot certainly holds for those who advocated expression in the eighteenth century, for they saw it as a communication of feeling from composer to audience. I shall discuss this basic tenet under three headings, each of which emphasizes a different aspect: (1) expression as imitation, (2) expression as power to arouse the listener, and (3) self-expression and spontaneous creativity. All three, I shall argue, remained within the affective-mimetic tradition, and none offered a conceptual foundation for the new instrumental music.

EXPRESSION AS IMITATION

For a large number of eighteenth-century writers, expression of the passions simply meant their imitation. Morellet states the position paradigmatically: "At least for the present problem, I regard the terms 'to express' and 'to paint' as synonymous—perhaps they always are. Since all [musical] painting is imitation, to ask whether music is expressive and wherein its expression lies means to ask whether music is imitative and in what manner" (114).[1] The reverse, namely, that musical imitation is necessarily expression, was stated in Cahusac's *Encyclopédie* article on expression: "Imitation [in music] is not and cannot be anything but the genuine expression of the sentiment that one intends to paint."

Whether the British critics also equated expression with imitation is a matter of debate. I side with Rogerson and Schueller (*Sist.* 198), who suggest that the British introduced the term *expression* to denote the imitation of affects and restricted musical imitation to the mimicry of natural sounds (Rogerson 74–77). In this view, expression is merely an extension of the seventeenth-century imitation of affects. A second line of thought holds that the British concept of expression represented a decisive departure from mimesis. In Wellek's *Rise of English Literary History* (51–52), as well as in his later works, Harris, Avison, Beattie, Adam Smith, and Sir William Jones are said to have raised increasingly powerful objections to musical mimesis. The argument has been generally adopted and may be found, for example, in Lipking (219), Scher, Lessem, the *New Grove* article on expression (6:325). I intend to show that the reputation of the British critics is inflated, for they have not contributed significantly to a new aesthetics.

EXPRESSION AS POWER TO AROUSE PASSIONS

The notion that the expression of a musical piece is to be gauged by the emotions aroused in the listeners has become difficult to maintain, and aestheticians today tend to agree with the delightful words of Bouwsma that sadness relates to music like redness to apple rather than like burp to cider (100). In other words, the affect of sadness is not a result of music but a quality we ascribe to it.

Many eighteenth-century writers thought differently, and they introduced the term *expression* to account for the power of music to sway the passions. In the words of Avison, which shall stand here for many similar formulations,[2] genuine musical expression "is such an happy Mixture of Air and Harmony as will affect us most strongly with the Passions or Affections which the Poet intends to raise" (69).

Now, as we have seen, swaying the passions was already the pragmatic dimension of affect theory, and the concept could have been fitted into that tradition. Many writers, for instance Webb (28, 43), did just that, but Harris, Beattie, and others proposed expression as a kind of replacement for imitation. These writers reject the imitation only of external noises, movements, and objects, not the general concept of mimesis. None of the champions of expression actually proposed thereby a new aesthetics.

The British Critics

Avison's *Essay on Musical Expression* brandishes the concept in its very title and has therefore been singled out as the key document of its history,[3] although, as Rogerson (88) remarks, the essay barely departs from a conventional and somewhat vague theory of imitation held by Dubos and others. In my view, Avison was unorthodox in one respect only, one for which he has not received due credit, namely, in defending harmony and polyphony against the dominant melodic and monodic practice.

Avison introduces expression to replace rhythm in the traditional tripartite division of music, which also included melody and harmony. But since he defines expression as "a combination of melody and harmony, and no more than a strong and proper application of them to the intended subject" (22), he makes the logical error of positing the combination of two elements as a third basic element.[4]

The important question, however, is what Avison says about expression in the body of his essay. For practical purposes we may characterize this work as a comparative study on the expressive, melodic, and harmonic styles. Now, Avison defines expressive style as the "unaffected Strain of Nature and Simplicity" (70), but the subsequent treatment discusses faulty imitations rather than successful expressions. The list of restrictions on imitation is rather conventional: music can imitate only sound and, to some extent, motion; the voice should not imitate (60–61); motionless and soundless objects, ungraceful motions and disagreeable sounds should not be imitated (66–67); finally, the "finest instrumental Music may be considered as an Imitation of the vocal" (117).

Some imitations are faulty because they imitate unworthy subjects (e.g., the barking of a dog), and others because they appeal to the understanding. Since imitated passions are, as a rule, neither vulgar nor intellectual, this principle does not clash with the traditional representations of affect theory, or with Avison's demand that true expression must "affect the Heart and raise the Passions of the Soul" (57–58). Indeed, Avison explicitly states that imitations that "coincide" with expression are "admitted universally" (62). His skimpy advice on how to write expressive music (74–75, 112–19) contains accordingly only traditional remarks on the affective value of keys, instruments, and other elements of music. His rejection of intellectual, emblematic representations can hardly be called an advocacy of a new aesthetics.

The issue on which Avison most clearly dissents from the received opinion of his day concerns the relative weight of melody and harmony. Though he admits the historical priority of melody, he considers harmony to be the "most important Circumstance which adorns, and supports the whole Performance" (22), and "the very Cement of all musical Composition" (31). Hence he is much softer on the sins of "too close Attachment to Harmony, and Neglect of Air" than on "the present fashionable Extreme of running all our Music into one single Part, to the utter Neglect of all true Harmony" (30). He admires the polyphonists and contrapuntists of the sixteenth century who had a "great Depth of Knowledge in the Construction of their Harmony . . . to which they often add a considerable Energy and Force of Expression" (43). Although their intellectual pieces "amuse the Understanding, and amaze the Eye, but can never touch the Heart, or delight the Ear" (44–45), Avison intends to rehabilitate Palestrina, the "Father of Harmony," and he believes that fugues are the "most noble and diffusive" species of composition (75). Just here, in Avison's defense of harmony and counterpoint, is a glimpse of a genuine departure from mimesis. For in the "full Music" of equal voices he finds a variety of expression (76) that arranges, "in beautiful Order, the distinguished Parts of a Composition" (80).

Avison is usually cited as the most prominent of the British writers concerned with expression, but his narrowing of the concept of imitation is actually deeply indebted to Harris's *Discourse* (1744). Harris starts from the general premise that the arts imitate either the natural world or "the Passions, Energies, and other Affections of Minds" (55–56). But music can "imitate only Sounds and Motions" (57), and even these only imperfectly, for it cannot individualize the represented objects, movements, or affects. Hence musical imitation is inferior to painting (69) and poetry (81).[5]

Is this a rejection of mimesis? And, if so, what new aesthetics does it suggest? We must postpone the answer temporarily, for the implications of Harris's position become fully evident only in Beattie's *Essays* (written in 1762 but not published until 1776), which poses a series of persuasive rhetorical questions designed to strike music from the list of imitative arts (118–25). Does a devotional song have to imitate the sounds of a devotional exercise? Is music truly imitative if a text is needed to explain it? Does the pleasure of listening depend on the quality of imitation? Is it not true that many good imitations are bad music? Can instrumental music be called truly imitative? These questions appear to signal Beattie's decisive departure from mimesis, but their inconsequentiality becomes evident when Beattie, following Harris and Avison, restricts musical imitation to the agreeable representation of sounds and motions (122). Since "imitative Music" always "imitates natural sounds and motions" (128), the musical representations of affects must reproduce the audible sounds of joy, lament, or anger—and Beattie has a justifiably low opinion of these. Handel's *Te Deum*, he remarks, does not imitate the sounds emitted by people venerating God (119).

Yet Beattie believes that music has a great power "of raising a variety of agreeable emotions in the hearer" (119). What is the source of that power? Not, to be sure, sounds of wailing or rejoicing, which are, for him, the only musical imitations of emotions: "An air may be pastoral, and in the highest degree pleasing, which imitates neither sound nor motion, nor any thing else whatever" (133). But, Beattie continues, there exists "some relation at least, or analogy, if not similitude, between certain musical sounds, and mental affections" that lends power to the expressive rousing of passions. Evidently, this is precisely what theorists of the affects always held. Indeed, Beattie, like Webb (6 ff.) and others, reaffirms the heart of affect theory, and he even continues to assign emotional values to keys and intervals; but since in his terminology imitation is restricted to the mimicry of sounds and does not include the representation of inaudible psychic events, he must use another term for it. Though he must call it expression instead of imitation, this associative representation of passions remains for him the highest aim of music. Upon closer inspection, Beattie's radical rejection of imitation reveals itself therefore as a definitional trick.

That Beattie and others had rejected mimesis nominally rather than in substance was recognized already in the eighteenth century by Twining, in a "dissertation" of 1789 attached to his translation of Aristotle's *Poetics*. Music, of course, is inferior to poetry when it tries to reproduce actual sounds and motions, because "of all the powers of Music, this of raising ideas by direct resemblance is confessed to be the weakest, and the least important" (45). But why do Harris and others restrict imitation to the reproduction of sound and motion (46), and why should the rousing of passions exclude their imitation, if for Twining's witnesses, Aristotle and Plato, the expressive "power over the affections" was synonymous with imitation (47)? They meant by mimesis not the imitation of external sounds and objects but precisely what we distinguish from it under the term *expression*, namely, the representation of affects (46). Twining seems to side with the ancients, for he asserts that "music can be said to imitate, no farther than as it expresses something" (44).

Now, Twining admits that associative and instrumental imitations are imprecise and not reproductions in the narrow sense, but he makes an early and unusually warm defense of them in a longer footnote:

> Music, here, is not imitative, but . . . merely suggestive. But, whatever we may call it, . . . in the best instrumental Music, expressively performed, the very indecision itself of the expression . . . produces a pleasure, which . . . [is] one of the most delicious that Music is capable of affording. [49]

Twining, then, turns imprecision and vagueness into the virtue of "suggestiveness." To suggest is to stimulate the imagination, to generate ideas and emotions that are unique to the character and experience of the listener. While this does not amount to a demand that music be stricken from the list of the imitative arts (Abrams 14), it frees music from the task of mediating to the listener precisely defined contents. In this sense we see here a step toward a Romantic aesthetics.

Like Beattie, Twining, and others, Robertson attacks only naturalistic sound imitations. His premise is different, however, for he believes that art idealizes and ennobles (11), and music is an "engine which lifts men the highest up above nature" (444). Mimetic representations must therefore idealize nature somewhat in the sense of Batteux, although the Frenchman would not have found anything "unclean and shocking in Nature," and he did not ask composers to give nature notes "she had never uttered" (8). In direct response to Batteux, Robertson finds opera "the most perfect and exalted entertainment," because it represents "not merely Nature, but the beautiful and sublime, added to Nature," even without resorting to the supernatural and the marvelous (354–55). While Robertson vehemently condemns "roaring of winds, cataracts of rivers, buzzing of flies, hopping of frogs" in music (444), he approves of the imitation of passions as long as they transform inarticulate and often unpleasant emotional sounds into "uplifting" form. Robertson's wistful conclusion reveals a Platonic ethical defense of mimesis: although it may have become more perfect, "Music, from once having been the friend of Virtue, and the companion of Philosophy . . . has now become chiefly the Amusement of Mankind" (451).

Adam Smith's essay *Of the Imitative Arts* (1795), finally, denies imitation only to instrumental music:

> The imitative powers of Instrumental are much inferior to those of Vocal Music; its melodious but unmeaning and inarticulated sounds cannot, like the articulations of the human voice, relate distinctly the circumstances of any particular story, or describe the different situations which those circumstances produced; or even express clearly, and so as to be understood by every hearer, the various sentiments and passions which the parties concerned felt from these situations. [159–60]

To cite such passages of the essay as evidence of Smith's decisive departure from musical mimesis is unjustified. He does say that "Imitation is by no means essential" to instrumental music (175), but this is not intended as praise. If instrumental melody and harmony "signify and suggest nothing," this means not only that they do not imitate ("signify") but also that they are not expressive (they do not "suggest" anything to the listener). In truth, nonimitative instrumental music remains, for Smith, inferior to the "necessarily and essentially imitative" music of the voice (152). In praise of the voice Smith can even extol, as we have seen in the previous chapter, the repetition of words in opera, which he considers a faithful reproduction of a mind haunted by passion: "It is by means of such repetitions only, that Music can exert those peculiar powers of imitation which distinguish it, and in which it excels all the other Imitative Arts" (155). This excellence of the voice in representing passions highlights the poverty of instrumental music: it can merely support such imitations (169–70), or, when imitating on its own, it needs explanations, like baroque emblems (161).

Only at the very end of a long list of shortcomings does Smith abruptly arrive at the important positive insight that instrumental music appeals to the imagination by activating memory and inviting anticipation. But he glosses too quickly over this potentially momentous idea and concludes that although "instrumental Music can produce very considerable effects" without imitation, "its powers over the heart and affections are, no doubt, much inferior to those of vocal Music" (171).

Evidence hardly warrants, then, the claim that the British concept of expression moved music aesthetics beyond, or even to the edge of, mimesis. The British critics criticized some forms of imitation, namely, naturalistic and instrumental imitations, but their outlook remained traditional.

SPONTANEOUS CREATIVITY AND SELF-EXPRESSION

Eggebrecht posits expression as the shibboleth of a musical Sturm and Drang stretching from 1740 (about thirty years before the start of the literary movement of that name) until the emergence of the classical style of Mozart and Haydn around 1780. In this view, expressive music used sharp dynamic, thematic, and harmonic contrasts, structured musical time freely, individualized instrumental parts, and manifested a craving for elemental experiences (*Ausdrucks-Prinzip* 325). Yet these new means per se do not constitute the real novelty; this novelty lies rather in their manner of application, as means to break up traditional forms to further self-expression. If baroque mimesis expressed something typical and objective, the new expression is an intense self-expression that cares little about balanced form (325).

Eggebrecht richly documents this shift from objective to subjective expression, but he does not demonstrate that it amounted to a departure from mimesis. To begin with, even stylized expressions had a personal dimension, for the originally alien affects had to be appropriated: the composer could move his listeners only if he had already experienced the represented passion (Matheson 108).[6] More important, the growing insistence that composers, performers, and listeners "live" the emotions actually served to improve verisimilitude in representing emotions. If, as Burney records, C. P. E. Bach was inspired and played like a "possessed" one (*Germ.* 2:270), his presentation was understood as imitation. According to Bach's own manual for players, "Since a musician cannot move unless he is moved, he must be able to project himself into all the affects which he wants to arouse in the listeners; he makes them understand his passions and moves them thereby best to com-passion" (85).

Several other shifts in style also improved imitative fidelity. For instance, younger composers sought to render emotional conflicts more faithfully by frequent and gradual shifts of emotion, using a wider dynamic range of sounds and enriching the orchestra. The new realism also advocated what Mozart practiced in his ensemble singing, namely, the simultaneous or successive portrayal of several emotions. This represented a change with respect to the traditional view that variety was just an anodyne to boredom that had to be subordinated to the principles of unity and simplicity. Mattheson, as well as Heinichen and Scheibe, still held that minor or secondary affects were not to divert the composer's steady gaze from the primary one (*Capellm.* 145), and Lessing still insisted in the *Hamburgische Dramaturgie* of 1767–68 that the tempo of a movement had to remain unchanged, "for one piece can only express one thing." Lessing even demanded an affective unity between movements: "A symphony which expresses in its various movements different, contradictory passions is a musical monstrosity; a single passion must dominate in a single symphony, and each movement must seek to express in sounds and arouse in us the same passion in different variations."[7] But the changes in style and taste loosened affective unity and worked toward a more subtle psychological realism. Quantz, who found variety to be the pleasure of music (275), advocated a "steady alternation of forte and piano" (106) and the use of loud dissonances to highlight "the excitement of alternating passions" (227). C. P. E. Bach remarked that the musician "has barely quieted down one [affect before] he arouses another, so that he constantly alternates the passions" (85).

This newly won flexibility in rendering emotional flux actually raised music's ranking among the imitative arts. Forkel noted that "the modulation of passion is best expressed and imitated by means of modulating sounds" (*Gesch.* 8). Music, according to Webb, can "catch the movements of passion as they spring from the soul; painting waits until they rise into action, or determine character" (39). For him, pleasure was no longer "the result of any fixed or permanent condition of the nerves and spirits" but something arising from "a succession of impressions" (47). The temporality of sounds, the possibility of imitating the ebb and flow of passions by means of modulations of pitch, loudness, and tempo now became a virtue rather than a liability. Heydenreich observed that emotions endure, have a continuous spectrum of intensity, flip over into their opposite, or shade into adjacent feelings. The signs of passions must therefore be finely graded, sustainable, and diverse—criteria best met by sounds, "which copy feeling and passion with generally comprehensible veracity and irresistible effect in the heart. No other sign can match them therein, and music is therefore the only art which can copy feelings and passions in the full sense of the word" (166).

If music became the best imitative art in terms of the criteria established by theories of expression, this was due not only to the proliferation and individualization of musical affects. In the changing conception of man, the very notion of the soul had slowly cast off its substantive, changeless character to assume a dynamic temporal existence. Eggebrecht actually acknowledges that the expressive style and its theory tried to capture this newly conceived emotional life with more supple means, by choosing "expressive realism" as his final formula for the musical Sturm und Drang.

In sum, the individualization of expression that Eggebrecht regards as the hallmark of Sturm und Drang improves rather than abandons musical mimesis. It remains to be seen, however, whether Herder and Heinse, the two major figures in Eggebrecht's musical Sturm und Drang, actually subscribed to a theory of self-expression. As I shall show, neither of them can be said to have advocated a consistent expressive theory of music.

Herder

In a letter of September 20, 1770, to his bride, Herder described himself as "a sensitive soul with the most clumsy and coarse hands for the piano." Nevertheless, this dilettante contributed significantly to German thoughts on music, by means of the sensualism and psychologism of his youthful *Critische[s] Wäldchen* (1769) and later by developing a unique notion of cosmic harmony. Attending these strands, however, we shall find no coherent theory of spontaneous expression.[8]

The *Wäldchen* ("Little Woods") was conceived as a series of forays into the woods (and thickets) of contemporary aesthetics. The fourth one, sketched early in 1769 and revised during Herder's sojourn in France later that year, was originally intended as a critique of an aesthetics by Riedel but became largely a treatise on music. Unfortunately it remained unfinished and was published only posthumously.

Herder's strong aversion to abstract thought disposed him toward sensualism and even pantheism. His empirical and inductive aesthetics of the senses gave priority to touch over temporally or spatially mediated impressions (4:54). He believed that the beauty of sound is inferior to visual splendor because its trace vanishes "like the ship in the sea, the arrow in the air, and the thought in the soul," though its intoxicating intensity compensates for its evanescence by penetrating us more deeply than the rays of light (4:47, 90). Herder's physiology of aesthetics starts with sense data but intends to go beyond pure physics and mathematics to study the impact of the data on the soul. For physical acoustics quantifies sound but explains nothing "about simple sound itself, nothing about its energy upon the ear, nothing of its grace" (4:90).

Unfortunately, Herder's "philosophy of sonorous beauty" (4:91) never achieved its aim of studying the metamorphosis of sound into feeling, for the fourth Wäldchen got bogged down by the critical task of showing that the calculus of sounds is irrelevant to the pleasure aroused by a single forcefully impinging sound. Even if the overtones produced harmony, which Herder doubted, they could still not account for the impact of music, because they are derivative of the primary impact of sheer sound (4:94). Judging tonal relations, like judging distance, is merely a cold, intellectual echo of the powerful primary sensations that constitute the "indivisible" primary data of music: "No principle based on relations and proportions can possibly account for the genuine, first, and original pleasure of the ear. . . . Aggregates of sound cannot be understood and explained unless the material parts of the aggregate are understandable and explainable" (4:96).

Hence Herder explicitly inverts the theory that the overtones generate emotional impact (4:94–95). Sounds without overtones, which are sheer noise for Rameau, are for Herder the "simple and powerful" tones (*Ton*) that constitute the aesthetic value of music. The harmonics ("sound," or *Schall*) are merely derivative. In Herder's "musical monadology" (4:114) chords are "the result of a composition, hence a dry concept of the mind; the three jointly heard sounds are essential only as individual elements; the conjoining itself is only a state. What should it explain?" (4:113). The mathematics of music, therefore, deals only with derivative aggregates, whereas acoustics knows "only about the external, composite phenomena and of motions caused by them." Herder's "inner physics of the spirit" would start with the emotional quality of simple sounds (4:98), for everything depends on "simple, effective feeling" (4:97).

The primacy of sensations undergirds Herder's historical thesis that the "expressions of passion, in irregular, bold, powerful accents of feelings" must have preceded the music of pleasing sounds (4:114–17).[9] Like Rousseau, Herder projects this state onto the Greeks, because he believes that "harmonic-scientific music was nothing and lively expression everything" for them (4:119). Our "sound-art (*Tonkunst*) of relations and intellect" (4:120) developed because we no longer revel in "tone-pleasure" (*Wollust;* 4:113). We invent gothic, heavy harmonies and learned relations because we have become deaf to accents and tones that penetrate the soul (4:109–11). Next to the intellectualization of music through harmony, the second great sin of modern music is to represent the external world. For if music "quits her empire of feeling and emulates the painting eye, she is no longer music but a cacophony of sounds" (4:138–39). In the later *Adrastea*, it is one of the three major sins of music to dally with painting objects instead of expressing emotions (23:567).

Much of this is clearly derivative of Rousseau, whose writings on music (save the *Essai*) Herder must have come to know during the revision of the *Wäldchen* in France. But the voice is unmistakably Herder's: the sensualism would have been anathema to Rousseau, and the atomization of aesthetic pleasure into momentary sensations clashes with Rousseau's sense of melodic form. And the distance between Herder's holistic sense of a physical union with nature and Rousseau's perception of music as a language of inner space only widens when Herder becomes preoccupied with cosmic music and ceases to attack mathematics. Indeed, when in *Kalligone* one of the discussants agrees with Rousseau's objections to Rameau and attacks mathematical music in the manner of Mattheson, his partner responds with the Leibnizian formulation that the pleasure of music may be unconscious counting: if nature is ordered by relations, "why should we not count if there is no music without counting? Especially, if nature had made this counting so easy that we needed no effort and no calculation on paper, and, just by accepting these golden coins, we were showered with a wealth of emotions, as if with waves of joy. Nature herself would, then, count for us" (22:66–67).[10]

Yet, this new perspective is not straightforward Pythagoreanism as Wiora believes, for Herder does not subscribe to its central tenet that the physical sounds merely indicate an unheard order behind them.[11] The sensualism of Herder's youth persists in his later desire to grasp the cosmic order in living sounds so that numbers and proportions become superfluous. This sensualism is actually reinforced by his shift from an ego-centered aesthetics to a nature-centered one that exalts music in the manner of Rameau as a universal voice of "sonorous bodies." Resonance, the response of other bodies to this voice, reveals a universal sympathy in nature and indicates that sound is never just empty vibration but a communication that "expresses something internal, moves something interior" (22:62). Sound is the "voice of nature" (22:181) speaking from the interior of agitated elastic bodies, "loudly or softly communicating to other harmonious bodies their suffering, resistance, or summoned forces" (22:63).

Kalligone and Herder's other late writings display two new ideas that have not been fully appreciated: namely, that sounds are nature's general reactive force, and that the human voice is just a participant in a kind of universal concert. The new controlling image of stasis and equilibrium is diametrically opposed to creative eruptions: "Everything wants to persist in its being and reconstitute itself" according to the "high laws of immutable nature" (22:65). Accordingly, Herder's attention is devoted to sound reception rather than sound emission; he understands music not as an irresistible expressive burst but rather as a restorative response to forces that disturb inner balance. Listening is just sympathetic resonance, a passive response whereby bodies agitated by sounds reestablish their peace: "They sense they are moved by proportions, and they are pleasantly swayed by them; they are compelled to return to their peace in the same proportion" (22:180). The dominant metaphors are therefore the aeolian harp and the inner "spiritual clavichord" that resonate in harmony with the sounds impinging upon us (22:68, 24:440). It is difficult to see how these notions could be fitted into a Sturm und Drang theory of subjectivity.

Herder's notion that "no artist ever invented a sound or gave it a power which it did not possess in nature and his instrument" (22:180) recalls Batteux but gains a new meaning within Herder's cosmic holism. He means by it, first, that "every sound in nature is music" so that man is not the principal music maker, merely a "general participant" in nature's creative concert (22:179–80) that subsumes individual genius. But if the voice is just one among many sources of sound, new perspectives open on instrumental music. Indeed, Herder remarks that music has gained a field of its own in overtures and sonatas, for here, "unrestrained by any other art, it spreads its wings and often takes its highest, wildest flight" (23:560). While a fusion of the arts is still Herder's vision, he approves of the new voice that the instruments display: "Music has acquired its own unique art form without words, just by and through itself" (22:185).

Thus Herder's thoughts on music elude the reductive label of "expressionism." Both the sensualism of the *Wäldchen* and his later "pantheistic Pythagoreanism"—to coin an oxymoron—focus on listening rather than expressive creation. Herder reminds us not that music is personal but that "we live in an 'Odeum,' a hall of eternal harmonies" (22:65). This sense of cosmic music paves the way for the revival of Pythagoreanism in Romanticism, though Herder appreciates the universe of sound in its physical majesty rather than its mathematical abstraction, and he remains generally uninterested in form.

Heinse

Though Heinse is little known outside German-speaking countries, he was an important figure of the Sturm und Drang and an unusually sensitive interpreter of music. In contrast to Herder and other writers, he had considerable empirical and technical knowledge of music, and his writings are distinguished by valuable concrete commentaries on specific pieces. It remains to decide whether these writings reveal "a watertight, mostly original and partly astonishing system of expressive musical meaning" (Eggebrecht, *Ausdrucks-Prinzip* 341).

Heinse's taste was formed between 1780 and 1782 in Venice and Rome, where he could still delight in the by then declining sensuous splendor of the Italian opera so congenial to the artistic-hedonistic vision of his chef d'oeuvre, the novel *Ardinghello*. His abiding love for the soaring melodies of Jomelli and Traetta prevented Heinse from appreciating fully Gluck's expressive style and the new instrumental music, though he recognized their power, and his late novel *Hildegard von Hohenthal* (1795–96) articulated these conflicts by means of dialogues.

The story tells how the aristocrat Hildegard develops under the tutelage of Lockmann, a young bourgeois conductor, from a musical dilettante into a ravishing singer, occasionally encouraging Lockmann's amorous overtures but finally marrying an English lord. The lengthy conversations on music that burden this threadbare plot often involve

Reinhold, an older architect, who corresponds to Heinse in age and in his love for Italian operas, though both Eggebrecht and Hugo Goldschmidt identify Lockmann with the authorial voice because Lockmann's views are frequently lifted from Heinse's diaries.[12] But if we heed Eggebrecht and take the fictional context seriously, we will also have to note the ironic perspective on the young protagonist that precludes regarding him simply as Heinse's mouthpiece, especially since the dialogues remain ultimately inconclusive.

Reinhold is a rhetorician of music who believes that linguistic intonation offers the best principle of melody (5:228). He may ignore Rousseau's moral objections while listening to the castrati, but he insists that we listen to what is said, not to "the tone in which it is said" (5:16, 228). Hence he subscribes to all the traditional objections to instrumental music: we must know its meaning in advance (5:229–30); instrumental concerts are "pastime and play, a tightrope dance of sounds" (5:230), a "tickling of the ear, like tobacco for the nose and the tongue" (5:240). Music without words is like a flower without fragrance, something general without individual content (5:236).

For Lockmann, too, "Music is merely a human art; man created it of himself and it owes but little to the rest of nature. The human voice is its first source, good vocal music is the model for all music, and language is inseparable from it" (6:39). However, Lockmann's ideal music is the expression of fierce passions, and he finds this often tempered by both words and melody (5:230–31). In contrast to Marmontel and the later Rousseau, he prefers "expressive power" to "sheer beauty." "Every sound is the result of our momentary existence" (5:239), so music becomes "the most sensuous representation of the soul and, so to speak, the truest image of its pure, self-motivating essence" (5:112–13). Music is "spiritual wealth" displaying itself in sound, which "widely disseminates inwardness and immateriality into the air" (6:39). In making music, "we toss out a part of life that is within us" (5:243).

This expressivity, however, curiously blends affect theory and incipient Romanticism. Lockmann explains the chords and their combinations in terms of traditional references to Pythagoras, Rameau, Tartini, and Kirnberger. Character reveals itself by resonating to certain chordal combinations, which means that our emotions correlate with "pure music." The sheer modulation of pitch, intensity, duration, and sequence "assails our nerves and all parts of our ear, altering thereby our inner feelings. . . . The total person resounds, so to speak, and emotions well up in proportion to the generating tonal ratios and masses. Our feeling itself is nothing but an inner music, ceaseless vibration of the vital nerves" (5:24). Hence Lockmann appreciates harmonic complexity as a means of individualizing the emotions and their conflicts (5:253), and he regards it as even more important than pleasing melodies and powerful rhythms (6:37).

Lockmann's reference to pure music shows that he considers the passions intrinsic to musical structure. To compose is to find musical correlatives to the emotions, to synchronize feeling with pure music without the help of language. In finding language inadequate, Lockmann's expressive theory moves toward Romanticism. Language is just "the garment of music" that is cast off while singing, to reveal, by means of the voice, humanity in a "natural state" (5:237). Music expresses "what language can often intimate only roughly and awkwardly" (6:39), and it speaks more eloquently than any language in moments of jubilation (5:243). The instruments, in turn, express all sounds and motions in nature: they provide "the sea and the air wherein it [the voice] swims and spans its wings" (5:241).

Hildegard sides with Lockmann but goes even further by charging that Reinhold's enchantment with the beautiful voices of Italy has prevented him from appreciating instrumental music. The instruments strengthen and define the singers' expression and portray their silent feelings. They even offer "a delightful and entertaining play of the imagination" that pleases the ear (5:241–42). Vocal music is only a branch of an untranslatable "pure and general art," music "in and for itself" (6:38, 40). Her praise of Haydn's symphonies and quartets finally forces Reinhold to acknowledge that the composer is the phoenix of instrumental music and the pride of Germany (5:242).

Lockmann and Hildegard certainly reveal Heinse's sensitivity to the new music, but their ideas do not congeal into a coherent expressive theory. Lockmann eclectically ranges from a traditional affect theory to a rationale of an instrumental music that no longer expresses linguistic contents, while Hildegard may have learned from Kant to appreciate, though not very deeply, what a play of harmony may mean. Textual as well as extrinsic evidence warns against attributing just one of these ideas to Heinse or writing off Reinhold as Heinse's representative of the old guard. Reinhold's fictional opponents smile about his "odd views," but they are "struck by the truth in them" (5:230). As

Reinhold aptly remarks, the heroine's physical beauty and sensuous voice belie the abstract theories she imbibes from Lockmann. Indeed, starting with the opening luscious scene of Hildegard bathing nude in the garden, which Lockmann spies from a distance, the young tutor appears as a poor devil who can impress her mind but never possess her body, which obeys no theory. It seems probable that Heinse chose a fictional context in order to stage a quasi-dramatic confrontation between the ideas he entertained. Far from offering a unified theory of expressive music, he constructed rather a dialogue in the manner of Diderot.

Sir William Jones

Jones' *Essay* of 1772 elaborates a theory of spontaneous expression which is so wrought with internal contradictions that it can hardly be said to weave the threads of the expressive tradition "into an explicit and orderly reformulation of the nature and criteria of poetry and the other poetic genres" (Abrams 87).

Using "naturalness" as a norm for imitations of passion, Jones finds elaborate forms objectionable because "no man, truly affected with *love* or *grief,* ever expressed the one in an *acrostick,* or the other in a *fugue*"; such "unnatural" forms, which exemplify the "false taste" of the "dark ages," should be banished now that people are enlightened (558). Representations of passions are equally objectionable because feigning (that is, imitating) a passion requires an unnatural distance from it: "A man who is *really* joyful or afflicted cannot be said to *imitate* joy or affliction. . . . *Petrarch* was, certainly, too deeply affected with real *grief* . . . to *imitate* the passions of others" (557). Jones is driven to the conclusion therefore that spontaneous outbursts of powerful emotions in poetry and music leave no room for reflection or control. The greatest effect of poetry and music "is not produced by *imitation,* but by a . . . principle; which must be sought for in the deepest recesses of the human mind" (550).

Such a theory of spontaneous creativity is open to general objections, but for now it will suffice to point out that Jones' own interpretation of poetry and music in part negates his demand for immediacy. For Jones' "language of the violent passions," which is "not an *imitation* of nature, but the voice of nature itself" (553–54), turns out to be a stylized expression "in exact measure, with strong accents and significant words." Similarly, true music, which is "no more than poetry, delivered in a succession of harmonious sounds" (555–56), must be "exactly measured, pronounced, in a common voice, in a just cadence, . . . sung in due time and measure, with a pleasing tune" (553). Like d'Alembert, Jones calls upon artists to work "not by *imitating* the works of nature, but by assuming her power, and causing the same effect upon the imagination, which her charms produce to the senses" (560). But since this expressive arousal of passions in the listener is linked to a spontaneous expression of the emotions, Jones remains within the bounds of mimesis.

Having arrived at the end of a key chapter, it will be useful to restate my negative answer to the question of whether eighteenth-century expressive theories of music replaced mimesis, or, to use Abrams's metaphors, whether the aesthetics of the lamp provided an alternative to that of the mirror. My survey of the three major meanings of the term *expression* in the eighteenth century shows that writers who entertained expressive notions either remained within the mimetic tradition or went beyond both mimesis and expression. Nowhere have we encountered a well-formulated, coherent new aesthetics of expression. It will be the task of the remaining chapters to show what other approaches to music offered genuinely new ideas.

12 TOWARD AUTONOMOUS MUSIC

Is mere Sound a thing of nought? Does it not place an image before you? Do not you see it passing by? its very speechlessness filling you with attention? Numeris & Modis, say the ancients themselves, less acquainted with it, inest quoedam tacita vis.

—Robertson 447

Now that expressive theories of music have been shown to be modifications of traditional mimesis, we can expose the genuine roots of the aesthetic shift in music: (1) sensualist aesthetics, (2) the mathematics of music, and (3) the principle of unity in variety. These dislodged music from its mimetic context and pushed it toward autonomy.

SENSUALISM AND FORMALISM

Diderot became dissatisfied with the aesthetics of tonal relations when he saw that it could not be turned into a science, but, given his strong inclination toward materialism, it is unclear why he did not adopt an aesthetics of sheer physical pleasure. Why did his materialism surface only as eroticism in fiction and not as sensualism in aesthetics? Could the pleasure of art not be merely visceral and void of intellectual meaning, as Lamettrie had claimed? Diderot's answer was negative, probably because of his intellectual bent, but others moved cautiously toward the affirmation of the pleasure principle in music. Blainville, whose *Histoire* (1767) staunchly defended Rameau's theory of harmony, suggested as early as 1754 that symphonies, trios, overtures, and concertos "often entertain us even though the composer did not propose any painting or character." However, Blainville assigned such simply amusing instrumental music to the *genre sonabile* and the childhood of music (*L'Esprit* 8). Beattie thought that "part of the pleasure, both of melody and harmony, arises from the very nature of the notes that compose" music (138), admitting that "the mind may be agreeably affected by mere sound, in which there is neither meaning nor modulation" (139).

Boyé and Chabanon

The generation after Diderot, notably Boyé and Chabanon, became more forceful advocates of sensualism in music by recognizing the kinship of imitation with expression and rejecting both. Boyé, pseudonymous author of *L'Expression musicale* . . . ("Musical Expression Relegated to the Ranks of Chimeras"; 1779), thought that musical imitations of language were boring. True melody, like Gluck's "J'ai perdu mon Euridice," was so indeterminate that any text could be fitted to it. A concert had to be a genuine feast for the ear: "The principal object of music is to please us physically, without troubling the mind to search for useless comparisons in it. One absolutely must regard music a pleasure of the senses and not of the mind. As soon as we try to attribute the cause of its impressions on us to a moral principle we lose ourselves in a labyrinth of extravagances" (23–24).

This sensualism discards in one fell swoop imitation, expression, and didacticism in music. In fact it rejects the analogy between composition and haphazard dribblings of paint on a canvas (24) only because Boyé thinks that painting, unlike music, is imitative. The "goose pimples" and shivers of musical pleasure (26) have no intrinsic relation whatsoever to passions felt by the composer or to feelings experienced in "real" life; if this were not the case, lovers of martial music would be a threat to peace (31–33). Pure music is for Boyé elemental sound, to the point that he has nothing to say about form.

Chabanon's break with the imitative tradition was equally radical. His early *Eloge* for Rameau admires the composer but criticizes the naturalistic imitations of his overtures (25) and dodges the discussion of his theory, because "it is too arid and studded with mathematics to be included" (50). Chabanon's defense of nonrepresentational instrumental music starts from the premise that the orchestral composer has no external resources:

No subject inspires and guides his ideas; one knows not where he obtains them. He makes something out of nothing, and this is creation in the proper sense. Once he has found the motif, he submits to the absolute necessity of continuing it without changing its character or its dynamics. . . . This first idea must become the generator of several other ones which belong to it without resembling it, and embellish it without effacing it. In sum, our mind favors no idea and our heart no feeling when we listen to pure symphonic music; the agitation must arise entirely from the force of sounds. [22–23]

Chabanon's anonymous article in the *Mercure de France* applies these principles by sensitively contrasting Rameau's *Castor* with the new instrumental style of the Mannheim school. Rameau's pieces are cast in a single mood ("sont d'une teneur"; 161), whereas Stamitz, Holzbauer, and others employ a host of new instruments, many of them not yet in use in Rameau's time, to produce subtle transitions between loud and soft. The new wealth, the constantly changing tone and mood of the new orchestral expression, demonstrates to Chabanon that it is no longer sensible to ask what a piece means. The composer's intentions and the listener's interpretations are superfluous, for "a beautiful song, like a beautiful face, carries its own effect, a pleasure that does not depend on imitation but is given by the intimate relation that the song and the face have with our senses" (162).

Chabanon's main work, *De la musique*, the first part of which was published in 1779, is the first fully persuasive argument in favor of nonrepresentational instrumental music. The title indicates that the author devotes much attention to the relation of music to words, languages, poetry, and the theater, but his primary concern is to show that music is a natural and universal language (2–3) that is not based on convention (129). Chabanon follows Rameau in claiming invariable laws for music, and he disagrees with Rousseau's cultural and historical approach. One would expect him therefore to favor harmony. Indeed, he believes that harmony furnishes melody's "geometric reason" (4), and he acknowledges that music as a mathematical science has been subject to the same calculations throughout all societies and ages. In this sense, harmonic proportions delineate our emotions, and, as Chabanon puts it in a remarkable phrase, "the mathematicians have encoded the reason of our pleasure" (*les mathematiciens ont chiffré la raison de nos plaisirs*) (130–31).

But Chabanon stays away from the war between Rameau and Rousseau. In contrast to Rameau, he considers harmony a mere complement (30), and he departs from Rousseau by denying that melody and song express language, feeling, or any other content. Instruments can sing as well as the voice (35), and musical imitation can offer only the pleasure of having overcome a difficulty (49–50). Music, unlike language, did not originate in imitation (40–46), and it lacks the means to practice it (55–56). Hence Chabanon condemns musical painting, including expression, which he regards simply as the painting of sentiments (70). At best, music can imitate the "roaring of angry waves" (61).

Musical rhetoric is equally misguided, because language is not the "mother of song" (72). Aristoxenos was right when he observed that language glides over sounds whereas musical intervals are fixed and calculable. On historical as well as structural grounds music is therefore independent of language (70–71, 75), and one should not try to trace national traditions in music to differences in language (84). Melody should follow neither words, which subjugate it, nor some preverbal, inarticulate cries of passion (101). Pleasure does not depend on inexplicable analogies between the affects and certain elements of music (107–08).

In sum, Chabanon unburdens musical pleasure both of representation and of moral or cognitive tasks. But his reasons differ from those of Kant a few years later. Kant, as we shall see, emancipates aesthetic judgment not only from pure and practical reason but also from pleasant sensations, which offer only physical pleasure. For Chabanon, pure sensations remain the only source of pleasure: sounds do not express, "do not carry any signification, do not speak to the mind, they exist for the ear alone" (26); they are "the song itself" (168). As in the case of Herder, the "harmoniously combined sounds" of music are the "immediate pleasure and voluptuous sensations" for the ear (50), and the pleasure of harmony is simply the sum of the pleasures drawn from individual sensations. Chabanon advocates a "theory of our most delicate sensations and our most exquisite tastes" (354).

Chabanon may be best appreciated therefore as a critic of traditional mimetic and expressive precepts in music and the first to fully recognize the possibility of nonrepresentational music. But although he persuasively questioned the old, he was not sophisticated enough philosophically to firmly establish the new, and his ideas were overlooked even during his lifetime,[1] which must have been in part due to his unabashed advocacy of the pleasure principle. Furthermore, Chabanon's theory of pure sensations had little to say about form, proportion, and organization, which became so important in the emerging Classical and Romantic styles. Finally, a theory that designated "tender affections and happy situations" as most appropriate for music (139–40) suited a gallant style but not the new pathos of a Beethoven or the metaphysical claims that the Romantics attached to music. Nevertheless, Chabanon's thought was pioneering and deserves kinder attention.

MATHEMATICAL FORMALISM

In music there is little beyond itself to which we need, or indeed can, refer to heighten its charms. If we investigate the principles of harmony, we learn that they are general and universal; and of harmony itself, that the proportions in which it consists are to be found in those material forms, which are beheld with the greatest pleasure, the sphere, the cube, and the cone, for instance, and constitute what we call symmetry, beauty, and regularity; but the imagination receives no additional delight; our reason is exercised in the operation, and that faculty alone is thereby gratified. In short, there are few things in nature which music is capable of imitating, and those are of a kind so uninteresting, that we may venture to pronounce that as its principles are founded in geometrical truth and seem to result from some general and universal law of nature, so *its excellence is intrinsic, absolute, and inherent*, and, in short, resolvable only into His will, who has ordered all things in number, weight, and measure. [Hawkins XX, my emphasis]

Hawkins's Preliminary Discourse exemplifies the impulse that mathematics gave to the emancipation of music. It is hardly surprising, of course, that the Enlightenment should have taken a mathematical approach to music, for it has been traditionally characterized as the age that consistently extended the application of mathematics to the widest range of knowledge and life. For older as well as newer scholars, including Adorno and Foucault, the Enlightenment represents the dominion of number, *mathesis universalis*, combinatorial art.

In light of these general interpretations it is quite surprising that Hawkins's text is rather unique and that the body of eighteenth-century mathematical writings on music, especially in the 1750s and 60s, is relatively slender. There are several reasons for this. Above all, we have to distinguish the different images and methods of mathematics that acquired broader cultural significance. Mathematics has been traditionally conceived of as the ideal deductive science with ineluctable conclusions. This great model for rationalist systems, which was still the inspiration for Rameau and even Hawkins, gradually lost its

attraction in the eighteenth century with the rise of empiricism and
the Newtonian analytic method. By mid-century, Diderot, Buffon,
and others were attacking the esprit de système for attempting to im-
pose a deductive mathematical order on the profusion of the empirical
world. As Cassirer has shown, scientific interest shifted from physics
and mathematics to the biological sciences and natural history. Part of
Rameau's trouble with the philosophes must be attributed to this
change in the wider intellectual climate.

But the weakening of the rationalist and deductive mathematics that
had inspired medieval and baroque theories of music has relatively little bearing on the history I am tracing here. For the theory of instrumental music and the principles of a new aesthetics were largely inspired by the image of mathematics as a "construction" that starts with
axiomatically adopted generating principles rather than with "facts of
nature" and terminates in a self-contained structure. Thus C. P. E.
Bach may have been right when he wrote to Forkel that his father,
Johann Sebastian, was "no lover of the dry mathematical stuff," yet the
latter's music, especially the late fugues and canons, undeniably have
an austere and abstract structural grandeur that can be called mathematical. Whether Johann Sebastian did calculate while composing or
use number symbolism is a matter of ongoing scholarly discussion; it
is in any case quite certain that he used a method of variation and
combination.

My central chapters on Rameau and the philosophes attempted to
show a conflict in each of the major figures. In Rameau, the conflict
was between the two mathematical concepts I have just described: the
deductive system, in which music was a representation of natural relations, and a combinatorial and constructive system, manifest in his
concept of tonality and his method of generating chords from thirds.
Ultimately the philosophes rejected Rameau because he himself leaned
more and more toward the deductive model, but, as I have tried to
show, the second model continued to motivate the aesthetic considerations of each of the philosophes. The principles underlying Diderot's
concern with rapports, d'Alembert's interest in the construction of
new chords, and Rousseau's project for a new notation continued to
be fruitful in the minds of the philosophes well after the specific projects had been surrendered.

Confronting the relatively slender volume of mathematical literature on music during the later eighteenth century—I have omitted a

larger but minor body of writing that naively continued to cling to the outmoded deductive model—we ought to remember therefore that the idea of mathematics worked mostly "underground," embedded in the writings of figures who were not explicit adherents of the mathematical method.

Leibniz

If the Pythagorean tradition stayed alive during the eighteenth century, this was largely due to Leibniz. Though he wrote very little about music, in a letter to Goldbach of April 1712 he coined the century's most famous phrase on music: "Musica est exercitium arithmeticae occultum nescientis se numerare animi"—"Music is an unconscious exercise in arithmetic in which the mind does not know it is counting" (*Epistolae* 241).[2]

The formula is founded upon a broad philosophical distinction between unconscious perceptions and conscious apperceptions in Leibniz' *Monadology* (par. 14). According to Leibniz, our knowledge is unavoidably imperfect for two major reasons. First, the grand design of the universe cannot be guessed from its fragmentary image in each monad, just as a spot in a painting resolves itself close up into meaningless strokes ("On the Radical Origin of Things," *Phil. Pap.* 489). Second, sense perceptions, including those of art, give us only a confused knowledge of things, because we do not fully understand the mechanism involved. Art always involves therefore a "je ne sais quoi." The essay "On Wisdom" (*Phil. Pap.* 425–26) argues, however, that the pleasure of music must also have a sufficient reason, and this consists of the order of harmony that is transmitted to us by means of the vibrations of the instrument and the air. Listening to music we enjoy its "regular though invisible order," its harmony between the parts and the whole (unity in plurality) without understanding it. This intuitive grasp of a mathematical order is "counting without being aware of it." In the end, "even the pleasures of sense are reducible to intellectual pleasures, known confusedly. Music charms us, although its beauty consists only in the agreement of numbers and in the counting, which we do not perceive [comprehend] but which the soul nevertheless continues to carry out, of the beats or vibrations of sounding bodies which coincide at certain intervals" (*Phil. Pap.* 641).

Unlike his followers Wolff and Baumgarten, who searched for normative laws of beauty, Leibniz himself did not try to formalize musical knowledge, perhaps because he shared Descartes's skepticism and anticipated the Romantics, who considered the unseen order of music as eternally elusive. By characterizing music as an "imitation of that universal harmony which God has placed in the world" (Haase 25), Leibniz transmitted the Pythagorean heritage to the Romantics, and it is hardly accidental that the epitome of Romantic aesthetics, Schopenhauer's *The World as Will and Representation*, had only to paraphrase Leibniz: "Music is an unconscious exercise in *metaphysics* in which the mind does not know it is philosophizing" (sect. 52, 1:264; my emphasis).

Euler

Like Descartes and Leibniz, Euler was a great mathematician fascinated by music. Apart from the youthful treatise *Tentamen* (1739), he wrote several essays on music, and he gave unusual attention to it in his brilliant popularization of science, the *Letters to a Princess of Germany*. Euler's reputation in mathematics ensured a wide circulation for his studies of music, though even mathematicians of music criticized them for disregarding musical practice.[3]

Euler described his *Tentamen* in a letter of May 25, 1731, as an attempt to show that music was a branch of mathematics; by this he meant both a study of intervals and an investigation of the foundations of musical pleasure. The *Tentamen*, subtitled "Attempt at a New Theory of Music founded on Physical and Metaphysical Knowledge applied to the True Principles of Harmony," set out to show that "there must be a theory, based on securest principles, which can explain why a piece of music pleases or displeases" (1:200). In contrast to Leibniz, Euler invokes the metaphysical principle of sufficient reason (1:223, 11:22) to find specific explanations for pleasure. Cultural conditioning is insufficient reason (1:223); next to qualities in the sound itself, the reasons must lie in the senses and the judgment of the mind (1:223). We perceive a sound if we register distinctly the beats upon our ear and recognize their rule of order. Connoisseurs of music are endowed with delicate ears and high intelligence; by means of these they discover and judge the order of vibrations (1:224).

According to Euler's second metaphysical principle, perfection pleases in proportion to its degree. The perception of internal organization and of the order of parts represent for Euler, unlike Descartes, criteria for grounding subjective pleasure in quantifiable criteria. They involve no mimetic principles, only mathematical rules for the internal structure, including the broader principles of symmetry, contrast, and repetition. In this respect Euler's mathematical theory is related to aesthetic theories based on the principle of "unity in multiplicity," as we shall see in the next section.

According to these metaphysical principles, "a song will please us if we recognize the order of its sounds" (1:226). For Euler, as for Rameau, pitch and time are the quantifiable elements of musical order (1:226, 11:23), though he treats only pitch (1:202).[4] The vibration theory of pitch is stated with beautiful clarity in the *Letters*. "If a chord is to please, we must perceive the proportion between the quantities of the simple sounds. . . . In this manner we reduce the perception of chords to a consideration of numbers" (1:246). The greater the consonance, the more easily the ear discovers the ratio (for this depends on the smallness of the numbers involved), and the pleasure is commensurate with the degree of order discovered (11:14–15). The major insight drawn from these questionable metaphysical presuppositions is that consonances and dissonances differ only in degree, and that the border between them is indistinct (1:508, 517).[5]

Euler nevertheless recognizes that intervals and metric rules do not suffice to explain musical pleasure and that "something else is needed that nobody has yet developed" (11:23), namely, an understanding of larger musical forms: "The composer must follow in his composition a certain plan or design, which he should execute by means of real and perceptible proportions; and if a connoisseur hears this piece and understands, apart from the proportions, the very plan and design envisioned by the composer, he will feel the satisfaction that is pleasure when beautiful music strikes intelligent ears" (11:23). Here, perhaps for the first time, a mathematician of music broadens his concept of form to include the overall structure. The statement is actually a powerful pre-Romantic affirmation of form, though, unfortunately, Euler immediately slips back into the mimetic discourse of his age by adding: "This pleasure arises therefore from guessing, so to speak, the views and sentiments of the composer, whose execution, if considered happy, fills the mind with agreeable satisfaction."

Mizler

As editor of the *Musikalische Bibliothek* and president of the Society for the Promotion of the Musical Sciences (*Sozietät der Musikalischen*

Wissenschaften) (1738–), Mizler was an indefatigable missionary for the mathematical study of music during the 1730s and 40s.[6] After writing a dissertation on the philosophical foundations of music, the second edition of which he dedicated to his teacher, J. S. Bach, he published a treatise on thoroughbass "according to the mathematical method," in which he described a composition machine based on Leibniz's ars combinatoria. But Mizler's lectures on music theory brought him so little success in Leipzig that he moved to Poland in 1743 and eventually became a physician, though he continued to publish his *Bibliothek* intermittently until 1754.

The *Musikalische Bibliothek* was to become a library of mathematical-scientific treatises on music for training learned musicians. Mizler scorned "mere historical knowledge" (1.4:56) and criticized Scheibe's unsystematic patchwork of remarks, but he developed the foundations of his own system unsystematically, by way of lengthy reviews and by attaching polemical commentaries to essays by others. Culling his scattered remarks, one learns that he regarded mathematics in the Pythagorean manner as "the heart and soul of music"; music was "sonorous mathematics" (2.1:53, 55). Being a rationalist, he no longer believed in number symbolism and the harmony of the spheres, but he adopted Leibniz's view that we perceive subconsciously the mathematical structure of music (2.1:60).

Mizler's musical society had only about twenty members, because admission was selective, and several famed authors, among them Leopold Mozart, declined to join. Telemann entered in 1739 as the sixth member, by submitting a *New Musical System* for admission.[7] Handel was awarded honorary membership; Graun joined in 1746, although his letters to Telemann (e.g., of June 20, 1747, and November 9, 1751) frequently criticize mathematical approaches to music. J. S. Bach joined the society only in 1747, apparently upon the urging of Mizler, by submitting the canon "Vom Himmel hoch da komm ich her."

Hawkins

Burney's graceful and entertaining but superficial history of music beat Hawkins's solid treatise at the cash register when they appeared almost simultaneously, in part I suspect because of Hawkins's unabashed and elitist preference for learned harmony over imitative melody. While Hawkins acknowledged that the arts offered in addition to an "original and absolute" pleasure a relative one that issued from the love of truth and resulted in imitation (XX), he thought that the second fell outside the domain of music, even if eminent musicians, like Handel, made use of it: "These powers of imitation, which admittedly exist, . . . constitute but a very small part of the excellence of music. . . . The truth is, that imitation belongs more properly to the arts of poetry and painting than to music" (XX).

Thus far Hawkins agrees with Harris (whom he extensively quotes) and other British critics of musical mimesis, and he even shares their disdain for the superficiality and empty virtuosity of contemporary instrumental music (XLI–XLII, 919). But in his case the criticism is not meant to be a defense of vocal and affective music. Rather, he extols harmonic, nonrepresentational compositions that make use of sophisticated harmony and structure in the manner of Corelli, Bononcini, Gemianiani, and Handel (XLII). Corrupted taste, "the vanity and emptiness of that music with which we now are pleased," cannot be cured by a Rousseauistic return to monodic and melodic music (Hawkins was a fierce "progressivist" champion of modern music) but only by a "sober reflection on the nature of harmony, and its immediate reference to those principles on which all our ideas of beauty, symmetry, order and magnificence are founded" (919).

By championing formal organization without specific mimetic content, Hawkins prepared, then, the ground for the appreciation of classical instrumental music. His sentiments were shared by some disciples of Bach, including Bach's student Kirnberger and his first biographer, Forkel. Though Forkel planned a rhetoric of music, as we have seen, he actually wanted to turn it into a distinctly nonverbal idiom and thought that "nothing has contributed more to the broadening and concretization of artistic expression in music than the invention of harmony" (Gesch. 13). He regarded harmony as "the logic of music" (24) which could raise this art to its peak of perfection (16), while rhetoric was only one of its auxiliary sciences (35).

FROM UNITY IN VARIETY TO AUTONOMY

We started to explore the aesthetics of unity in variety with the young Diderot, who drew upon André, Crousaz, Hutcheson, and probably Shaftesbury. But the idea that beauty was dependent on the symmetry, proportion, and interrelation of parts was held by diverse other writers as well, including Baumgarten, Moses Mendelssohn (176–77),

Beattie (156), and Sulzer (art. "schön"). While mimetic aesthetics judges art by the success of reproduction, a consistent judgment based on unity in variety values only qualities in the object.

One of the first to explore these premises was Malcolm, who in his 1721 treatise held that modern music was superior to ancient music and that "the modern Concerts must undoubtedly be allowed to be Entertainments worthy of our Natures," not because they move the passions to serve morality and virtue but because their form offers intellectual pleasure:

> If it be not a low and unworthy Thing for us to be pleased with Proportion and Harmony, in which there is properly an intellectual Beauty, then it must be confessed, that the modern *Musick* is more perfect than the ancient. But why must the moving of particular Passions be the only Use of *Musick*? If we look upon a noble Building, or a curious Painting, we are allowed to admire the Design, and view all its Proportions and Relation of Parts with Pleasure to our Understanding, without any respect to the Passions. . . . If one altogether ignorant of Painting looks upon the most curious Piece, wherein he finds nothing extraordinary moving him, because the Excellency of it may ly in the Design and admirable Proportion and Situation of the Parts which he takes no Notice of: Must we therefore say, it has nothing valuable in it, and capable to give Pleasure to a better Judge? What, in *Musick* or *Painting*, would seem intricate and confused, and so give no Satisfaction to the unskilled, will ravish with Admiration and Delight, one who is able to unravel all the Parts, observe their Relations and the united *Concord* of the Whole. . . . The Ancients studied only how to move the Heart . . . but we have also a new Art, whose End is rather to entertain the Understanding, than to move particular Passions. . . . Their End was to please and move the People, which is better done by the Senses and the Heart than by the Understanding. [598–601]

Malcolm knew that the harmony of parts was a Pythagorean concept, yet he regarded its musical materialization as a distinctly modern achievement, because only the moderns, according to him, had divorced the interrelation of parts from affective and moral considerations. Whether this is true is not at issue here; what matters is that Malcolm prophetically discarded the principles of affect theory and boldly asserted that *intellectual* aesthetic pleasure could be drawn from the contemplation of form. In contrast to Boyé and Chabanon, who departed from mimesis and didacticism to adopt an anti-intellectual, hedonistic attitude, Malcolm and his colleagues advocated a pleasure of taste that must be learned, though it has no educational purpose.

Diderot and the German rationalist aestheticians—Wolff, Baumgarten, and Moses Mendelssohn—relied on this intellectual quality of taste when they attempted to construct an objective aesthetics. For Mendelssohn, "The perception of sensuous perfection is called beauty" (176); more specifically, "Everything that can be presented to the senses as a perfection can also become an object of beauty." Such perfections include "the concordance of sounds and colors, the order in the parts of a whole, their similarity, variety, and agreement, their transpositions and transformation into other shapes" (177). Mendelssohn explicitly fuses this formal principle of perfection with mimesis, by requiring (as did Batteux even earlier) that artistic imitations possess formal symmetries and overall harmony: "The imitation must incorporate through art all the requirements of a beautiful object. First it must have therefore a variety of parts. . . . Furthermore, these parts must harmonize, form a whole in the senses, which means that the order and regularity of their succession must strike the senses" (180). Mendelssohn's criteria for beauty in music include therefore "the sensuous order, the concordance of the individual sounds in a whole, the reciprocal relation of the parts to each other, imitation, and, finally, the sentiments and passions of the human soul which usually manifest themselves through sounds" (184).

Mendelssohn uses eclectic criteria, and he still wants to make the idea of unity in variety a part of an objective aesthetics. An article dedicated to Mendelssohn and published in 1785 took the decisive step of divorcing the internal and autonomous order of art from objectivist considerations. Its young author, Karl Philipp Moritz, entitled it "On the Concept of Self-Contained Perfection" (*Über den Begriff des in sich selbst Vollendeten*). "Self-contained perfection" was deliberately meant to replace Batteux's "imitation."[8]

Moritz was a step ahead of the others, for he recognized that the assault of sensualism on mimesis had weaknesses of its own. How are we to distinguish utilitarian from aesthetic pleasure if "the basic principle of the imitation of nature as the final purpose of the arts has been discarded and subordinated to the purpose of pleasure" (203)? Moritz's answer is a distinction based in part on the object, in part on our attitude toward it. The primary pleasure of useful objects is to imagine the benefits of their use, "as if I made myself the center to which I refer all parts of the object" (203). In contrast, if I contemplate something beautiful, I roll back the purpose from myself into an object of self-contained perfection: I enjoy it for its own sake, not for my own purposes (204). The beautiful engages our attention completely, "temporarily diverts it from ourselves and effects that we seem to lose ourselves in the beautiful object; and just this losing, this forgetting ourself, is the highest degree of pure and selfless enjoyment granted to us by the beautiful" (206).

Aesthetic contemplation resembles, then, the self-denial of mystic contemplation and Aristotelian pity, but it differs from both by asking for identification with a lifeless object. Since the detachment from self leads to no emotional or intellectual identification with another, Moritz's aesthetic state suppresses all forms of expression.

Yet this self-abandonment does not enhance our attention to the object's constitution, for the inner purposiveness that replaces outer purposiveness (use) cannot be defined in terms of rules for the interrelation of parts. Moritz never seriously entertains the possibility that inner perfection can be measured objectively. In this sense as well, Moritz moves from rationalist aesthetics toward Romantic organicism and Kant's disinterested and noncognitive aesthetic contemplation.

Moritz also has a new perspective on the artist's relation to his work. The selflessness demanded from the audience must find its antecedent in the artist's creative self-denial: reaching for success and recognition results in a social compromise and a less than perfect work. For this reason too, the artistic self-denial demanded by the autonomy and inner purposiveness of the work precludes self-expression or the communication of ideas and feelings: "The perfection of your work should fill all your soul during your work. . . . The true artist will attempt to introduce the highest inner purposiveness or perfection into his work. . . . He will already have reached his actual purpose with the completion of his work" (209).

Moritz made a few remarks on music in his novel *Andreas Hartknopf*, but he is more important for his general aesthetic ideas, which played a formative role during the final decade of the century. Although there is no evidence that Kant knew Moritz's work, the kinship between the two is undeniable. More important, Reichardt, Wackenroder, and Tieck attended the lectures that Moritz gave in Berlin as "Professor of the Beautiful Arts and the Relevant Science of Mathematics" (*Professor der schönen Künste und der dahin gehörigen Wissenschaft der Mathematik*)!

13 KANT AND THE ORIGINS OF FORMALISM

Having seen how Rameau, Diderot, Chabanon, and Euler were groping for a justification of instrumental music but were held back by
their insistence on determinate meaning and content, one is struck
by the revolutionary definitions in section 16 of Kant's *Critique of
Judgment*: while "dependent beauty" presupposes concepts of the
represented object and its perfection, "free beauty" does not. Examples of free beauty include not only flowers, birds, and seashells but also "delineations à la grecque, foliage for borders or wallpapers [which
mean nothing in themselves]," and, most important, musical "phan-
tasies (i.e., pieces without any theme) and in fact all music without
words." According to Kant, pure taste judges free beauty "according
to the mere form."

We suddenly seem to find here an aesthetic formalism that could
justify instrumental music and allow an emancipation of music from
language. Indeed, on the basis of such passages, Kant's Third Critique
has often been hailed as the first work to announce the principles and
possibilities of formalism. Bröckel, for instance, writes that Kant's theory is best exemplified in abstract art and atonal music, which did not
yet exist at his time (486–87).[1] While Bröckel takes an extreme view,
others see the principles of the modern arts anticipated in the Third
Critique, either partially or by implication. According to Cohen, for
instance, "The characterization of aesthetic content as form is of fundamental importance for the aesthetics of the Critiques." Cohen finds
form to be "the liberating term for all of the problems Kant poses"
(360), and he even extrapolates from the Kantian text to conclude:
"Music, more than any other art, is symbolic, because individual objects, be they natural or moral, do not constitute its content. . . . The
inexhaustible harmonic interconnection of the thematic world of
thought is the material of musical symbolism" (319). "Music alone creates a new world as its content. . . . The sounds and the effects do not

strive to be anything but inner materials. And they alone construct inwardness as their own world that wants to be only inwardness" (334).

Others accept Kant as a father of formalism but find the principles of the Third Critique eclectic. Marschner discovers in it Hanslick's formalism of "absolute music," as well as a clashing, content-oriented music aesthetics. Moos strikes it even richer, for he finds formalism, sensualism, and naturalism in Kant's text. Nonformalist readings are distinctly in the minority. Klinkhammer believes that Kant unconditionally recognized and preferred absolute music (33) but sharply separates Kant from Hanslick and the mathematical formalists (44–46). More recently, Dahlhaus (*Kant* 344) has praised and Schueller (*Kant* 219) has criticized Kant for using cultural and psychological as well as formal criteria to judge music.

Some of these critical disagreements arise from Kant's inconsistencies, but most of them result from ahistorical perspectives. My own close reading of the relevant passages relies on the broad parameters and insights we have gained on eighteenth-century music aesthetics, which set the stage, so to speak, for Kant's hesitancy. I attribute his hesitation to a culminating and decisive clash between the verbal and mathematical interpretation of music that he was unable to resolve, though he significantly furthered the eventual acceptance of nonmimetic theories of art and music.

Kant's "free beauty" must be judged according to its form because it contains no concepts. This establishes the autonomy of the purest aesthetic objects, but it does not prove that such objects are for Kant highest art. In fact, he specifically states in section 52 that "if the beautiful arts are not brought into more or less close combination with moral ideas, which alone bring with them a self-sufficing satisfaction," mere sensations will make "the spirit dull, the object gradually distasteful, and the mind . . . discontented with itself and peevish." To be sure, beauty is denied here to mere "material sensation (charm or emotion)" and not to pure form, but since the latter is as void of moral ideas as the former, the argument holds for both. Schueller resolves the issue by suggesting that Kant's moral rigor prevented him from embracing a formalism he would have preferred on purely aesthetic grounds. But if, as Schueller says, "Kant has distinguished taste from cognition and found taste wanting" (*Kant* 236), one must assume a schizophrenic split between his aesthetic and ethical concerns that some key passages of the Third Critique do not support. In contrast to

Klinkhammer (32–33), Reed (573), and others, I believe that concepts are quite germane to Kant's notion of beauty, that he hesitates about music precisely because he assigns a specific role to concepts in art but cannot find concepts or their equivalent in music. Music is a problem for Kant not in spite of but rather because of his general aesthetics. It even becomes a kind of touchstone for it.

REPRESENTATION AND AESTHETIC IDEAS

We may tackle the issue by turning to Kant's theory of representation. The "Copernican revolution" defines the limits beyond which the mind cannot represent to itself anything securely but reverses the traditional view within those limits by claiming that the human mind is more than a passive mirror to nature:

> Hitherto it has been assumed that all our knowledge must conform to objects. But all attempts to extend our knowledge of objects by establishing something in regard to them *a priori*, by means of concepts, have, on this assumption, ended in failure. We must therefore make trial whether we may not have more success in the tasks of metaphysics, if we suppose that objects must conform to our knowledge. . . . If intuition must conform to the constitution of the objects, I do not see how we could know anything of the latter *a priori*; but if the object (as the object of the senses) must conform to the constitution of our faculty of intuition, I have no difficulty in conceiving such a possibility. [BXVI–XVII]

The First Critique proceeds to show that the constructivism in mathematical representation can serve as a model for all a priori synthetic knowledge. This constructivism in cognitive representation was bound to become relevant to the treatment of artistic representations in the Third Critique, even if Kant refrained from assigning cognitive value to the latter. For if, as Kant says, the mind makes a creative contribution to representation, if representations are synthesized by the imagination and the a priori forms of the mind, faithful reproduction becomes problematic and verisimilitude should no longer be the central aesthetic concern. Hence Kant nowhere demands that artistic representations copy the original exactly and he does not believe that aesthetic pleasure consists in comparing the image with its physical or psychic prototype. Furthermore, as he explains in section 52 of the *Metaphysics of Morals*, he has general ethical reservations about imitation (6:479–80), though elsewhere he admits that a certain degree of imitation is inevitable in all spheres of human activity (15:340–41). Finally, Kant does not assign to taste the function of evaluating the adequacy of the signifier to the signified. Art deserves to be ranked with science and morality because its signifiers are used freely and creatively. The critical enterprise demands that art be more than a mere image of nature or expression of a subjectivity.

At first sight, Kant seems to concentrate in the Third Critique on the nature and claims of taste at the expense of artistic representation. He certainly devotes more attention to the evaluation of art than to its mode of creation and its ontology. But creativity is nevertheless its focus, because it is now posited also in the receptive mind. Aesthetic judgment is no longer based on the represented objects or ideas alone but on the internal sense of harmony that results from "the play of the mental powers" (sect. 15). The creative, spontaneous activity of the mind, most clearly delineated in sections 43–54 on genius and aesthetic ideas, is the mode of receiving as well as making art, and Kant's most significant achievement in aesthetics is perhaps to show that this individual creativity can claim, if not demonstrate, universal validity.

In this sense, the heart of Kant's essay is the treatment of genius and its production of aesthetic ideas. Since genius is "the talent (or natural gift) which gives the rule to art" and "the innate mental disposition (*ingenium*) through which nature gives the rule to art," Kant believes in a theory of subconscious creativity that precludes the possibility of describing scientifically how art is produced. The originality of genius cannot be copied; its exemplary products serve merely as "a standard or rule of judgment for others" (sect. 46).

An aesthetic idea is the animating principle (*Geist*) of a work created by a genius; it is a "representation of the imagination which occasions much thought, without however any definite thought, i.e., any *concept*, being capable of being adequate to it; it consequently cannot be completely encompassed and made intelligible by language" (sect. 49).[2]

Taken by itself, this definition seems to support the formalist concept of free beauty. By emphasizing the verbal and conceptual indeterminacy of aesthetic ideas, Kant denies foundation to any science of the beautiful and seems to liberate artistic expression from the burden of direct communication. Aesthetic ideas in art are merely a source, a generating force that engenders in the observer's mind "much thought" not contained in the object itself.

Commentators have noted that aesthetic ideas seem especially well suited to explaining wordless instrumental music. However, such interpretations do not take into account other passages which reestablish the centrality of concepts and clarify why Kant has not given music the high regard that the cited passage would warrant. Somewhat earlier in section 49 he states, for instance, that an aesthetic idea is "a representation of the imagination associated with a given concept, which is bound up with such a multiplicity of partial representations in its free employment that for it no expression marking a definite concept can be found; and such a representation, therefore, adds to a concept much ineffable thought, the feeling of which quickens the cognitive faculties." Hence aesthetic ideas may go beyond concepts, but they must be associated with them. As Cohen observes, "Aesthetic ideas rely on a sharpness and an exactitude of which only verbal concepts are capable" (311).

Kant's examples for aesthetic ideas are not very illuminating. He notes that artists may represent impalpable objects and events (e.g., hell, eternity, creation) or concepts of experience (e.g., death, envy, love). In the latter case, the representation must be more complete than reality; the aesthetic idea is placed under a concept but "occasions in itself more thought than can ever be comprehended in a definite concept and consequently aesthetically enlarges the concept itself in an unbounded fashion." This turns the Leibnizian category of plenitude into a criterion of aesthetic ideas: the more they urge the mind beyond experience, opening up the realm of the possible and providing a "completeness" that concepts are lacking, the better they are. Yet without concepts there can be no aesthetic play, because the imagination "is free to furnish the understanding with an unsought abundance of undeveloped material" only "in agreement with" a concept.

If aesthetic ideas rely on concepts, though in a noncognitive, associative manner, then poetry seems to be their best artistic medium. Indeed, Kant unhesitantly declares in section 53 that poetry is the first among the arts because "it expands the mind by setting the imagination at liberty and by offering—*within the limits of a given concept* and amid the unbounded variety of possible forms accordant with it—that which unites the presentation of this concept with a wealth of thought to which no verbal expression is completely adequate, and so rising aesthetically to ideas" (my emphasis). Barrows rightly says therefore that "conceptlessness" is "a principle that vanishes when Kant undertakes his discussion of art, and with it vanishes the restriction of attention to the object's form" (*Study* 119).

AFFECTS AND CONCEPTS IN MUSIC

Why does Kant not take a verbal approach to music if concepts are indispensable to aesthetic ideas? How does music fit into the Kantian scheme of things?

To begin with, the tie between music and language is mere association: "Every expression of speech has in its context a tone appropriate to the sense. This tone indicates more or less an affection of the speaker and produces it also in the hearer, which affection excites in its turn in the hearer the idea that is expressed in speech by the tone in question" (sect. 53). In other words, the conventional use of language associates musical sounds with words (or statements), and music utilizes then these links to convey affective meaning. Such associations between sound and meaning are set mechanically as it were by tradition and allow no free play with concepts. Affect theory, which relies on mechanical associations, cannot accommodate a free imagination. Dahlhaus rightly says therefore that Kant's reference to affect theory is historically accidental and systematically unnecessary (346).[3]

It remains to be seen whether music can free the imagination and stimulate and sustain a play of the faculties in some other manner. Such a play, though less valuable than one with concepts, could still place musical pleasure above the mere charm of sensory stimulation.

Indeed, Kant is most interested in seeing whether the mathematical structure underlying musical harmony could generate a play with form and allow for a perception of beauty and universal communicability. When he distinguishes the aesthetic sphere from the cognitive and moral on the one hand and the merely sensuous on the other, he does not enforce the two separations with equal vigilance, for knowledge and morality retain an indirect role in the autonomous aesthetic judgment, while considerations pertaining to matter are unconditionally excluded from it. As Cohen remarks, the *Aufhebung* of content into form is accomplished fully with respect to nature but only partially with respect to morality (232–33).

This antisensualist thrust in Kant's aesthetics explains the presence of Pythagorean elements in his music theory: he identifies harmony and consonance (rather than physical sound) with the essence of music; he regards the harmony of the faculties, their balanced and free play with each other, as the essence of the aesthetic state and the feeling of harmony "in the play of the mental powers" as the ground of aesthetic judgments (sect. 15). In other words, Kant inherits and decisively reformulates Pythagoreanism. In that tradition, musical harmony was thought to mirror a static cosmic harmony; in Kant's scheme of things, the order related to art is not cosmic but mental, not prior to art but a result of it, not static but a "play." The continued relevance of the Pythagorean tradition to Kant's undertaking is nevertheless indicated by the spiderweb of musical metaphors—"harmony," "play," "tuning" (*Stimmung*), and so on—in terms of which the Third Critique is spun.

What did this Pythagoreanism in Kant's aesthetics imply for the role of mathematics in music? Did he hold that music, as all of nature, is determined and objectified by mathematics (Cohen 318)?

Kant's rejection of the verbal approach to music did not lead him into the opposing camp of the mathematicians. The issue is broached in section 14 with the question of whether single colors and tones are charming or beautiful. Kant claims that aesthetic judgments can pertain only to pure colors and tones and only to their form, not to their material substance. Euler's vibration theory of light and sound suggests to him the possibility of formal judgment.[4] If perception of color and sound involves not only sensation but also "by reflection the regular play of impressions," then pure colors and sounds could be reckoned as "the formal determinants of the unity of a manifold of sensations, and thus as beauties." In other words, reflection on the form of the vibration in a single musical note could provide the basis for its aesthetic judgment.

Unfortunately, the resolution of the conditional clause is ambiguous: in the first two editions (1790 and 1793), Kant doubts very much that we register such a play (*woran ich doch gar sehr zweifle*), while in the third edition of 1799 the *sehr* is replaced by a *nicht*, thereby inverting the original meaning, and asserting now that Kant doubts *not* that the vibrations produce a play with form. Some commentators, including Cohen, ignore this confusing textual situation, whereas others (including Bernard, one of the major English translators) mix up the facts. Windelband's detailed philological study of the issue in the Akademie-Ausgabe of Kant's works notes that although Kant was apparently not directly involved in the corrections of the third edition, he probably gave his general consent to the changes (5:526). Windelband shows with a battery of passages that the third edition expresses Kant's position and cannot be a misprint. Though commentators agree with Windelband, the case is not quite settled,[5] for the passages from Kant's other works show only that he subscribed to the vibration theory of sound, and Guyer (423) is right in saying that this belief has little bearing on the aesthetic question. Kant himself says that single tones merely enable form to become "more exactly, definitely, completely intuitable"; only harmonic musical composition "constitutes the proper object of the pure judgment of taste."[6]

Since the aesthetic value of music does not hinge on the quality of single sounds, we have to turn to other passages in the Third Critique, but before doing so, it may be instructive to look at some of the early statements, which are seldom brought to bear on issues in the Third Critique. The most important of these are contained in the Philippi transcriptions of Kant's 1772 lectures on logic, in which Kant already distinguishes between physical sound and "form of appearance" in music. He specifically sides with Rameau and the mathematicians of music by ascribing form to harmony and matter to melody. On physical sound, opinions may differ, but "concerning the form of music, a concert that is harmonious must sound good to everybody" (24/1:348–49). This anticipates his critical position that only musical form (harmony) can lay claim to universal validity, though Kant still hopes here that the universality can be objectively certified by means of the mathematics of harmony (24/1:352–53). This legacy of Leibniz and Euler instills in Kant a mathematical and intellectual appreciation of music: its beauty consists of proportion, "in which music is richer and more exact than any other kind of beauty" (24/1:357–58).

By the time of the Third Critique, Kant no longer believed that harmonic proportion, and form in general, could yield objective criteria for aesthetic judgments, and this must be one of the reasons why concepts come to play a new role in his idea of music. Comparing the arts, he assumes that aesthetic ideas "must be occasioned by a concept of the object represented" (sect. 51). Hence he tentatively ranks the arts according to their analogy "with the mode of expression of which men avail themselves in speech." This necessarily works against music. Indeed, music (together with the art of color, i.e., Castel's color organ) belongs to the third category of "beautiful play of sensations . . . which admits at the same time of universal communication."

It remains uncertain "whether colors or tones (sounds) are merely *pleasant* sensations or whether they form in themselves a *beautiful* play of sensations" (my emphasis). On the negative side, the time interval between the vibrations in a tone are probably too short to be registered in our judgment, and thus "only pleasantness and not beauty of composition, is bound up with colors and tones" (sect. 51). Two arguments form the positive side: first, aesthetic judgments could be based on the mathematical ratios of the oscillations; second, tone-deaf people are capable of judging music, and hence musical notes "are to be regarded . . . as the effect of a judgment passed upon the form in the play of diverse sensations."[7] Kant seems to be swayed by the positive arguments: "Either, *as we have done*, we must explain it [music] as the beautiful play of sensation (of hearing), or else as a play of pleasant sensations. According to the former mode of explanation, music is represented altogether as a beautiful art; according to the latter, as a pleasant art (at least in part)" (sect. 51, my emphasis).[8]

This very tentative appreciation of music as an aesthetic (instead of a merely pleasant) art is reaffirmed also in section 53. Music ranks immediately after poetry in terms of its affective power, but this power has nothing to do with concepts or mathematical form: "Although it [Music] speaks by means of mere sensations without concepts, and so does not, like poetry, leave anything over for reflection, it yet moves the temperament [Gemüt] in a greater variety of ways and more intensely, although only transitorily. It is, however, rather enjoyment than cultivation . . . and in the judgment of reason it has less worth than any other of the beautiful arts."

The number of qualifications in this passage indicates how uncertain Kant is on this point. Nor does the subsequent key paragraph bring clarification on the question of whether verbal association or mathematical form is more important in music. As we have seen, the affects (*Reiz und Bewegung des Gemüts*) are communicated in music by means of their conventional (and mechanical) association with words. Mathematics has no role in rousing the affects. But whenever aesthetic ideas are attached to the affects, mathematical form becomes crucial:

The form of the composition of these sensations (harmony and melody) only serves instead of the form of language, by means of their proportionate accordance, to express the aesthetical idea of a connected whole. . . . This can be brought mathematically under certain rules, because it rests in the case of tones on the relation between the number of vibrations of the air. . . . To this mathematical form, although not represented by determinate concepts, alone attaches the satisfaction that unites the mere reflection upon such a number of concomitant or consecutive sensations with this their play, as a condition of its beauty valid for every man. It is this alone which permits taste to claim in advance a rightful authority over everyone's judgment.

In sum, the limited role of mathematical form accounts in part for Kant's skeptical view of music. He admits that music has an intense emotional appeal, but this does not turn it into an art. To be sure, mathematical form makes the communication of aesthetic ideas in music possible, but in Kant's view this is not why people listen to it. Music remains for him primarily an art of physical sound. Mathematics underlies the universal communicability and aesthetic judgment of music, but ultimately it acts only as a surrogate for concepts.

And so music ranks lowest among the arts if judged "by the culture they supply to the mind" (sect. 53). While painting and sculpture are "permanent self-commendatory" vehicles for promoting the union of concepts with sensibility and the urbanity of the higher cognitive powers, music is lacking in urbanity. Like laughter, it may promote physical well-being and may further "the vital bodily processes, the affection that moves the intestines and the diaphragm . . . so that we can thus reach the body through the soul and use the latter as the physician of the former" (sect. 54). But, Kant complains—probably in reference to devotional exercises in the jail adjacent to his apartment—music "extends its influence further than is desired (in the neighborhood), and so as it were obtrudes itself and does violence to the freedom of others who are not of the musical company" (sect. 53). The protest against "noise pollution" represents one of the rare cases in which we can trace Kant's theory to personal experience. Lacking urbanity remains his stigma for music.

Kant belittles music for its alleged conceptual poverty and asocial character. On both counts, the upcoming Romantic generation dissented from him. Apart from Michaelis's poor attempts at popularization, the reactions to his theory of music were generally unfavorable, and in *Kalligone* Herder sharply attacked Kant's inconsistencies: beautiful art is supposed to appeal to us without interest, merely by means of its purposiveness; yet Kant actually ascribes to music a "therapeutic shaking of the diaphragm and a healthy digestion in a disinterested, pure aesthetic play of ideas" (22:73). In Herder's view, sympathetic resonance, not detachment, is the listener's aesthetic state. In words from the *Merchant of Venice* (5.1), the urbanity of music lies in its orphic, humanizing power: "Since nought so stokish, hard and full of rage / But music for the time doth change his nature."

The ability to produce change lies in the very temporal character of music. As Schueller and Dahlhaus note, Kant neglects the temporality of music; more precisely, he considers the evanescence of the notes a source of music's inferiority (sect. 53). For the mature Herder, the emotional power of music is manifest in the awakened associative memories and, more important, in the anticipation and recognition of recurrent musical phrases. The very evanescence of notes makes their return delightful (22:189), but this delight will only be shared by those who can rivet their attention to the temporally unfolding inner structure of music. Herder's sharpest critique of Kant is that in the end he did not respect the autonomy of music:

> If you—who look down upon music of mere sound and cannot gain anything from it—find nothing in music without words, stay away from it. Regard it as a play, wherein purposive-purposeless live instruments practice. But you, musicians, write the words upon the entrance of your music hall in the manner of Plato: "None may enter without the company of the muses"!
>
> How hard it was for music to develop itself into an art of its own and part from its sisters, the words and gestures, is shown by the slow movement of its history. A compelling means was necessary to make it independent and to liberate it from alien aid. [22:186]

That "compelling means" was for Herder *Andacht*, devoted attention.

14 AN EPILOGUE ON ROMANTICISM

I regard this art [of music] . . . as the algebraic formula of all the others, and . . . from my earliest youth onward I have related all my general thoughts on poetry to sounds. I believe that the thoroughbass contains the most important disclosures about poetry.

—Kleist to Marie von Kleist, summer 1811

I have tried to show how eighteenth-century music theories and debates slowly prepared the way for a Romantic music aesthetics that could accommodate instrumental music. Aesthetics is therefore a central link between Romanticism and music. As Dahlhaus says, "Romantic poetics is just as much nourished by the idea of absolute music as, vice versa, the idea of absolute music by romantic poetics" (*abs. Mus.* 70). Although the term *absolute music* was coined only by Wagner, it was undoubtedly implied already by Romantic notions of music, and, as Rosen notes in his polemic with Scruton on the entry "absolute music" in the *New Grove*, "the same concept, expressed in different terms" existed already around 1800.

To attempt even to sketch here all dimensions of the relationship between Romanticism and music would not only be impossible but also inconsistent with my focus on philosophical issues. I shall have to forego therefore such tempting and exciting topics as the birth of the lied and Romantic opera, the relationship between musicians and Romantic poets, the "Romantic" nature of specific compositions, and even the image of music and musicians in Romantic literature. There are excellent studies on these subjects, and though there is room for more, I shall not try to fill the gap. My main purpose is to show that this recognition of instrumental music went hand in hand with a revival of Pythagoreanism, a new mathematical metaphysics of music. Since I shall discuss only the most important representatives, I should mention here that Romantic Pythagoreanism embraces many divergent works, including pseudo-scientific speculations by Ritter on the music of the spheres (45 ff.) and Gotthilf Heinrich Schubert's efforts to revive Kepler's harmonic speculation, to name only two.

An adequate treatment of these matters has been delayed for a long time by emotive-expressive interpretations of Romanticism. While it has been generally granted that German Romantics were the first to appreciate symphonic music, the reasons for this have not been well understood. Schäfke (*Gesch.* 328 ff.), for instance, conventionally reduces Romanticism to an irrational and mystic opposition to the Enlightenment, which obscures his valid insight that the Romantic tendency toward abstraction and formalism counteracted indulgences in emotional outbursts. Schering denounces the Romantic drive toward abstraction and its separation of music from language in an unfortunately tainted right-wing vocabulary (*Kritik*, esp. 26–27). Becking regards music-dominated settings by Schubert and others as evidence for the divergence of musical and literary Romanticism. Even Dahlhaus's earlier article on Romantic music aesthetics and Viennese classical music is remarkably negative. Although it draws a clear line between Sturm und Drang and Romantic music aesthetics, it also finds a gap between the new music and Romantic aesthetics, and it concludes that the metaphysical formulas of the Romantics missed the spirit of Viennese classicism (181).

Dahlhaus's excellent study on the idea of absolute music, which starts where my treatment will have to stop, takes a significantly more positive view of the relation between the new music and the new aesthetics, and much of what it says, especially on "absolute music and absolute poetry" (the title of Dahlhaus's concluding chapter) extends my epilogue in important ways. By showing how the revitalization of Pythagorean and mathematical interpretations motivated the change from an aesthetics of affects and expression to an aesthetics of structure, my purpose is to combat what Dahlhaus calls one of the most resilient prejudices of intellectual history, namely, "that Romantic aesthetics was an aesthetics of emotions and that of rationalism one of structure" (*abs. Mus.* 74).

Of course, a monolithic Romantic aesthetics, whether structure- or emotion-oriented, is just as much a figment of the historian's imagination as a unified aesthetics of the Enlightenment. As we have seen, the new aesthetics was anticipated and prepared in a number of eighteenth-century works. In turn, what we glibly call Romantic music aesthetics had no adherents among the French or English Romantics; in Germany, August Wilhelm Schlegel, Schelling, Jean Paul, and others held a predominantly affective theory of music, and residues of that theory crop up in virtually all Romantic writings. Finally, even the new aesthetics was Janus-faced, inasmuch as it was a metaphysics in the Pythagorean and mystic sense, as well as a "constructivist" demythologized aesthetics. Music is in both cases associated with mathematics, form, and symmetry, but in the Pythagorean conception these remain representations of a cosmic order, whereas in constructivism the idea of imitation is surrendered completely.

These backward- and forward-looking faces of the new music aesthetics blend into each other all too easily, as the two meanings of *absolute music* indicate.[1] On the one hand, the new music is perceived as absolute because it reaches out from the empirical world toward some absolute and final entity. If, in Schleiermacher's sense, religion is a perception (*Anschauung*) of the universe, Pythagorean music is an organon of religion. On the other hand, absolute music is—already in Romanticism and certainly in its later variants—a demythologized, formalist, and l'art-pour-l'art conception, based on the premise that art is a pure play with form. Absoluteness here means self-referentiality. The ambiguity is disconcerting but not illogical: as Schäfke writes, the drive toward abstraction and away from matter is common to formalism and mysticism (*Gesch.* 380). The conjunction of Pythagorean mysticism and formalism is evident in many modern artists, perhaps most clearly in Kandinsky.

If these qualifications and ambiguities will not allow us to designate the new aesthetics as an all-inclusive and homogeneous single paradigm, the ideas that follow do represent, nevertheless, a definite turning point in the history of ideas on music.

SCHILLER AND KÖRNER

Schiller, who was in many respects the father of the Romantics, was still too close a follower of Kant to assume a Romantic view of music. To be sure, he claimed in a letter to Körner of May 25, 1792, that his poems originated in music: "When I sit down to make a poem, its musicality far more often hovers before my soul than the clear concept of its content, about which I am frequently divided." The remark anticipates Poe's commentary on the making of "The Raven," but it should not be taken as an affirmation of indeterminacy in music. As Schiller declared in his review of Matthisson's poetry, as well as in his essay *On Naive and Sentimental Poetry* (20:455–56), the composer was "a genuine painter of the soul," whose task it was to find external correlatives to movements in the soul. He softened this conventional affect theory by suggesting that music could represent only the form of feelings, since their contents were unrepresentable (22:271).

According to the twenty-second letter *On the Aesthetic Education of Man*, "in a truly successful work of art the contents should effect nothing, the form everything." The paragraph preceding this sentence shows, however, that Schiller's formalist credo was accompanied by Kantian doubts about music's ability to offer more than merely sensuous pleasure. To reflect upon musical pleasure would be mistaken, writes Schiller, for "even the most ethereal music has, by virtue of its material, a still greater affinity with the senses than true aesthetic freedom really allows."

While Schiller prepared his letters on aesthetic education, his friend Körner wrote an essay for Schiller's *Die Horen* entitled "On the Representation of Character in Music" (*Über Charakterdarstellung in der Musik*), which restates the aesthetics of unity in variety in terms of a tension between shifting emotions (pathos) and permanent character (ethos) (98). If the composer follows the emotional flux, he will produce cacophony, but if he represents a single affect, he will depart from verisimilitude, for the soul experiences "nothing but variety and constant change" (99). What is to be done?

Körner actually never gives a clear answer to this question, although he seems to prefer the representation of character. The real significance of the essay lies in his claim that not all music represents character or emotions. There was a primitive age, he writes, "when dance, music, and poetry were not considered representations of a definite object" and were "not means to an end but an end in themselves" (102–03). That Körner should regard these self-contained arts as free expressions of the artist seems paradoxical, but the important part of his view is his belief that even modern music, which he considers essentially representational, ought to include passages that retain this older freedom. In such parts one should not expect concrete representations but readily accept vagueness: "This very indeterminacy is welcome to the imagination because it safeguards better its free play" (104).

Körner's merit is to suggest, however tentatively, that vagueness in music is no shortcoming but a positive power that can release a Kantian free play. Schiller, who sided more with Kant's negative view of music, responded that the power of music sprung from its material (rather than formal) aspect and suggested that Körner devote more attention to it (22:295).

WACKENRODER AND TIECK

The outbreak of the Romantic enthusiasm for music is usually dated to Wackenroder and Tieck's rediscovery of old church music in South Germany, but the two had already been exposed to contemporary music and its theory earlier in Berlin, where Wackenroder had studied with Zelter, frequented Reichardt's house, and attended Moritz's lectures. He was already familiar with Forkel's studies (365) (the ones listed in my Bibliography) and later attended his lectures in Göttingen. As early as May 5, 1792, Wackenroder wrote to Tieck that he enjoyed concert music in two ways. The first, "genuine" pleasure consisted "of the most attentive concentration on the sounds and their progression, the complete surrender of the soul to this sweeping flood of feelings, and a removal and separation from every disturbing idea and all alien sensory impressions" (283). But music could also induce and sustain a certain activity in his mind:

> I no longer hear then the feeling that dominates the piece, but my thoughts and fantasies are, so to speak, carried away by the waves of the song and often lose themselves in distant corners. Strangely, once in this mood I can also best reflect on music as an aesthetician while listening; it seems as if general ideas would cut themselves loose from the sentiments generated by the piece, which then quickly and clearly present themselves to my soul. [284]

The two states seem to correspond to Goethe's pure and affective music, but Wackenroder, without making it explicit, seems to reverse the priorities and regard the first, nonintellectual reaction as the more musical. The utter concentration on "sounds and their progression" generates "thoughtless" states of mind.

The reflection precedes Wackenroder and Tieck's *Herzensergiessungen eines kunstliebenden Klosterbruders* ("Outpourings of an Art-loving Friar") of 1797 and *Phantasien über die Kunst* ("Fantasies about

Art") of 1799, works whose titles indicate a sentimental and religious rather than a nonrepresentational art. The *Outpourings* are partly to blame if Romanticism is often reduced to naive rapture, yearning for the infinite, and emotional rebellion against the intellect.

Yet we should not identify Wackenroder with the fictional friar overhastily, especially not in the pieces on music, which are either on or by an acquaintance of the friar, the musician Joseph Berglinger. In these doubly-mediated narratives a modern rift appears between art and life, utilitarianism and intrinisic aesthetic value, which is largely absent from the more pious pieces on painting that are usually placed in the Renaissance.[2]

Berglinger is no primitivist, for he believes that the "coarse medium" of passionate sounds had to evolve into an "artful system." The description of this development is spun into a Pythagorean myth of science and reason:

> The monotone light-ray of sound is split into a colorful sparkling fire of art, shimmering in all colors of the rainbow, but for this to happen several wise men had to descend first into the oracle caves of the most secret knowledge, where all-productive nature itself revealed to them the primal laws of sound. From these secret-laden vaults they brought to daylight the new teaching written in recondite numbers, which served to assemble out of a variety of individual sounds a tight and wise order. From this rich source the masters draw the greatest variety of tonalities. [218–19]

Mathematics reveals "an inexplicable sympathy" between tonal relations "and each fiber of the human heart" (219). Though mere concern with order may produce barren, scientific music, to scorn structure and surrender to sheer physical pleasure is equally undesirable. Music is the happiest artistic medium, because the composer's passion can melt "the profound science," so that an "ineffably precious work emerges, where feeling and science are as strongly and inextricably bonded as stone and color in enamel painting" (221).

This reemergent Pythagoreanism is accompanied by a distrust of language. Berglinger withdraws from worldly chaos and misery "into the land of music . . . where no babble of words and speech, no whirl of letters and monstrous hieroglyphic writing dizzy us" (204); there he will enter states of mind that verbal outpourings and fantasies can render only poorly. Tieck believes that reason and its inferences can never capture the essence of our innermost thoughts (248), and hence he concludes his "Töne" with a poetic exhortation to sink the securely moored vessel of language and brave the stormy seas of sound. Wackenroder's metaphor for music is a verbally indescribable turbulent stream that serves as a mirror to our inner life and a source of self-knowledge for our heart (223).

The metaphors of moving water indicate that the states of the soul can no longer be captured by stationary affects and corresponding verbal concepts. The poverty of language leaves the essence of music as well as the meaning of individual pieces inexplicable: "What do they want, these timorous and doubting sophists, who wish to have each of the hundreds and hundreds of musical pieces explained in words and cannot acquiesce that not all of them have utterable meanings like paintings? Do they strive to measure the richer language by the poorer one, and dissolve in words what disdains words? Or have they never had feelings without words?" (223).

The expressive poverty of language gives new prominence to instrumental music. As Tieck says in his essay on "Symphonien," vocal music "remains heightened declamation and speech." Music should not aspire to become language but make the most of its own powers: "Art is independent and free in instrumental music; it prescribes its own rules all by itself; it daydreams playfully and without purpose, and yet it satisfies and reaches what is highest; it completely follows its dark drives and expresses with its triflings what is deepest and most wonderful" (254). It follows that orchestral music may abandon its introductory and supplementary function and develop its own dramatic plot without texts and characters (255–57). The orchestra is the last and highest triumph of the instruments, for "instead of portraying a single sentiment, it projects a whole world, a complete drama of human affects" (226).

This liberation of music from the confinement of language has all too often been seen as Romantic irrationalism, a surrender to the chaos of emotions. Yet Pythagoreanism attributes to music a formative power, and Wackenroder envisions it as a mathematical structure that magically transforms matter into pure form:

From what kind of magic preparation does the scent of this splendid spectral world arise now?—I observe and find nothing but a wretched texture of numerical proportions, palpably represented in drilled wood and on frames of gut and brass wire.—This is almost more miraculous, and I am inclined to believe that God's unseen harp chimes in with our sounds and endows the human texture of numbers with heavenly force. [205]

All sonorous affects are ruled and guided by the dry, scientific number system, as if by the odd, magic-conjuring formulas of an old, fearsome magician. [224]

Both these passages offer a double optic on numbers: they are wretched and dry, yet they also perform miracles, as if deliberately hiding beneath their rags the wonders of a new world. It is mathematics that enables music to rid itself altogether of the burden of imitation; the "sounds which art has miraculously discovered and pursues along the greatest variety of paths . . . do not imitate and do not beautify; rather, they constitute a separate world for themselves" (245).

Thus Wackenroder's and Tieck's notion of music bridges inwardness and form. At least one piece in the collection, a remarkable fictional letter by Berglinger, fully articulates the ambiguity of this position, by describing Berglinger's agonizing hesitation between aestheticism and human involvement. For our purposes it suffices to note that music is not merely a vehicle of passion in this new conception but a higher and richer language, which expresses inwardness but also intimates, by means of mathematics, a higher order.

NOVALIS

Novalis's *Monologue* postulates an analogy between mathematics and poetic language that recalls the ideas of Wackenroder and Tieck:

Speaking and writing are actually odd matters; true talk is mere word play. One can only be astonished by the ridiculous, mistaken belief that we are talking for the sake of objects. Nobody seems to understand that language is unique because it cares only about itself. This is why it is such a wonderful and fertile secret—when we speak just for the sake of speaking we utter the most magnificent and original truths. But when we wish to speak about something definite, moody language makes us say the most ridiculous and twisted things. This too is the source of the hatred which so many serious people feel against language. If one could only explain to people that language behaves like mathematical formulas—they form a world of their own, they play only with themselves, express nothing but their own wonderful nature, and for this very reason they are expressive, just because of this they mirror the strange interplay of objects. [2:672]

Upon closer inspection, however, the differences become significant. For Wackenroder, as for most eighteenth-century writers, mathematical music meant a calculus of harmonic proportions. Novalis, who studied mathematics and made extensive notes on the relation between music, mathematics, and language, had a deeper insight into the significance of mathematics for the arts and the sciences,[3] though he could also speak in Pythagorean language: "All pleasure is musical, therefore also mathematical" (3:593).

Novalis's most ambitious and imaginative nonpoetic project was a collection of notes he entitled *Allgemeines Brouillon* ("General Outline"), a unique kind of encyclopedia that was to indicate the interrelation between all knowledge by means of analogies, combinations, and associations. Mathematics was at the heart of this project in several different senses. First, in a Kantian sense, it served as a model for all knowledge that was "constructive" rather than merely empirical. Furthermore, the combinatorial branch of mathematics, as developed by Leibniz and practiced in Leipzig when Novalis studied there, suggested an imaginative interlinking of the diverse arts and sciences, and it intimated a new way of thinking about art as a creative combination of nonreferential signs. Both aspects may be illustrated by an entry in the *Brouillon*, which attributes a common "combinatorial" structure to mathematics, music, and language:

> Musical mathematics.
> Doesn't music contain some combinatorial analysis and vice versa? Numerical harmonies—number acoustics—belong to combinatorial analysis. . . .
> Combinatorial analysis leads to number fantasias—and teaches the compositional art of numbers—the mathematical figured bass. (Pythagoras. Leibniz.) Language is a musical idea-instrument. The poet, the rhetorician, and the philosopher play and compose grammatically. A fugue is completely logical or scientific—it can also be treated poetically. The figured bass contains the musical algebra and analysis. The combinatorial analysis is the critical algebra and analysis—and the musical theory of composition relates to the figured bass as the combinatorial analysis to simple analysis.
> [3:360]

The dashes, typical for Novalis, indicate that his thought proceeds here associatively rather than deductively. The kinship between mathematics, music, and language is suggested by a transposition of their vocabularies: we are invited to contemplate combinatorial mathematics as an art of composing with numbers and, in agreement with the

passage from the *Monolog*, the poetic, rhetorical, and philosophic uses
of language as a (musical) play whereby grammar furnishes the rules
of "composition." For Friedrich Schlegel, in turn, instrumental music
is a text, not because it follows language but rather because it has a
vocabulary and grammar of its own:

> Whoever has a sense for the wondrous affinities between all the arts and
> sciences will at least not look upon the matter from the shallow perspective
> of so-called naturalness, according to which music is supposed to be just
> the language of sentiment, and such persons will not find it impossible that
> all pure instrumental music should have a tendency to philosophy. Must
> pure instrumental music not create a text for itself? And is the theme in it
> not developed, confirmed, varied, and contrasted as the object of medita-
> tion in a philosophical sequence of ideas? [2:254]

In Schlegel's fragment,[4] as well as in the game that Novalis's note
describes and simultaneously exemplifies, the primary value of words
lies not in their so-called vertical, semantic-referential dimension, but
in their horizontal, syntactic combination. Lacking a precise meaning,
they are mobile and suggestive. New contexts—for instance, the conjoining of combinatorial analysis and figured bass—will open unsuspected dimensions of meaning. Hence combinatorial play is both an
exercise of the imagination and an imaginative enlargement of our cir-
cle of knowledge.

Such an approach to the arts and the sciences throws a new light on
instrumental music. Writers were uneasy about it throughout the
eighteenth century because, in spite of efforts by theorists of the Affektenlehre, it had no precise semantics. Its signs could acquire precise
meaning only through marriage with words. Novalis ceases to worry
about the semantic imprecision of signs because he no longer assigns
them a representative function; instead, he exploits their ambiguity
and interpretability by placing them in new contexts: representation
may be said to be replaced by exploration.

Novalis has no doubts that music points toward a departure from
mimesis. He considers music as a "mathematics for the ear" (3:50), not
because it is a deductive science in Rameau's sense but rather because
"music has much in common with algebra" (3:319). In music as in algebra we take indeterminate signs and combine them according to certain rules that are specified by the field itself and not by the qualities of
some object that is to be represented. In this sense, music is "a general

N-language" (3:283). Symphonies, sonatas, fugues, and variations represent genuine, pure music (3:685, 691) that can only be compared with arabesques and ornaments (3:559), visual forms that have no content. Music is the least representational art, for the musician ignores the "rough and spiritless" (2:573) natural sounds and "takes the essence of his art from himself—he is free of even the faintest suspicion of imitation" (2:574). In the theater, which is still under its "tyranny," operettas and operas depart from naturalistic mimesis by stylizing the representations (3:691).

Wackenroder's music resounds where language becomes mute; Novalis's language continues to speak, but in the voice of music, by means of suggestions: "Every general, indeterminate sense contains something musical. It excites philosophical fantasies—without expressing a definite philosophical train of thought, any individual philosophic idea" (3:319). In this sense Novalis perceived in poetry a play of philosophical music (3:320) that harks back to the effect produced by Kant's aesthetic ideas. Applied to fiction, the break with mimesis should result in "narrations without connection yet with associations, like dreams" (3:572). The ideal narrative is now the tale whose wondrous, inexplicable, and chaotic events constitute a completely musical texture (3:458), a "musical fantasy" (3:454) without any immediately evident plot and moral.

Though Novalis speaks of musical fairy tales, the genre he envisioned already contained *Tristram Shandy, Jacques le fataliste*, and *Rameau's Nephew*, and it was to encompass the modern psychological and experimental novel, whose kinship to serial music has often been noted. Novalis's own fairy tales enunciate rather than embody his vision, as a brief look at the tales in his novel *Heinrich von Ofterdingen* shows. According to Novalis, the unfinished second part of *Ofterdingen* would have become a tale; the transformation is anticipated in a sequence of tales inserted in the first part that themselves form a progression, both in terms of content and narrative mode. That music should play a central and increasingly subtle role in them is hardly surprising.

I shall have to forego discussion of the stylistic evolution from concretion and directness toward indirection and allusion in favor of the more easily describable evolution of musical images. The first two tales, narrated by merchants, speak of the traditional affective power of music: in the first, the singer Arion saves himself from a ship by attracting with his singing a fish that carries him safely to the shore; in the second, the song of a lover wins the consent of his father-in-law to an already consummated marriage. In the final and most elaborate tale, told by a poet rather than merchants, music no longer has affective control over beasts and men but stands in an unmistakably Pythagorean relation to the forces of the universe. In the opening scene a king and his daughter play a game with cards that depict the "holy, profound symbols" of star constellations. The association between the card game and the cosmic movements becomes audible in a "music of the spheres":

> Soft but deeply moving music was heard in the air that seemed to originate from the wondrous interweaving of the stars in the hall and the other strange motions. The stars coursed around, now slow now fast, in constantly changing patterns; and following the movement of the music they imitated the figures of the cards in the most artistic way. Like patterns on the table, the music changed ceaselessly; and peculiar and difficult as the transitions not infrequently were, still only one simple theme appeared to unite the whole. [1:293]

In accordance with the *Monolog*, music originates in an aimless play that follows only its own intrinsic rules. Yet its very autonomy turns it into a microcosm to which the macrocosm will respond by resounding. But the relationship between game, music, and cosmos is associative rather than causal. The contentless game cannot "produce" the changes outside, and the mechanism of the relationships cannot be explicated. As a note says, the configurations and movements can be duplicated best in poetry rather than narrative prose: "Poems— merely mellifluous and full of beautiful words—but also without any sense and connection—at most individual strophes are comprehensible—they must be like so many fragments from most varied things" (3:572).

The absence of determinate meaning and even form, the reliance on mere suggestiveness, is now a virtue. Listener and reader are no longer passive recipients of a predetermined communication but themselves active participants in a game with indeterminate signs. The portrayal and arousal of determinate feelings is banished, for "affects are just something nasty, like illnesses" (3:560). The purpose of art is not to transmit determinate attitudes but to free the recipient: "All representations of the poet must be symbolic or moving. Moving here for stimulating generally. Symbolism does not stimulate directly, it induces self-contained activity. The latter stimulates and excites, the former touches and moves" (3:693). Obviously, orchestral music is best suited to induce "self-contained activity."

E. T. A. HOFFMANN

Wackenroder shrouded the new music in fictional and mythic images, whereas Novalis explored its implications for a new poetics. Hoffmann was largely responsible for the development of a new language of music criticism.[5] As a regular contributor to the *Allgemeine Musikalische Zeitung* in Leipzig, Hoffmann wrote a number of exemplary reviews of music and musical performances that contain no biographical facts or anecdotes, subjective impressions, or descriptions of affects, only general introductions and careful analyses of themes and structures. Treatises on music that had no concrete foundations in specific works (he considered, unjustly, *Hildegard von Hohenthal* an exemplar of this genre) he found boring (345).

Though it may seem paradoxical at first sight, there is no clash between the Romantic belief that music utters the ineffable, a belief that Hoffmann deeply shared, and the attempt to develop a new language in which to talk about music. Since Hoffmann's criticism is based on the premise that music is a completely independent medium, he makes no attempt to articulate what is untranslatable in music but discusses rather musical materials and their uses. Hoffmann's great review of Beethoven's Fifth Symphony (1810) praises music as the highest, perhaps the only, Romantic art, and instrumental music as its noblest expression, because it "scorns every help, every admixture of another art (poetry)" (34). Instrumental music is an intensification of vocal music, because music "had to break all the fetters of an alien art" (35).

The premise, if not the actual use, of the term *absolute music* enabled Hoffmann to hail the revolutionary novelty of classical instrumental music. Symphonies were formerly introductions, he writes, but "our great masters of instrumental music, Haydn, Mozart, Beethoven, gave the symphony a direction, so that it has become an independent whole and, simultaneously, the highest instrumental music—a kind of . . . opera of the instruments. The composer now has the freedom to utilize all the possible means which the art of harmony and the infinite variety of instruments in their different combinations offer, and thereby let the wonderful, secret magic of music powerfully move the listener" (145). Of course, symphonies are "the opera of the instruments" not because they sing (as Mattheson's generation would have expected) but rather because of their newly won prestige and popularity. Though Hoffmann retains a predilection for melody, he recognizes the power of harmony to move, and he sees in the fortepiano the representative instrument of the age because it is designed to produce powerful chords. Proportions remain "dead, stiff examples of calculation for grammarians without genius," but for the masters of harmony they are "magic preparations from which they release an enchanted world" (121).

Hoffmann continues to demand that music arouse the listener, and he admires Beethoven for his ability to move "the levers of horror, fear, shock, and pain" (36), but the role he assigns to emotions in music can no longer be accounted for in terms of affect theory or self-expression. On the one hand, he advises composers to avoid the "ridiculous aberrations" of those musicians who "tortured" themselves with the portrayal of "definite sentiments, nay, even occurrences" (34); on the other, he postulates that there must always be an aesthetic distance between the composer and his work.

For all its emotional intensity, Beethoven's music possesses sobriety, structure, and deep inner cohesion that reveal themselves only to the careful listener. The subjective objectivity of the Romantic genius must be distinguished from emotional outpourings. Beethoven does not pour himself into music; rather "he separates his self from the inner realm of sounds, and rules over this like an unrestricted lord" (37). As pedantic and superficial critics overlooked the organic unity of Shakespeare's plays and found them disorganized, so too "only a deeper penetration into the inner structure of Beethoven's music will perceive the master's high sobriety, which is inseparable from true genius and nourished by his continuous study of the art" (37, 119). More specifically, in Beethoven's Fifth Symphony that sobriety expresses "to a very high degree the romanticism of music" (50). The double demand for emotional intensity and sober detachment links Hoffmann's vision of Romantic music with the poetics of Friedrich Schlegel, Novalis, Keats, and Coleridge.

The distinction between pure self-expression and detachment corresponds to the difference between mannerism and style that Hoffmann defines in connection with Spontini's *Cortez*. A concrete style is compatible with absolute music, for it results from "the liveliest perception of a concretely limited region and its shapes. A true master has such a perception: with deep and clear inner eyes he sees those shapes, and he hears how in a single language of his homeland love and hate, rapture and desperation ring out. What is objective and rounded in itself is shaped from the innermost being of the master." Mannerism, on the other hand, is "the expression of a stereotypical subjectivity of the artist" (285), which results from the composer's capricious grasp of impressions that happen to come his way. The resultant work is a collage, a potpourri without style.

Ultimately, Hoffmann found even personal objectivity wanting in face of a music that was absolute because it was divinely inspired. While he was deeply moved by the "quintessentially romantic" art of instrumental music, he approached it with mixed moral and religious feelings. The inspiration of a Mozart or a Beethoven had to emanate from a source beyond the artist's subjectivity, yet it was of a secular nature. The ambiguity in Hoffmann's music aesthetics, which corresponds to his hesitation in matters of literature, results from the clash he perceived between the religious sources of music and its secular telos. His great essay *Old and New Church Music* (1814) defined music as a profoundly spiritual cult, whose origin "is to be sought and to be found only in religion and the church" (212); but he found this religious spirit expressed most purely in the sacred vocal music of Palestrina's time. In spite of, or rather because of, the advances made in technique, the instrumental music of Hoffmann's own age could not replicate this music. Palestrina was divinely inspired, and composition was for him a "religious exercise" (216). The music of his age was authentic because "no anxious striving for so-called effect, no artificial games and mimicry profaned what came pure from heaven" (218).

But "the most simple, choral-type songs of Allegri, Perti, Durante, Benevoli," this "only genuine, high church style" had to disappear (179), because the new, technical possibilities of instrumental music diverted composers from that majestic simplicity which constituted the glory of church music for Hoffmann (232). The decline of simple chant and song (230), which Hoffmann regrets for religious rather than aesthetic reasons, was inevitable: Mozart, Haydn, and especially Beethoven (whose *Missa Solemnis* Hoffmann did not live to know) no longer mastered this sacred idiom (227–28).

Hoffmann articulates here a Romantic rift between an aesthetic imagination awed by new possibilities in art and a religiously inspired conservative historical understanding. Like Novalis, whose *Christendom or Europe* probably informed Hoffmann's historical scheme, Hoffmann believes in the inevitable forward march of the *Weltgeist* (229–30, 235), and, since he seeks no quixotic restoration, he is left with only the vaguely articulated hope that in a triadic pattern of music history the fall from Palestrina's art will be followed by a sacred music on a higher level: the new instrumental art—which attained heights unimaginable to the old masters (230, 235)—will eventually engender a new religious music. Thus, while Hoffmann seems to agree superficially with the advocates of word-dominated music from Plato to Brown, his admiration for older church music is motivated by a very different disposition. These others found pure instrumental music empty and meaningless, whereas Hoffmann discovered in it the deepest expression of a modern disposition that he himself shared, but with equally profound misgivings. Not the superficiality but the very earnestness of the new voice disturbs him.

Hoffmann's interest in opera and his admiration for Gluck have different foundations, but they do not testify, any more than his love for older church music does, to a belief that words ought to dominate music. He admires the genuine unity of word, action, and text, as well as the dramatization of music in Gluck's operas. The operas of Lully and Rameau he finds monotonous because they aim at proper declamation; their style, for all its merit, strips music of "its power and magnificence" and uses it not "to allow the drama itself to shine forth but to lead and to accompany the words" (358). Gluck, on the other hand, "grasped the high splendor of music in its full essence and all of its qualities, with such power that genuine musical drama soared from his own interior like a brilliant meteor" (358). In this view, which differs from Gluck's self-understanding but agrees with his image in Hoffmann's first great story entitled *Ritter Gluck*, the source of genuine operas is music's "own inner being," not words.

The function of the text is therefore not rhetorical: "Not the word but thoughts ignited music, and it created not a series of notes defined by the order of words, but true melody, which, without doing the least harm to the fundament, proper declamation, brought thought into full and active life" (358). What Hoffmann admires in Gluck is concentration and autonomy. Whereas Sacchini and other Italians wanted merely to please and thought of music as an "accidental companion to the play" that seldom deserved independence, Gluck, like Beethoven, realized a dramatic unity of style that infused all parts of music with a single idea, so that the action "irresistibly advances from moment to moment" (69) without the intrusion of anything trivial, irrelevant, or designed for mere applause.

Hence, from Hoffmann's perspective, the function of the text in Gluck's operas is not to dominate the music but to advance its dramatic unity, not to reestablish a rhetorical style but to move it in the direction of absolute music. Not surprisingly, Hoffmann entertained the possibility that the advances made by instrumental music since the time of Gluck could emancipate the orchestra and turn it into a vehicle of action and voice (368). This anticipates Wagner, not in the sense in which Wagner saw himself—namely, as a reviver of a word-dominated music in the manner of Gluck—but in the sense of his musical practice, which, as Dahlhaus argues (*abs. Mus.* 24 ff.), is not the antipode but a logical development of absolute music.

More than any other music critic of his time, Hoffmann recognized the novelty and importance of Classical (for him Romantic) instrumental music and hailed it as the emancipation of music. But while he understood the new form and recognized its potentialities, he, like Wackenroder and Novalis, saw it also against the background of the vocal tradition of church music, opera, and lied that he continued to treasure. Hailing the emancipation of music, he desired to revive its original use in sacred cult. If his partisanship of a revolution was not radical and total but inextricably interwoven with revival and reinterpretation—if, in other words, his ideas on music cannot be pressed into an unequivocally defined epistème, paradigm, or Zeitgeist—there may be a lesson here that applies to the larger dimensions of music aesthetics and Romanticism as well.

MUSIC AND THOUGHTS ABOUT MUSIC

I have ended my consideration of Romantic music aesthetics with the ideas of Hoffmann because he was a bona fide musician and perhaps the first great music critic. But I wonder whether such professional credentials are necessary for the kind of questions I am considering. Would the words of Wackenroder, Novalis, and Hoffmann be more important had they been uttered by Haydn, Mozart, or Beethoven? That the composers wrote music and left it to the poets to articulate the meaning of their work does not make Romantic reflections less relevant: it only shows that practice and reflection on practice are different activities, especially in nonverbal fields like music. Had Romantic reflections on music completely missed the mark, they would not have caught on. The fact is that such reflections on music became the lens through which composers of the next generation perceived their art. As Dahlhaus says:

> Literature about music is no mere reflex of what happens in the musical praxis of composition, interpretation, and reception; it belongs in a certain sense to the constitutive moments of music itself. For inasmuch as music is not restricted to the acoustic substrate that underlies it, but emerges only through the categorial forming of what has been perceived, a change in the categorial system directly modifies the material of the very subject. [*abs. Mus.* 66–67]

The Romantics had discovered the epochal significance of a genre that until then had little prestige and that throughout the Romantic era constituted a quantitatively small part of the repertoire. Their vision has shaped ours ever since. Technical know-how is the prime requisite for composition, but the use and interpretation of any created object are, for better or worse, usually beyond the control of the creator. One task of interdisciplinary studies is to illuminate aspects of that larger context within which the creation as well as the uses and perceptions of created objects take place. If I have been able to show that reflections on literature and music are interdependent, we have advanced a small step in our understanding of what that larger context is for the arts.

APPENDIX: CHRONOLOGICAL TABLE OF THE PRINCIPAL EVENTS IN THE QUARREL BETWEEN RAMEAU AND THE PHILOSOPHES

1722	Rameau, *Traité de l'harmonie*
1726	Rameau, *Nouveau système de musique théorique*
1737	Rameau, *Traité de la génération harmonique*
1742	Rousseau, *Projet concernant de nouveaux signes pour la musique*
1745	Rousseau, *Les muses galantes* (ballet)
1749–50	Rousseau, Encyclopédie articles on music theory
1750	Rousseau, private letter to Grimm, praising Rameau
	Rameau submits his Mémoire to the Académie
1751	D'Alembert, *Discours préliminaire* to the *Encyclopédie*
	Rameau, *Démonstration du principe de l'harmonie*
1752	Rousseau, anonymous *Lettre à Grimm* with an attack on Rameau
	D'Alembert, *Elémens de musique*
1752–53	querelle des bouffons
1753	Rousseau, *Lettre sur la musique française*
1754	Rameau, *Observations sur notre instinct pour la musique*
1754?–?	Rousseau, *Essai sur l'origine des langues*
1755	Rameau, *Erreurs sur la musique dans l'Encyclopédie*
	Rousseau, *Examen de deux principes avancés par M. Rameau* (publ. posthumously)
1756	Rameau, *Suite des erreurs*
	D'Alembert and Diderot, prefatory note to the sixth volume of the *Encyclopédie*, defending Rousseau
1757	D'Alembert, articles *fondamental* and *gamme* in seventh volume of the *Encyclopédie*
	Rameau, *Réponse à MM. les Editeurs*
1760	Rameau, *Code de musique pratique*
	Nouvelles réflexions sur le principe sonore
	Lettre à M. d'Alembert
1760?–?	Diderot, *Le neveu de Rameau* (publ. posthumously)

1761   Polemic between Rameau and d'Alembert in the *Mercure de France*
1764   Death of Rameau
1767   Rousseau, *Dictionnaire de musique*

NOTES

Introduction

1 As quoted by Tardieu, "La peinture et les peintres, M. Paul Gauguin," *Echo de Paris*, May 13, 1895.
2 "Crise de vers," *Oeuvres complètes* (Paris: Gallimard, 1965), 365.
3 For a critique of the Affektenlehre, see the entries "Affections" and "Rhetoric and Music" in the *New Grove*, as well as Buelow's other works. Though it has become customary to translate the German *Affekten* as "affections," I prefer to use the unusual but bona fide English term "affects" in order to avoid the undesirable modern connotations of "affection."
4 Reductive categorizations have weakened several important studies of music theories. Dammann's book for instance, establishes such a tight network of philosophical, theological, and scientific ideas around German baroque music that the collapse of the system approaches a *Götterdämmerung*. A greater attention to the contradictions, tensions, and ambiguities within the baroque world view would have allowed a less cataclysmic dissolution. Serauky's book on musical imitation similarly suffers from limitations in Geistesgeschichte in that it neatly divides eighteenth-century music aesthetics into "the rationalism of the Enlightenment and the irrationalism of Romanticism" (XIII), discarding thereby the possibility of finding irrationalism in the Enlightenment or rationalism in Romanticism. Foucault has rightly criticized such total constructs of Geistesgeschichte, though his own history of epistèmes, divided by unbridgeable ruptures, is open to similar charges.

Neither does Thomas Kuhn's theory of scientific paradigms offer a useful model for understanding the history of aesthetics. For Kuhn divides the history of science into periods of so-called normal science, dominated by single paradigms, and intervening revolutionary periods. Critics of Kuhn have pointed out that the sciences usually entertain several simultaneous and conflicting paradigms. To import this model into the arts, which are usually even more pluralistic than the sciences, is mistaken. In treating the notion of absolute music, Dahlhaus rightly stresses that the concept was in constant competition with rival paradigms of music. Strictly speaking, therefore, he should not regard it as a Kuhnian paradigm for the Romantic and post-Romantic age (*abs. Mus.* 12). The alternate scheme I am proposing has greatly profited from critics of Kuhn, especially Laudan.

Chapter 1

1 On music, mathematics, and the Pythagorean tradition, see Bloch, Dammann, Guthrie, Haase, Heninger, Hollander, Junge, Ludwig, Ruhnke, Schäfke (*Gesch.*), Zenck, Ziller, and Zimmermann.
2 By harmony the Greeks did not mean chords and their progressions in our sense, only successive combinations of sounds in melodies and the modes. In Greek heterophony, instrumental accompaniments deviated from the melody only slightly.
3 Similarities in overall purpose and vision override, at least in our context, the conceptual and methodological differences between Kepler and Mersenne on the one hand and Fludd on the

other. Kepler considered Fludd an alchemist, hermeticist, and Paracelsist, himself a philosopher and mathematician exploring the "nature of things" (362).

4 The articles of Gerigk, Deutsch, Schering (*ars inveniendi*), and Ratner usefully enumerate the
combinatorial practices of the eighteenth century but tend to see them as an oddity and fail
to recognize their philosophical foundations and their role in anticipating serial and other
modern techniques. Foucault's *The Order of Things* posits the Leibnizian ars inveniendi as the
conceptual background of the whole classical age (57). My book *Symbolismus und symbolische
Logik* shows how combinatorial theories became the foundation of Romantic and Symbolist
poetics.

5 On Mattheson see Lenneberg, Cannon, and, above all, the volume on the 1981 Mattheson
symposium in Wolffenbüttel edited by Buelow and Marx. The latter also contains a bibliography of the secondary literature.

6 While at the Hamburg opera, Mattheson was a friend of Handel. Their stormy friendship
even survived a duel.

7 Schäfke (*Quantz* 225) claims that Heinichen was the first to attack the mathematical tradition
in music, but the 1711 edition of *Der General-Bass* calls for a general "weeding out of all musical quackery, metaphysical speculation, barbaric terminology, ridiculous divisions, anti-
quated and discarded rules, and similar unfruitful things" (19); only the 1728 edition contains
an explicit and sharp defense of the ear against abstract reason—with specific reference to the
works that Mattheson had published meanwhile (3–5). Scheibe (650 ff.) continued Mattheson's attacks and occasionally copied him.

Chapter 2

1 On music and language, see Combarieu, Dahlhaus, Georgiades, Gurlitt, and Winn.

2 Most writers, including Webb (130–32), and Arnaud (6–13) rejected the notion of a syllabic
rhythm, in which accents were simply indicated by longer notes. As Mattheson wrote, the
length of sound in music has a much finer gradation than that in poetry (*Capellm.* 170). Printz
(18), Marpurg (*Briefe* 1:477), and Rellstab all insisted that the textual accents coincide with
the musical "thesis and arsis," the down beat and up beat, of the measure. Some even allowed
a limited melismatic style with syllables stretched over several notes (Scheibe 359, Sulzer, art.
"Lied").

3 Mattheson (*Capellm.* 180–95), Marpurg (Briefe 2:309–79, 414), and Sulzer (art. "Accent in
der Musik").

4 Isidore's reference to martial trumpets suggests a debt to Quintilian. But Isidore cites the
biblical example of David instead of Orpheus or Linus. As Clement of Alexandria and
Cassiodorus (Strunk 61, 91–92) had argued earlier, classical accounts of music's power could
not be trusted.

5 Although Peacham, Mersenne, and many others believed in the possibility of a rhetorical music, curiously, only Germans wrote systematic treatises on it. The reasons for this are not
clear. Musical rhetoric is not included in the *Encyclopédie*. Arnaud proposed one in 1754, but,
as d'Alembert regretfully noted later (*Oe. inéd.* 157f), nothing came of it. The situation was
similar in England; as late as 1784 William Jones of Nayland suggested some rules that had
been in use for a long time in Germany (43).

6 See mainly Kretzschmar, Schering, Unger, and Brandes, though the Bach studies of
Schweitzer and Pirro also contributed to the revival of interest in rhetorical figures.

7 Draper has shown that in England, "'imitation' in the sense of copying was the common conception that the age gleaned from its dictionaries and rhetorics, as well as from the commentators of Aristotle." Especially in the early eighteenth century, theorists "advocated 'imitation' in the sense of copying models" (*Mim.* 375). But Draper underestimates the verbal and
rhetorical approaches to music, for he claims that "the vocal and even the operatic settings of

the early and middle eighteenth century are almost unrelated to the accompanying words" (393), and that "absolute music was characteristic of the age" (395)!

8 A promenade through rooms of a house was a favorite rhetorical technique to memorize parts of a speech.

9 Of the older studies on the subject, those of Unger and Brandes are the most exhaustive. For more recent studies, see Buelow's article on "Rhetoric and Music" in the *New Grove* and Vickers, who provides some correctives to it. Some of my examples are indebted to a delightful Dutch radio program on the subject, which has been published by Peter van Dijk and his colleagues under the title *Musiceren als Brugman* (Brugman was a proverbial fifteenth-century sermonizer).

Chapter 3

1 Aristoxenos claims that a "natural law," defined by the limits of the voice, allowed only two successive dieses (quarter-tone intervals) in a scale (185). For similar empirical reasons he discards the music of the spheres and other speculations. But the violence of Aristoxenes' attacks on Pythagoreanism obscures the rationalist premises of his empiricism. Since for him the "ultimate factor in every visible activity is the intellectual process" (195), the senses remain "inanimate instruments incapable of grasping the natural laws of harmony.

2 Hence the revival of music therapy, based on the biblical and classical belief that music, as a "cordial of a troubled mind" (Purcell) and "heaven's gift to lengthen life" (Peacham) could reharmonize the morbid imbalance of the humors. The link between music and medicine is underscored by the double meanings of "temperament," "harmony," "mood," or "tuning." Kircher discusses the affects under "Musica pathetica"; illnesses are for Niedt a *Verstimmung* ("mistuning") of the body (3:39) and for Mattheson just discords and dissonances (*Capellm.* 14). Both Baglivi and Kircher studied tarantism, the Apuleian belief that the tarantula's sting could be cured by an ecstatic and cathartic dance at the market.

3 In contrast to Schueller (*Pleasures*), I find the eighteenth-century associationist treatments of music, especially Hartley's, quite disappointing, precisely because they virtually ignore the role of memory in listening.

4 According to Schäfke (*Quantz* 233), Spinoza's notion that affects can be extinguished only by other affects (*Ethics* pt. 3) was equally important for affect theories of music. But Schäfke supports this only with a dubious passage from Krause (81–83).

5 Bach asked his friend Birnbaum, a professor in Leipzig, to respond to Scheibe's attack. Unfortunately, Birnbaum's lame defense focused on trivialities such as whether Bach should be addressed as a composer or a *Musikant*.

6 Sulzer collaborated with Kirnberger on the music articles in Sulzer's volume as far as the entry "Modulation." The articles after this were written by either Kirnberger or J. A. P. Schulz.

7 Hollander notes that the association between tonality and affect was reinforced by the linguistic accident that "the English derivatives of the Anglo-Saxon 'mod' (originally 'pride,' 'courage,' finally becoming 'feeling' generically) and the Latin 'modus' ('measure,' 'manner,' 'means,' 'structure,' 'pattern') fell together" (209). The resultant 'moode' was used until the end of the seventeenth century to denote both affect and church modality.

8 That words must make vague musical meanings concrete was held, for instance, by Harris (81), Beattie (147), Brown (223), Mendelssohn (192), and Körner (320).

Chapter 4

1 Diderot, who remarked that Batteux's work was "headless" because it did not define belle nature, was particularly uncharitable, but others were hardly more enthusiastic about the book. Though mimesis was the norm in the 1750s and 60s, Batteux's system was not the virtually unchallenged basis for French aesthetics, as the *New Grove* (art. "Expression") claims. Batteux

had no "system," and most advocates of mimesis criticized him, even if they frequently coopted his ideas.

The German responses by Gottsched, Johann Adolph Schlegel, Ruetz, Hiller, Ramler, Mendelssohn, and Klopstock were equally critical. The most thorough of them, Schlegel's annotated translation of Batteux, was twice reprinted in enlarged editions. Hugo Goldschmidt (*Musikästhetik* 134) hails Ruetz as one of the greatest aestheticians of the century, for responding to Batteux that music was "no copy of nature but the original itself" (293). But Ruetz merely means that music can produce natural sounds without imitating them by way of language. As a "universal language of nature," music incorporates all "ringing and singing" sounds absent from the more limited repertoire of language. In this, Ruetz barely goes beyond Batteux.

2 On imitation in the eighteenth century and in general, see Butor, Bukofzer (*Allegory*), Cazden, Darenberg, Draper (*Mim.*), Harry Goldschmidt, Frank, Schäfke (*Quantz*), Scher, Serauky (*Nachahm.*), and Winn. Serauky considers only the last three of the five imitations I have listed (XII).

3 Sulzer still recommends the imitation of models (art. "Nachahmung"). In England, according to Draper, the copying of models gave way in the second third of the century "to 'imitation' of Nature," while during the last third, "'imitation' became a less and less vital part of literary criticism" (*Mim.* 387). The division may be too tidy, but it suggests that literary developments ran parallel with, not behind, music.

4 Schweitzer, Pirro, and later Schering have shown that J. S. Bach frequently painted words, either directly or by means of figures and tropes. Bukofzer (*Allegory*) rightly remarks, however, that these studies make no clear distinction between naturalistic, allegorical, and symbolic imitations.

5 One finds a similar criticism of Handel in Beattie (127), Brown (219), Robertson (444), and Sulzer's article "Gemählde."

6 Engel, like Sulzer, considered music an emotive art and frowned upon portrayals of concepts (321, 325). He anticipated Kant by distinguishing "aesthetic ideas" from concepts, though he did not ascribe generating forces to the former.

7 Goldsmith admired Pergolesi for "knowing how to excite our passions by sounds, which seem frequently opposite to the passion they would express" (91–92); Rousseau noted that Italian music occasionally used tempi contrary to the required affect (*Ecrits* 305).

Chapter 5

1 For a chronology of Rameau's works and his debates with the philosophes, see my Appendix. Rameau explicitly endorses the Cartesian method in the opening section of the *Démonstration* (*Wr.* 3:169–71).

2 See texts by Marmontel, La Borde, and Hawkins, in Rameau *Wr.* 6:213–15, 3:466, and 5:385, respectively.

3 See, for instance, Serauky *Nachahm.* 32 and the introduction to the Rameau anthology *Musique raisonnée*. On Rameau see also Chailley, Doolittle, Ferris, Keane, Oliver, Pischner, Shirlaw, and Suadeau.

4 Although Rameau defended his principles with dogmatic fervor, he constantly changed his derivations and even some of his basic ideas. His experimental and innovative style in composition is seen in his enrichment of the orchestra with new instruments.

5 For instance, the perfect fourth (4:3) is simpler than the major third (5:4), but since Rameau considers the fourth an inversion of the fifth, he ranks it below the third. Rameau recognizes three primary consonances in the *Treatise*: the perfect fifth and the major and minor third; their inversions, the perfect fourth and the minor and major sixth, respectively, yield the secondary consonances (16 and 40).

6 As Shirlaw (81–84) and others have noted, Rameau uses two incompatible principles in the *Treatise* to derive chords: the division of the monochord through the first six numbers (the *senario*) and the repeated addition of thirds. The later, and different, derivations of the chords are no more consistent.

7 Bemetzrieder, for instance, follows this principle by describing music as an "art to shock the natural sounds [of the tonic chord] to render their return that much more agreeable" (Diderot *Oe.* 12:495).

8 According to Rameau, the fundamental bass moves best by ascending fifths or their inversion, descending fourths. Both movements link dominant to tonic and provide a bass for perfect cadences (*Treatise* 59–61).

Chapter 6

1 On the issues to be raised, see also Baud-Bovy, Duchet and Launay, Kintzler in Rousseau's *Ecrits sur la Musique*, Masson, Murat, Porset, Starobinski, and Wokler.

2 Although the *Essai* was a response to Rameau, Rousseau adopts here and in the letter to Burney (*Ecrits* 399) Rameau's view that single notes or even intervals have indeterminate meaning. As Rameau wrote in his criticism of the *Encyclopédie*, the interval c-f may signify, for instance, an apostrophe, a question, an exclamation, an affirmation, or a negation. Only harmony will specify the meaning, by means of cadences or modulations (*Wr.* 5:51–55).

3 Rousseau could not have known that Euler's notebooks contained sketches for a similar system (Euler 3.1:XIV). The idea of such a notation suggests itself more readily to the French, for whom the solmization syllables (ut, re, mi, etc.) have a fixed as well as a movable meaning. The fixed meaning simply represents the notes of the C-major scale, whereas the movable meaning represents the distance of a note from the fundamental note of any major or minor scale: the movable syllables thus form a pattern that can be transposed to any point of origin. Rousseau's contribution was to replace the meaningless syllables by numbers that encode the distance from the fundamental note.

4 This passage in the published version was probably a response to Rameau, who criticized the abstractness of Rousseau's system and the concomitant loss of visual power. In book 7 of the *Confessions* Rousseau admitted that Rameau was right.

5 According to Rameau's unconfirmed account, he was commissioned first but declined and merely requested that the articles be sent to him for evaluation.

6 However, the articles "duo" and "musique" contain references to events in the 1750s and must have been added later, by either Rousseau or the editors.

7 The articles "accord," "basse fondamentale," "cadence," "chiffrer," and "musique" concern themselves with Rameau's theory. Rousseau praised Rameau for reducing the number of chords by inversion, for distinguishing between thoroughbass and fundamental bass, and for introducing general principles into a formerly empirical and haphazard field. He still agreed that harmony, "the true foundation of melody and modulation," represented the great advance of modern over ancient music (art. "musique"). He qualified this with a critique of "harmonic chaos" in opera, but the suggestion of "thinning out" noisy full chords, a major anti-harmonist argument later, is made here only tentatively (art. "accompagnement"). The most substantial criticism of Rameau, concerning his tempering of the scale (art. "ton"), appeared after the composer's death.

8 In a letter to de Lalande of March 1768, Rousseau himself admitted that the dictionary was uneven, incomplete, and often derivative; among the fourteen articles he recommended, five were completely new, and three had undergone significant expansion.

9 Both Starobinski and Derrida show, from different perspectives, that "animal cries" are not the original language for Rousseau. As Derrida says, there is no degree zero for Rousseau, because "language is born out of the process of its own degeneration" (345).

10 Rousseau's comments on Gluck demonstrate that his notion of imitating language constitutes no rhetoric of music and contains no rhetoric of composition. Intonation was to be imitated to express passions, not concepts, and never at the expense of melody.

11 My reading is quite compatible, however, with de Man's allegorical interpretation of Rousseau and Romanticism.

Chapter 7

1 See Pappas (*querelle*) and Wachs. On d'Alembert, see also Bernard, Doolittle, Essar, and Jullien. My quotations from *Le Neveu de Rameau* rely on Jacques Barzun's translation, which appeared in *Rameau's Nephew and Other Works*, (Indianapolis: Bobbs-Merrill, 1964).

2 D'Alembert now favored the rival schemes proposed by Tartini and Serre, which proposed that the fundamental bass was engendered by the two upper voices. Tartini's theory soon became the rallying point for Rameau's opponents.

3 D'Alembert resented the fact that Rameau had changed the approved title, *Mémoire*, to *Démonstration*, which gave totally new claims to the paper. He also thought that Rameau wanted to make music the foundation of geometry. Although Rameau did not say this explicitly, in his last papers he attributed a Pythagorean metaphysical significance to musical harmony.

4 Rousseau's famous closing of chapter 16 in the *Essai sur l'origine des langues* restates d'Alembert's idea verbatim: "[the composer] does not represent things directly, but excites in the soul the same sentiments as the ones aroused while seeing them" (177). Webb (134) and Cahusac (art. "expression" in the Supplement to the *Encyclopédie*) adopted this idea from the article on imitation in Rousseau's *Dictionnaire*.

Chapter 8

1 On Diderot, see Bardez, Barricelli, Belaval, Chouillet, Crocker, Dieckmann, Duchet and Launay, Fabre's introduction to Diderot's *Oe. esth.*, Gamilschegg, Hugo Goldschmidt *Musikästhetik*, Heartz, Lang *Did.*, O'Gorman, Schlösser, Spitzer, Thomas, and Trilling.

Apart from the works to be discussed, Diderot's writings on music include the *Encyclopédie* articles on musical instruments, contributions to the querelle des bouffons, the third *Entretien sur le fils naturel* (1757), and scattered remarks on the musical scene. The extent of his contributions to Rameau's *Démonstration* (Rameau *Wr.* 3:XXXIX–XLI) are difficult to assess.

2 Neither is the pantomime a parodistic attack on Rousseau's expressive-imitative theory of music, as O'Gorman (152–53) believes. O'Gorman correctly notes the discrepancy between Lui's theory and his subsequent performance, but judging the theory flat and unoriginal does not yet prove that Diderot opposed Rousseau's music theory.

3 Bemetzrieder, who taught Diderot's daughter music, wrote a manual for playing the clavichord. In his preface to it Diderot admits that he improved Bemetzrieder's style, but his contribution probably included matters of substance as well. For this reason it has been included in the Assézat edition of Diderot's works.

Chapter 9

1 On Goethe, music, and Diderot, see Abert, Blume, Bode, Dreyer, Moser, Schlösser, Sternfeld, and Zoltai.

Chapter 10

1 According to Batteux, words constitute an "institutional language," whereas "gestures and sounds are like a dictionary of simple nature, which contains a language we all learn at birth" (264). See also Ruetz (293), Dubos (319 ff. and 467), Heinichen (19), Scheibe (771–72), Harris (81), Krause (*Verm.* 3:541), and Nichelmann (100).

2 When Lessing stated in his first draft of 1763 that painting used the natural signs of figure and color in space, and poetry the articulate sounds in time, Mendelssohn responded that the distinction was clearer between music and painting, for "the former is also served by natural signs, but imitates only by means of motions" (Lessing 6:564). He also commented that music should never overstep its supportive role and diminish the effect of poetry: "We rightly blame newer music that its artificialities are incompatible with any harmonious poetry" (6:581–82).

3 Yet Lessing did not break fully with the traditional view. His longest note for the second part recognizes arbitrary, natural, diachronic, and synchronic signs. But in discussing synthetic arts, Lessing considers only the traditional union of arbitrary and natural diachronic signs in vocal music, and he ignores the other possible combinations. In this traditional combination the tension is due to differences in tempo: the arbitrary signs of poetry condense meaning whereas musical sounds can represent passions only by constituting a sequence. Texts to be set must be prolix in order to allow music to keep up with language (6:653). Languages with many short words are therefore less fit for opera. Grimm was of the opposite opinion: a librettist must be "precise and economical" to fulfill opera's elementary demand for simplicity and appropriate choice of words; he "must completely surrender to the musician" and claim only a secondary role in shaping an opera (12:826).

4 The last question was a matter of national pride and ignited bitter debates between Vieville and Raguenet, the king's and the queen's corner in the opera (the querelle des bouffons), Agricola and Marpurg, Gluck and Piccini. Paul has shown that even twentieth-century French musicologists have tended to see the quarrel between Rousseau and Rameau in highly nationalistic terms. Daval's recent book is a case in point.

5 Only Grimm's *Encyclopédie* article on the "poème lyrique" took a different view, arguing that a few words set to music may have greater effect than all the magic poetry of the divine Racine, for verse tragedy "will always appear feeble and cold next to one that is animated by music."

6 Mattheson *Neu-Eröffn.* 166, Mizler 2.2:186–87, Krause *Poesie*, 371–73, J. E. Schlegel 163–64, and J. A. Schlegel 313.

7 *Gedancken* 77–78; see also Mattheson *Capellm.* 86 and Krause *Poesie* 374. Uffenbach assigned "hypothetical" probability and reality to opera (387, 395, 397).

8 Einstein *Gluck* 112–13. Garlington notes that with the exception of *Iphigénie in Aulis* Gluck continued to rely on the marvelous. His major contribution was to increasingly replace machinery by psychology (493–94).

9 As we shall see in the next chapter, this is spoken by a fictional character, but comes from Heinse's diaries.

Chapter 11

1 See also Dubos (484), Batteux (37), Sulzer (art. "Melodie"), Blainville (*L'Esprit* 71–72), and Forkel (*Gesch.* 55).

2 See also Harris (99), Beattie (136, 145), Gerard (60–61, 80), Sir William Jones (561), and Webb (28). The German term *Ausdruck* carried similar pragmatic meanings. Scheibe, for instance, believed that Ausdruck "should stimulate the mind" (92), while Sulzer, for whom melodic expressions were imitations (art. "Melodie"), claimed that Ausdruck belonged to "representations which are generated in the mind by means of external signs," sometimes referring to the cause of the representations, sometimes to their effects" (art. "Ausdruck").

3 On Avison, see Abrams, Darenberg, Lipking, Malek, and Schueller.

4 For Avison, expression is not "the power of exciting all the most agreeable passions of the soul" (Abrams 92), just an agent working through melody and harmony: if we add expression to melody and harmony "*they* assume the Power of exciting all the most agreeable Passions of the Soul" (my emphasis).

5 Harris has probably been more influential than Avison. At any rate, he seems to have been cited more frequently.

6 There were several variants of this idea: Scheibe (1:102) and Krause (*Verm.* 3:36) believed that composers must actually live the emotions while writing. Batteux's creative enthusiasm is a kin of Lui's self-abandonment: the artist's "soul passes into the things he creates: he is in turn Cinna, Augustus, Phaedra, Hippolyte"; he becomes Lafontaine's wolf, lamb, oak tree, or rose (34). The line between this late baroque mimesis and expression as found in Lepileur (108), Sulzer (art. "Ausdruck"), Heinse (5:46), or even Reichardt (108) is imperceptible.

7 Reichardt echoes this view as late as 1782: "Our most unnatural sonatas, symphonies, concerti, and other pieces of new music" indiscriminately mix joy and sadness by suddenly and frequently moving from one to the other (119).

8 On Herder, see Hugo Goldschmidt *Musikästhetik*, Huber, Jacoby, Marks *St. u. Dr.*, Moos *Philos*, Nufer, and Wiora *Beitrag*.

9 Hence Herder's interest in folksongs. They must, he wrote ten years later, "be heard, not seen; heard with the soul's ear that does not merely count and weigh individual syllables, but listens to its movement and swims along with it" (25:333).

10 Herder adds in a footnote that Leibniz's "unconscious counting" was not meant literally. In the earlier *Ideen* he calls musical consonance "the finest art of measuring" and says that when listening, the soul exercises "darkly" and through the senses (13:138).

11 A passage in *Gott* (1787), however, says that music is "a formula of necessary, eternal harmony," which could be enjoyed "even if I had no ear, even if I counted and calculated it merely with my intellect, abstracting from all of its physical pleasure" (16:520).

12 This forces Eggebrecht to discard all views of Lockmann that do not fit into Heinse's allegedly coherent theory of music, for instance, the Pythagorean elements (343). On Heinse see also Müller, Terras, and Wiora.

Chapter 12

1 As was to be expected, Grimm gave Chabanon's book a negative review. Hiller translated the first volume in 1781, but the echo was as weak in Germany as in France. Only Heydenreich responded positively, and even he rejected Chabanon's sensualism (98–99, 227–29). The entry on Chabanon in the *Dictionnaire des Biographies Françaises* is strikingly hostile and unfair to him.

2 Mersenne had already written that the soul counts the vibrations "without our awareness, or it senses the number that touches it" ("des sons" 23). Apart from the texts cited below, Leibniz made an important defense of opera in a letter of January 13, 1682, to Marci. Bokemeyer (Mizler *Bibliothek* 2.1:148–49) claims that the Hannover Library owns a manuscript by Leibniz on music, but this has not been found. Haase (24) mentions an unpublished correspondence with Konrad Henfling about music.

3 See Mizler *Bibliothek* 2:328–29; Mattheson *Plus Ultra* 3:539; Graun letter to Telemann, Nov. 9, 1751, in Telemann.

4 According to Euler, the rules of pitch are more difficult and may contain guidelines for time as well. The *Tentamen* reduces the temporal dimension of music to rhetorical rules and harmonic laws: since the sequence of notes must resemble the succession of ideas in speech, "one must follow the same rules in music as in the art of oratory" (1:242). But in fact Euler determines the order of notes or chords by converting them into simultaneous chords (chapters 5 and 6).

5 In Euler's table, which orders intervals by their degree of mathematical simplicity, the higher octaves (which Rameau regards as variants of the unison) are weak consonances. The twelfth (ratio 1:3) belongs, for instance, in the same category as the double octave and precedes in simplicity all higher octaves. For the mathematical details of Euler's system, see Busch and also Vogel in Euler II:XLVII ff.

6 On Mizler, see Birke and Wöhlke.

7 Telemann advocated the division of the octave into 55 commas; the proposal was criticized even in Mizler's *Bibliothek*.

8 Moritz's role in the development of an aesthetics of autonomous art has received growing attention recently. See, for instance, Bürger, Todorov, and Waniek.

Chapter 13

1 On Kant, see also Cohen, Crawford, Dahlhaus *Kant*, Guyer, Klinkhammer, Marschner, Menzer, Moos *Philos.*, Reed, Schlapp, Schueller *Kant*, Uehling, and Windelband's commentary in the *Akademie-Ausgabe*. I use Norman Kemp Smith's translation of Kant's First Critique and J. H. Bernard's for the Third, with modifications whenever necessary.

2 It will be remembered that according to the First Critique secure knowledge necessitates both perceptions (intuitions) and concepts: "Thoughts without content are empty, intuitions without concepts are blind" (B 75). Every concept of knowledge must therefore have a corresponding intuition.

   Aesthetic ideas may be thought of as counterparts to rational ideas: if the latter are concepts without corresponding intuitions, the former are intuitions (or representations of the imagination) which cannot be adequately captured by concepts: "An aesthetic idea cannot become cognition because it is an intuition (of the imagination) for which an adequate concept can never be found. A rational idea can never become cognition because it involves a concept (of the supersensible) to which no corresponding intuition can ever be given" (sect. 57).

3 The closing passage of section 42 approaches the relation between language and music differently: colors and sounds in nature may offer us "also reflection upon the form of these modifications of sense." However, the examples show that Kant still thinks of communication in terms of convention: white lilies suggest innocence, red roses sublimity, and "the song of birds proclaims gladness and contentment with existence. At least so we interpret nature, whether it has this design or not." Kant does not indicate how such attributions of meaning to natural objects relate to aesthetic judgments.

4 He read the *Letters to a Princess of Germany* (24/1:353).

5 According to Klinkhammer, Kant rejected Euler's theory (44–46); according to Aster, he actually changed his mind (476). Only Dahlhaus (*Kant* 342) disagrees explicitly with Windelband.

6 Like Rousseau, but for different reasons, Kant belittles color and values outline. Rousseau compares outline to melody because both imitate; color does not contribute to imitation. Kant compares outline (*Zeichnung*) to harmonic composition and characterizes both as formal properties; color merely gratifies the senses and cannot make the object beautiful and worthy of contemplation.

7 The latter, obscure point was the subject of a correspondence between Kant and a certain Christian Friedrich Hellwag, who suggested in a letter of December 13, 1790, that music could generate a beautiful play of impressions, not only a pleasant one (*Briefe* 238). Kant responded on January 3, 1791, that he had a friend in mind who could not distinguish one musical piece from another, even though he learned to play the piano (*Briefe* 245). His point seems to be that those who cannot enjoy music physically can still do so intellectually.

8 Heydenreich took the opposite position the same year. Citing Chabanon's sensuous, direct appreciation of music and Leibniz's theory of unconscious counting, Heydenreich defines the first of the four modes of beauty as follows: the eternal and calculable laws of harmony directly determine our pleasure, without reason's intervention or even without our understanding those laws. We recognize mathematical relations in music because of an involuntarily aroused sense of pleasure, not the other way round (99).

Chapter 14

1 On the tension between Pythagoreanism and formalism in absolute music, see Dahlhaus (*abs. Mus.*, esp. 33, 43, and 45).

2 We must also distinguish the contributions of Wackenroder and Tieck. The authorship of the "Fragment aus einem Brief Joseph Berglingers," which is the most untraditional of the pieces, is debated, though it probably belongs to Wackenroder. I will concentrate on "The Wonders of Tonal Art" (*Die Wunder der Tonkunst*) and "The Peculiar Inner Essence of Music and the Psychology of Contemporary Instrumental Music" (*Das eigentümliche innere Wesen der Tonkunst, und die Seelenlehre der heutigen Instrumentalmusik*) by Wackenroder and "The Sounds" (*Die Töne*) and "Symphonies" (*Symphonien*) by Tieck. I shall not discuss Wackenroder's "Miraculous Oriental Tale of a Naked Saint" (*Ein wunderbares morgen-ländisches Märchen von einem nackten Heiligen*), which anticipates Schopenhauer, because it raises different questions.

3 See my *Symbolismus und symbolische Logik* on this subject.

4 Schlegel may have gotten this idea from Forkel, but his break with affect theory is more radical. The analogy between language and music involves no imitation or representation, only an analogy between their respective vocabularies and grammatical structures.

5 On Hoffmann and music, see Lichtenhahn, Miller, Moos, and Salmen.

WORKS CITED

Primary Texts

Addison, Joseph. *The Spectator*. Oxford: Oxford UP, 1965.

Adlung, Jacob. *Anleitung zu der musikalischen Gelahrtheit*. Erfurt, 1758. Facs. rpt. Kassel: Bärenreiter, 1953.

d'Alembert, Jean Lerond. *Elémens de musique, theorique et pratique, suivant les principes de M. Rameau*. Paris, 1752. Facs. rpt. Geneva: Slatkine, 1967.

———. *Oeuvres complètes*. 5 vols. Paris, 1821. Facs. rpt. Geneva: Slatkine, 1967.

———. *Oeuvres et correspondances inédites*. Paris, 1887. Facs. rpt. Geneva: Slatkine, 1967.

Algarotti, Francesco. *An Essay on the Opera*. 1755. Glasgow, 1768.

André, Yves Marie. *Essai sur le beau*. Paris, 1741.

Aristotle. *Politics*. Trans. Ernest Barker. Oxford: Clarendon, 1946.

———. *Metaphysics*. Trans. Hippocrates Apostle. Bloomington: Indiana UP, 1966.

Aristoxenos. *Harmonics*. Ed. Henry Macran. Oxford: Clarendon, 1902.

Arnaud, Abbé François. *Lettre sur la musique à M. le Comte de Caylus*. Paris, 1754.

Augustine. *Confessions*. In *Basic Writings*. N.Y.: Random, 1948. 1:3–256.

———. *Musik*. Trans. Carl Johann Perl. Paderborn: Schöhning, 1940.

Avison, Charles. *An Essay on Musical Expression*. 1752. London, 1753.

Bach, Carl Philipp Emanuel. *Versuch über die wahre Art das Clavier zu spielen*. Berlin, 1753.

Bach-Dokumente. Ed. Werner Neumann and Hans-Joachim Schulze. 3 vols. Kassel: Bärenreiter, 1963–72.

Batteux, Charles. *Les Beaux Arts réduits à un même principe*. 1746. Paris, 1747.

Bayly, Anselm. *The Alliance of Musick, Poetry and Oratory*. London, 1789.

Beattie, James. *Essays*. 1776. 3d ed. London, 1779.

Bemetzrieder, Anton. *Leçons de clavecin, et principes d'harmonie*. 1771. Diderot *Oeuvres complètes* 12:171–534.

Bernhard, Christoph. *Die Kompositionslehre Heinrich Schützens in der Fassung seines Schülers Christoph Bernhard*. Ed. Joseph Müller-Blattau. Leipzig: Breitkopf, 1926.

Blainville, Charles Henri. *L'Esprit de l'art musical, ou Réflexions sur la musique, et ses différentes parties*. Geneva, 1754.

———. *Histoire générale, critique et philologique de la musique*. Paris, 1767.

Boethius. "The Principles of Music." Trans. and ed. Calvin Martin Bower. Diss. Peabody College for Teachers, Columbia U, 1966.

Boileau, Nicolas. "Prologue d'opéra." *Oeuvres*. 2 vols. Paris: Garnier, 1969. 2:227–37.

Boyé (Pascal Boyer ?). *L'Expression musicale mise au rang des chimères*. Amsterdam, 1779. Facs. rpt. Geneva: Minkoff, 1973.

Brossard, Sébastian de. *Dictionnaire de musique*. Paris, 1703.

Brown, John. *A Dissertation on the Rise, Union, and Power, the Progressions, Separations, and Corruptions, of Poetry and Music*. London, 1763. Facs. rpt. N.Y.: Garland, 1971.

Burmeister, Joachim. *Musica poetica*. Rostock, 1606. Facs. rpt. Kassel: Bärenreiter, 1955.

Burnett, James (Lord Monboddo). *On the Origin and Progress of Language*. 6 vols. London, 1773–92. Facs. rpt. N.Y.: Garland, 1970.

Burney, Charles. *The Present State of Music in Germany, the Netherlands and United Provinces*. 2 vols. London, 1773. Facs. rpt. of the 1775 ed. N.Y.: Broude, 1969.

———. *A General History of Music from the Earliest Ages to the Present Period*. 4 vols. London, 1776–89.

Buttstett, Johann Heinrich. *Ut, Mi, Sol, Re, Fa, La Tota Musica et Harmonia Aeterna, Oder Neu-eröffnetes, altes, wahres, eintziges und ewiges Fundamentum Musices, entgegen gesetzt Dem neu-eröffneten Orchestre*. Erfurt, 1716.

Chabanon, Michel-Paul Guy de. *Eloge de M. Rameau*. Paris, 1764.

———. "Observation sur la musique, à l'occasion de Castor." *Mercure de France* Apr. 1772:159–79.

———. *De la musique considérée en elle-même et dans ses rapports avec la parole, les langues, la poésie et le théâtre*. Paris, 1785.

Chastellux, François-Jean de. *Essai sur l'union de la poésie et de la musique*. The Hague, 1765.

Condillac, Etienne Bonnot de. *An Essay on the Origin of Human Knowledge*. 1746. London, 1756.

Crousaz, Jean-Pierre de. *Traité du beau*. Amsterdam, 1715.

Dennis, John. "Essay on the Opera's after the Italian Manner." 1706. *Critical Works*. Ed. Edward Niles Hooker. 2 vols. Baltimore: Johns Hopkins UP, 1939–43. 1:382–93.

Descartes, René. *Musicae compendium*. 1650. Darmstadt: Wissenschaftliche Buchgesellschaft, 1978.

———. *Les passions de l'âme*. 1649. Paris: Vrin, 1970.

———. *Correspondance*. Ed. Ch. Adam and G. Milhaud. 8 vols. Paris: Alcan, 1936–63. Facs. rpt. Nendeln: Kraus, 1970.

Diderot, Denis. *Oeuvres complètes*. Ed. J. Assézat. 20 vols. Paris: Garnier, 1875–77.

———. *Oeuvres esthétiques*. Paris: Garnier, 1968.

——— et al., ed. *Encyclopédie ou Dictionnaire raisonné des sciences des arts et des métiers*. 17 vols. Paris, 1751–65.

Dubos, Jean Baptiste. *Réflexions critiques sur la poésie et la peinture*. 1719. Paris, 1770. Facs. rpt. Geneva: Slatkine, 1967.

Engel, Johann Jakob. *Über die musikalische Malerei*. 1780. *Schriften*. 12 vols. Berlin, 1801–06. 4:297–342.

Estève, Pierre. *Nouvelle découverte de principe de l'harmonie, avec un examen de ce que M. Rameau a publié sous le titre de Démonstration de ce principe*. Paris, 1752.

Euler, Leonhard. *Opera omnia*. 73 parts. Ed. Ferdinand Rudio et al. Leipzig: Teubner, 1911– .

Feind, Barthold. *La Costanza Sforzata*. Hamburg, n.d.

———. "Gedancken von der Opera." *Deutsche Gedichte*. Stade, 1708. 74–114.

———. *Das Römische April-Fest*. Hamburg, n.d.

Fludd, Robert. *Utriusque cosmi historia*. Oppenheim, 1617.

Forkel, Johann Nicolaus. *Musikalisch-kritische Bibliothek*. 3 vols. Gotha, 1778–79. Facs. rpt. Hildesheim: Olms, 1964.

———. *Allgemeine Geschichte der Musik*. 2 vols. Leipzig, 1788–1801.

Friedrich II. *Oeuvres*. 32 vols. Berlin, 1846–57.

Gaultier, Denis. *La Rhétorique des Dieux*. MS. 1652. Paris: Droz, 1932.

Gerard, Alexander. *Essay on Taste*. 1759. Edinburgh, 1780. Facs. rpt. Menston: Scolar, 1971.

Gerstenberg, Heinrich Wilhelm von. "Über Recitativ und Arie in der italienischen Sing-Komposition." *Vermischte Schriften*. 3 vols. Altona, 1815–16. 3:352–81. Facs. rpt. Frankfurt: Athenäum, 1971.

Goethe, Johann Wolfgang von. *Werke* (Weimarer Ausgabe = *WA*). 143 vols. Weimar: Böhlau, 1887–1919.

———. *Werke* (Berliner Ausgabe = *BA*). Berlin (East): Aufbau, 1961– .

———. *Briefwechsel zwischen Goethe und Zelter in den Jahren 1799 bis 1832*. 3 vols. Leipzig: Reclam, 1902.

Goldsmith, Oliver. "On the different Schools of Music." 1759. *Collected Works*. Ed. Arthur Friedmann. 5 vols. Oxford: Clarendon, 1966. 3:91–93.

Gottsched, Johann Christoph. *Versuch einer Critischen Dichtkunst*. 1730. Leipzig, 1751. Facs. rpt. Darmstadt: Wissenschaftliche Buchgesellschaft, 1962.

Grétry, André-Ernst-Modeste. *Mémoires ou Essais sur la musique*. 3 vols. Paris, 1797.

Grimm, Friedrich Melchior. *Correspondance littéraire, philosophique et critique*. 16 vols. Paris, 1877–82.

Hanslick, Eduard. *Vom musikalisch-Schönen*. 1854. Facs. rpt. Darmstadt: Wissenschaftliche Buchgesellschaft, 1976.

Harris, James. *Three Treatises*. 1744. London, 1786.

Hartley, David. *Observations on Man: His Frame, his Duty and his Expectations*. London, 1749. Facs. rpt. Gainsville, Scholars, 1966.

Hawkins, Sir John. *A General History of the Science and Practice of Music*. 1776. London, 1853. Facs. rpt. N.Y.: Dover, 1963.

Hayes, William. *Remarks on Mr. Avison's Essay on Musical Expression*. London, 1753.

Heinichen, Johann David. *Der General-Bass in der Composition*. Dresden, 1728.

Heinse, Wilhelm. *Sämmtliche Werke*. Ed. Carl Schüddekopf. 10 vols. Leipzig: Insel, 1902–25.

Herder, Johann Gottfried. *Sämmtliche Werke*. Ed. Bernhard Suphan. 33 vols. Berlin, 1877–99.

Heydenreich, Carl Heinrich. *System der Aesthetik*. Leipzig, 1790.

Hiller, Johann Adam. "Abhandlung von der Nachahmung der Natur in der Musik." Marpurg *Beyträge* 1:520–43.

Hoffmann, E. T. A. *Schriften zur Musik*. Ed. Friedrich Schnapp. Munich: Winkler, 1977.

Home, Henry (Lord Kames). *Elements of Criticism*. Edinburgh, 1762.

Hudemann, Ludwig Friedrich. "Gedanken von den Vorzügen der Oper vor Tragödien und Comedien." Mizler *Bibliothek* 2.3:120–51.

Hutcheson, Francis. *An Inquiry into the Original of our Ideas of Beauty and Virtue.* 1725. London, 1729.

Jacob, Hildebrand. *Of the Sister Arts.* London, 1734. Facs. rpt. Los Angeles: Clark Memorial Library, 1974.

Jones, William (of Nayland). *A Treatise on the Art of Music.* Colchester, 1784.

Jones, Sir William. "Essay on the Arts, Commonly called Imitative." 1772. *Works.* 6 vols. London, 1799–1801. 4:549–61.

Kant, Immanuel. *Gesammelte Schriften* (Akademie-Ausgabe). 30 vols. Berlin: de Gruyter, 1966–75.

———. *Briefwechsel.* Ed. Otto Schöndörffer. 2d ed. Hamburg: Meiner, 1972.

Kepler, Johannes. *Harmonices mundi,* 1619. *Welt-Harmonik.* Trans. Max Caspar. Munich: Oldenburg, 1939. Facs. rpt. Munich: Oldenburg, 1967.

Kircher, Athanasius. *Musurgia universalis, sive ars magna consoni et dissoni.* Rome, 1650.

Kirnberger, Johann Philipp. *Die Kunst des reinen Satzes.* Berlin, 1771.

Körner, Christian Gottfried. "Über Charakterdarstellung in der Musik." *Die Horen* 5 (1795):97–121.

Krause, Christian Gottfried. *Von der musikalischen Poesie.* Berlin, 1753. Facs. rpt. Leipzig: Zentralantiquariat, 1973.

———. "Vermischte Gedanken." Marpurg *Beyträge* 1:550–59, 3:19–144, 530–43.

Kuhnau, Johann. *Musikalische Vorstellung Einiger Biblischer Historien.* Leipzig, 1700. Facs. rpt. N.Y.: Broude, 1953.

Laborde, Jean Benjamin. *Essai sur la musique ancienne et moderne.* Paris, 1780. Facs. rpt. N.Y.: AMS, 1978.

Lacépède, Bernard-Germain-Etienne de la Ville sur Illon. *La poétique de la musique.* Paris, 1785.

Lecerf de la Viéville de Freneuse, Jean-Laurent. *Comparaison de la musique italienne et de la musique française.* 3 vols. Brussels, 1704–06.

Leibniz, Gottfried Wilhelm. *Epistolae.* Ed. Christian Kortholt. 3 vols. Leipzig, 1734–42.

———. *Philosophical Papers and Letters.* Ed. Leroy E. Loemker. 2d ed. Dordrecht: Reidel, 1970.

Lepileur, d'Apligny. *Traité sur la musique, et sur les moyens d'en perfectionner.* Paris, 1779.

Lessing, Gotthold Ephraim. *Werke.* Ed. Herbert G. Göpfert et al. 8 vols. Munich: Hanser, 1970–78.

Lockman, John. *Rosalinda.* London, 1740.

Ludwig, Christian Gottlieb. "Versuch eines Beweises, dass ein Singspiel oder eine Oper nicht gut seyn könne." Mizler *Bibliothek* 2.1:1–27.

Mainwaring, John. *Memoirs of the Life of the late George Frederic Handel.* London, 1760.

Malcolm, Alexander. *A Treatise on Musick, Speculative, Practical and Historical.* Edinburgh, 1721. Facs. rpt. N.Y.: Da Capo, 1970.

Marmontel, Jean François. *Essais sur les révolutions de la musique en France.* Paris, 1777.

Marpurg, Friedrich Wilhelm. *Des critischen Musicus an der Spree erster Band.* Berlin, 1750. Facs. rpt. Hildesheim: Olms, 1970.

———. *Kritische Briefe über die Tonkunst.* 3 vols. Berlin, 1760–64.

———, ed. *Historisch-kritische Beyträge zur Aufnahme der Musik.* 5 vols. Berlin, 1754–78. Facs. rpt. Hildesheim: Olms, 1970.

Mattheson, Johann. *Das Neu-Eröffnete Orchestre.* Hamburg, 1713.

———. *Das beschützte Orchestre.* Hamburg, 1717.

———. *Das forschende Orchestre.* Hamburg, 1721.

———. *Critica musica.* 2 vols. Hamburg, 1722–25. Facs. rpt. Amsterdam: Knuf, 1964.

———. *Grosse General-Bass Schule.* Hamburg, 1731. Facs. rpt. Hildesheim: Olms, 1968.

———. *Der vollkommene Capellmeister.* Hamburg, 1739. Facs. rpt. Kassel: Bärenreiter, 1954.

Meier, Georg Friedrich. *Anfangsgründe aller schönen Wissenschaften.* Halle, 1754. Facs. rpt. Hildesheim: Olms, 1976.

Mendelssohn, Moses. *Ästhetische Schriften in Auswahl.* Ed. Otto F. Best. Darmstadt: Wissenschaftliche Buchgesellschaft, 1974.

Mersenne, Marin. *Harmonie universelle.* 2 vols. Paris, 1636–37. Facs. rpt. Paris: CNRS, 1963.

Michaelis, Christian Friedrich. *Ueber den Geist der Tonkunst. Mit Rücksicht auf Kants Kritik der ästhetischen Urtheilskraft.* Leipzig, 1795. Facs. rpt. Brussels: Culture et Civilisation, 1970.

Mizler, Lorenz Christoph. *Anfangsgründe des General Basses nach mathematischer Lehr-Art abgehandelt und vermittelst einer hierzu erfundenen Maschine auf das deutlichste vorgetragen.* Leipzig, 1741.

———. *Neu eröffnete Musikalische Bibliothek.* 4 vols. Leipzig, 1739–54. Facs. rpt. Hilversum: Knuf, 1966.

Möser, Justus. "Harlequin oder Vertheidigung des Groteske-Komischen." 1761. *Sämmtliche Werke.* Ed. B. R. Abeken. 10 vols. Berlin, 1842–43. 9:63–106.

Morellet, Abbé André. "De l'Expression en Musique." *Mercure de France* Sept. 1771:113–43.

Moritz, Karl Philipp. "Über den Begriff des in sich selbst Vollendeten." 1785. *Werke.* 2 vols. Berlin: Aufbau, 1973. 2:203–10.

Mozart, Leopold. *Versuch einer gründlichen Violinschule.* 1756. Facs. rpt. of the 1787 ed. Leipzig: Breitkopf, 1956.

Muratori, Ludovico. "Gedanken von Opern" (sel.). Mizler *Bibliothek* 2.2:161–98.

Nichelmann, Christoph. *Die Melodie nach ihrem Wesen sowohl als nach ihren Eigenschaften.* Danzig, 1755.

Nicolai, Christoph Friedrich. *Briefe über den itzigen Zustand der schönen Wissenschaften in Deutschland.* Berlin, 1755.

Niedt, Friedrich Erhardt. *Musikalische Handleitung oder Gründlicher Unterricht.* 3 vols. Hamburg, 1700–17.

Nietzsche, Friedrich. *The Birth of Tragedy.* 1872. Trans. Walter Kaufmann. N.Y.: Random, 1967.

Novalis. *Schriften.* Ed. Paul Kluckhohn and Richard Samuel. 2d ed. 4 vols. Stuttgart: Kohlhammer, 1960–75.

Plato. *The Collected Dialogues.* Ed. Edith Hamilton and Huntington Cairns. N.Y.: Random, 1961.

Pluche, Abbé Antoine. *Le spectacle de la nature.* 9 vols. Paris, 1732–50.

Porée, Charles. "Gedanken von der Oper." Mizler *Bibliothek* 2.1:28–37.

Potter, John. *Observations on the Present State of Music and Musicians*. London, 1762.

Printz, Wolfgang Caspar. *Phrynis Mitilenaeus, oder Satyrischer Componist*. 1676–79. Dresden, 1696.

Quantz, Johann Joachim. *Versuch einer Anweisung die Flöte traversiere zu spielen*. 1752. 3d ed. Breslau, 1789. Facs. rpt. Kassel: Bärenreiter, 1953.

Quintilian, Marcus Fabius. *Institutio oratoria*. Trans. H.E. Butler. London: Heinemann, 1933.

Raguenet, Abbé François. *Parallèle des Italiens et des Français en ce qui regarde la musique et les opéras*. Paris, 1702.

Rameau, Jean-Philippe. *Complete Theoretical Writings*. Ed. Erwin R. Jacobi. 6 vols. N.Y.: American Institute of Musicology, 1967–72.

——. *Treatise on Harmony*. Trans. Philip Gossett. N.Y.: Dover, 1971.

——. *Musique raisonnée*. Textes choisis, présentés et commentés par Catherine Kintzler et Jean-Claude Malgoire. Paris: Stock, 1980.

Reichardt, Johann Friedrich. *Briefe, die Musik Betreffend. Berichte, Rezensionen, Essays*. Leipzig: Reclam, 1976.

Rellstab, Johann Carl Friedrich. *Versuch über die Vereinigung der musikalischen und oratorischen Declamation*. Berlin, 1786.

Ritter, Johann Wilhelm. *Fragmente aus dem Nachlasse eines jungen Physikers*. 1810. Ed. Friedrich von der Leyen. Frankfurt: Insel, 1946.

Robertson, Thomas. *An Inquiry into the Fine Arts*. London, 1784. Facs. rpt. N.Y.: Garland, 1971.

Rousseau, Jean-Jacques. *Correspondance complète*. Ed. R. A. Leigh. 40 vols. Geneva: Droz, 1965– .

——. *Dictionnaire de musique*. Paris, 1768. Facs. rpt. Hildesheim: Olms, 1969.

——. *Ecrits sur la musique*. Paris, 1838. Facs. rpt. Paris: Stock, 1979.

——. *Oeuvres complètes*. 4 vols. to date. Paris: Gallimard, 1959– .

——. *Essai sur l'origine des langues où il est parlé de la mélodie et de l'imitation musicale*. 1781. Paris: Nizet, 1970.

Ruetz, Caspar. "Sendschreiben eines Freundes an den andern." Marpurg *Beyträge* 1:273–311, 318–25.

Saint-Evremond, Charles de. "Sur les opéras." 1705. *Oeuvres en prose*. Ed. René Ternois. 4 vols. Paris: Didier, 1962–69. 3:149–64.

Scheibe, Johann Adolph. *Kritischer Musikus*. 1738–40. 2d ed. Leipzig, 1745. Facs. rpt. Hildesheim: Olms, 1970.

Schiller, Friedrich. *Werke. Nationalausgabe*. 43 vols. to date. Weimar: Böhlau, 1943– .

Schlegel, Friedrich. *Kritische Friedrich-Schlegel-Ausgabe*. Ed. Ernst Behler. 22 vols. to date. Paderborn: Schöning, 1958– .

Schlegel, Johann Adolph. *Einschränkung der schönen Künste auf einen einzigen Grundsatz von Batteux*. Leipzig, 1751.

Schlegel, Johann Elias. *Aesthetische und dramaturgische Schriften*. Ed. Johann von Antoniewicz. Heilbronn, 1887. Facs. rpt. Nendeln: Kraus, 1968.

Schopenhauer, Arthur. *The World as Will and Representation*. 1819. 2 vols. N.Y.: Dover, 1969.

Schubart, Christian Friedrich Daniel. *Ideen zu einer Ästhetik der Tonkunst.* 1806. In *Gesammelte Schriften und Schicksale.* 8 vols. Stuttgart, 1838–40. Vol. 5. Facs. rpt. Hildesheim: Olms, 1972.

Schubert, Gotthilf Heinrich. *Ansichten von der Nachsteite der Naturwissenschaft.* Dresden, 1808. Facs. rpt. Darmstadt: Wissenschaftliche Buchgesellschaft, 1967.

Schumann, Robert. *Aus Kunst und Leben.* Ed. Willi Reich. Basel: Schwabe, 1945.

Serre, Jean-Adam. *Essais sur les principes de l'harmonie.* Paris, 1753. Facs. rpt. N.Y.: Broude, 1967.

———. *Observations sur les principes de l'harmonie.* Geneva, 1763. Facs. rpt. N.Y.: Broude, 1967.

Smith, Adam. "Of the Imitative Arts." *Essays on Philosophical Subjects.* London, 1795. 133–79.

Steffani, Agostino. *Send-Schreiben darinn enthalten, wie grosse Gewissheit die Music aus ihren Principiis, und Grund-Sätzen habe.* 1695. Amsterdam, 1699.

Stravinsky, Igor. *Stravinsky: An Autobiography.* N.Y.: Simon and Schuster, 1936.

Sulzer, Johann Georg. *Allgemeine Theorie der schönen Künste.* 1771–74. 4th ed. 4 vols. Leipzig, 1792–99. Facs. rpt. Hildesheim: Olms, 1967.

Telemann, Georg Friedrich. *Briefwechsel.* Leipzig: Deutscher Verlag für Musik, 1972.

Twining, Thomas. "Dissertation On the Different Senses of the Word Imitative, as applied to Music by the Antients, and by the Moderns." *Aristotle's Treatise of Poetry.* London, 1789. 44–61.

Uffenbach, Johann Friedrich. "Von der Würde derer Singgedichte, oder Vertheidigung der Opern." Mizler *Bibliothek* 3:377–408.

Vogt, Mauritius. *Conclave thesauri magnae artis musicae.* Prague, 1719.

Vossius, Isaac. "Vom Singen der Gedichte und von der Kraft des Rhythmus." 1673. Forkel *Bibliothek* 3:5–107.

Wackenroder, Heinrich. *Werke und Briefe.* Heidelberg: Schneider, 1967.

Walther, Johann Gottfried. *Musikalisches Lexicon.* Leipzig, 1732. Facs. rpt. Kassel: Bärenreiter, 1953.

———. *Praecepta der Musikalischen Composition.* MS. 1708. Leipzig: Breitkopf, 1955.

Webb, Daniel. *Observations on the Correspondence between Poetry and Music.* London, 1769.

Werckmeister, Andreas. *Musicae mathematicae Hodegus Curiosus, oder Richtiger Musicalischer Wegweiser.* Frankfurt, 1686.

———. *Musikalische Paradoxal-Discourse.* Quedlinburg, 1707.

Zarlino, Gioseffo. *Le Istitutioni harmoniche.* Venice, 1558. Facs. rpt. N.Y.: Broude, 1965.

Secondary Literature

Abert, Hermann. *Die Musikanschauung des Mittelalters und ihre Grundlagen.* Halle: Niemeyer, 1905.

———. *Goethe und die Musik.* Stuttgart: Engelhorn, 1922.

———. "Wort und Ton in der Musik des 18. Jahrhunderts." *Archiv für Musikwissenschaft* 8 (1923):31–70.

Abrams, Meyer. *The Mirror and the Lamp. Romantic Theory and the Critical Tradition.* N.Y.: Norton, 1958.

Aden, John. "Dryden and Saint Evremond." *Comparative Literature* 6 (1954):232–39.

Anderson, Warren D. *Ethos and Education in Greek Music*. Cambridge: Harvard UP, 1966.

Aster, E. von. Rev. of vols. 5 and 6 of the Akademie-Ausgabe of Kant's Works. *Kant-Studien* 14 (1909):468–76.

Augst, Bertrand. "Descartes's Compendium on Music." *Journal of the History of Ideas* 26 (1965):119–32.

Baldensperger, Fernand. *Sensibilité musicale et romantisme*. Paris: Presses Françaises, 1925.

Bardez, Jean-Michel. *Diderot et la musique: valeur de la contribution d'un mélomane*. Paris: Champion, 1975.

———. *La gamme d'amour de J.-J. Rousseau*. Geneva: Slatkine, 1980.

Barricelli, Jean-Pierre. "Music and the Structure of Diderot's 'Le Neveu de Rameau'." *Criticism* 5 (1963):95–111.

Barrows, Dunham. *A Study in Kant's Aesthetics*. Lancaster: Science P, 1934.

———. "Kant's Theory of Aesthetic Form." *The Heritage of Kant*. Ed. G. T. Whitney and David F. Bowers. Princeton: Princeton UP, 1939. Facs. rpt. N.Y.: Russell, 1962. 359–75.

Basch, Victor. *Essai critique sur l'esthétique de Kant*. 1896. Paris: Vrin, 1927.

Becking, Gustav. "Zur musikalischen Romantik." *Deutsche Vierteljahrsschrift für Geistesgeschichte und Literaturwissenschaft* 2 (1924):581–615.

Belaval, Yvon. *L'Esthétique sans paradoxe de Diderot*. Paris: Gallimard, 1956.

Benary, Peter. *Die deutsche Kompositionslehre des 18. Jahrhunderts*. Leipzig: Breitkopf, 1961.

Bernard, Jonathan. "The Principle and the Elements: Rameau's Controversy with d'Alembert." *Journal of Music Theory* 24 (1980):37–62.

Betz, Siegmund. "The Operatic Criticism of the 'Tatler' and the 'Spectator'." *Musical Quarterly* 31 (1945):318–30.

Birke, Joachim. *Christian Wolffs Metaphysik und die zeitgenössische Literatur- und Musiktheorie: Gottsched, Scheibe, Mizler*. Berlin: de Gruyter, 1966.

Bloch, Ernst. "Über das mathematische und dialektische Wesen der Musik." 1925. *Gesamtausgabe*. Frankfurt: Suhrkamp, 1969. 10:501–14.

Blume, Friedrich. *Goethe und die Musik*. Kassel: Bärenreiter, 1948.

Blumröder, Christoph von. "'Streben nach Musikalischen Verhältnissen . . .' Novalis und die romantische Musikauffassung." *Die Musikforschung* 33 (1980):312–18.

Bode, Wilhelm. *Die Tonkunst in Goethes Leben*. 2 vols. Berlin: Mittler, 1912.

Bouwsma, O. K. "The Expression Theory of Art." *Philosophical Analysis*. Ed. Max Black. 2d ed. Englewood Cliffs: Prentice-Hall, 1963. 71–96.

Brandes, Heinz. *Studien zur musikalischen Figurenlehre im 16. Jahrhundert*. Berlin: Triltsch. 1935.

Bröckel, Walter. "Was bedeutet die abstrakte Kunst?" *Kant-Studien* 48 (1956–57):485–501.

Broeckx, Jan L. "De mythe van de specifiek muzikale expressie: Naar aanleiding van Alan Tormey's 'Concept of Expression' toegepast op de musiek." *Revue belge de musicologie* 32–33 (1979–80):232–50.

Brown, Calvin S. *Music and Literature: A Comparison of the Arts*. Athens: U of Georgia P, 1948.

Buelow, George J. "Music, Rhetoric, and the Concept of Affections: A Selective Bibliography." *Notes* 30 (1973):250–59.

————, and Hans Joachim Marx, eds. *New Mattheson Studies*. Cambridge: Cambridge UP, 1983.

Bukofzer, Manfred. *Music in the Baroque Era*. N.Y.:Norton, 1947.

————. "Allegory in Baroque Music." *Journal of the Warburg Institute* 3 (1939–40):1–21.

Bürger, Christa. *Der Ursprung der bürgerlichen Institution Kunst*. Frankfurt: Suhrkamp, 1977.

Bus, Antonius Johannes Maria. "Der Mythus der Musik in Novalis' Heinrich von Ofterdingen." Diss. U of Amsterdam, 1947.

Busch, Hermann Richard. *Leonhard Eulers Beitrag zur Musiktheorie*. Regensburg: Bosse, 1970.

Butor, Michel. "La musique, art réaliste." *Répertoire II. Etudes et conferences 1959–63*. Paris: Minuit, 1964. 27–41.

Cannon, Beekman C. *Johann Mattheson; Spectator in Music*. New Haven: Yale UP, 1948. Facs. rpt. Hamden (Conn.): Archon, 1968.

Cazden, Norman. "Towards a Theory of Realism in Music." *Journal of Aesthetics and Art Criticism* 10 (1951):135–51.

————. "Realism in Abstract Music." *Music and Letters* 36 (1955):17–38.

Chailley, Jacques. "Rameau et la théorie musicale." *La Revue Musicale,* numéro spécial 260 (1964):65–95.

Chouillet, Jacques. *La formation des idées esthétiques de Diderot 1745–1763*. Paris: Colin, 1973.

Cohen, Hermann. *Kants Begründung der Aesthetik*. Berlin, 1889.

Combarieu, Jules. *Les rapports de la musique et de la poésie considérées au point de vue de l'expression*. Paris, 1894.

Cowart, Georgia. *The Origins of Modern Musical Criticism: French and Italian Music, 1600–1750*. Ann Arbor: UMI Research P, 1981.

Crawford, Donald W. *Kant's Aesthetic Theory*. Madison: U of Wisconsin P, 1974.

Crocker, Lester. *Two Diderot Studies; Ethics and Esthetics*. Baltimore: Johns Hopkins UP, 1952.

Dahlhaus, Carl. "Zu Kants Musikästhetik." *Archiv für Musikwissenschaft* 10 (1953): 338–47.

————. "Musica poetica und musikalische Poesie." *Archiv für Musikwissenschaft* 23 (1966):110–24.

————. *Musikästhetik*. Cologne: Gerig, 1967.

————. "Romantische Musikästhetik und Wiener Klassik." *Archiv für Musikwissenschaft* 29 (1972):167–81.

————. *Die Idee der absoluten Musik*. Kassel: Bärenreiter, 1978.

————. "Musik und Text." *Dichtung und Musik. Kaleidoskop ihrer Beziehungen*. Ed. Günter Schnitzler. Stuttgart: Klett, 1979. 11–28.

————. "Kleists Wort über den Generalbass." *Kleist Jahrbuch* 1984:13–24.

Dammann, Rolf. "Zur Musiklehre des Andreas Werckmeister." *Archiv für Musikwissenschaft* 11 (1954):206–37.

———. *Der Musikbegriff im deutschen Barock.* Cologne: Volk, 1967.

Darenberg, Karl H. *Studien zur englischen Musikaesthetik des 18. Jahrhunderts.* Hamburg: Cram, 1960.

Daval, Pierre. *La Musique en France au XVIIIe siècle.* Paris: Payot, 1960.

Deditius, Annemarie. *Theorien über die Verbindung von Poesie und Musik: Moses Mendelssohn, Lessing.* Diss. U of Munich, 1918. Liegnitz: Seyffarth, 1918.

Derrida, Jacques. *De la grammatologie.* Paris: Minuit, 1967.

Deutsch, Otto Erich. Comment [on "Mit Würfel komponieren."] *Zeitschrift für Musikwissenschaft* 12 (1929–30):595.

Dieckmann, Herbert. "Die Wandlung des Nachahmungsbegriffs in der französichen Ästhetik des 18. Jahrhunderts." *Studien zur Europäischen Aufklärung.* Munich: Fink, 1974. 275–311.

Dijk, Peter van, Gerard van der Leeuw, and Jos Leussink. *Musiceren als Brugman; de verbindingen tussen muziek en retorica in de 17e en 18e eeuw.* Hilversum: KRO, 1983.

Donington, Robert. *The Rise of the Opera.* N.Y.: Scribner's, 1981.

Doolittle, James. "A Would-be Philosophe: Jean-Philippe Rameau." *PMLA* 74 (1959):233–48.

Draper, John W. "Aristotelian Mimesis in Eighteenth-Century England." *PMLA* 36 (1921):372–400.

———. "Poetry and Music in Eighteenth Century Aesthetics." *Englische Studien* 67 (1932–33):70–85.

Dreyer, Ernst-Jürgen. "Musikgeschichte in Nuce. Goethes dritte grundsätzliche Äusserung zur Natur der Musik." *Jahrbuch des freien deutschen Hochstifts* 1979:170–98.

Duchet, Michele, and Michel Launay, eds. *Entretiens sur 'Le Neveu de Rameau.'* Paris: Nizet, 1967.

Duchez, Marie-Elisabeth. "Principe de la mélodie et origine des langues. Un brouillon inédit de Jean-Jacques Rousseau sur l'origine de la mélodie." *Revue de Musicologie* 60 (1974):33–86.

Ecorcheville, Jules. *De Lulli à Rameau 1690–1730. L'Esthétique musicale.* Paris: Fortin, 1906. Facs. rpt. Geneva: Slatkine, 1970.

Edelhoff, Heinrich. *Johann Nikolaus Forkel. Ein Beitrag zur Geschichte der Musikwissenschaft.* Göttingen: Vandenhoeck, 1935.

Eggebrecht, Hans Heinrich. "Das Ausdrucks-Prinzip im musikalischen Sturm und Drang." *Deutsche Vierteljahrsschrift für Literaturwissenschaft und Geistesgeschichte* 29 (1955):323–49.

———. *Studien zur musikalischen Terminologie.* Wiesbaden: Steiner, 1955.

Einstein, Alfred. *Gluck.* 1936. London: Dent, 1954.

———. "The Conflict of Word and Tone." *Musical Quarterly* 40 (1954):329–49.

Essar, Dennis. *The Language, Theory, Epistemology, and Aesthetics of Jean Lerond d'Alembert.* Studies on Voltaire and the Eighteenth Century 186. Oxford: Voltaire Foundation, 1976.

Ferris, Joan. "The Evolution of Rameau's Harmonic Theories." *Journal of Music Theory* 3 (1959):231–56.

Finney, Gretchen L. "Ecstasy and Music in Seventeenth-Century England." *Journal of the History of Ideas* 8 (1947):153–86.

———. "'Organical Musick' and Ecstasy." *Journal of the History of Ideas* 8 (1947):273–92.

Flaherty, Gloria. *Opera in the Development of German Critical Thought*. Princeton: Princeton UP, 1978.

Flasdieck, Hermann. *John Brown (1715–1766) und seine Dissertation on Poetry and Music*. Halle: Niemeyer, 1924.

Forchert, Arno. "Polemik als Erkenntnisform: Bemerkungen zu den Schriften Matthesons." Buelow *New Mattheson Studies*. 199–212.

Foucault, Michel. *The Order of Things*. 1966. N.Y.: Random, 1970.

Frank, Paul L. "Realism and Naturalism in Music." *Journal of Aesthetics and Art Criticism* 11 (1952):55–60.

Friedländer, Max. "Goethe und die Musik." *Jahrbuch der Goethegesellschaft* 3 (1916):277–340.

Fubini, Enrico. *Gli enciclopedisti e la musica*. Torino: Einaudi, 1971.

Gamilschegg, Ernst. "Diderots Neveu de Rameau und die Goethesche Übersetzung der Satire." 1953. *Ausgewählte Aufsätze*. 2 vols. Tübingen: Niemeyer, 1962. 2:299–333.

Garlington, Aubrey S. "'Le merveileux' and Operatic Reforms in 18th-Century French Opera." *Musical Quarterly* 49 (1963):484–97.

Georgiades, Thrasybulos. *Musik und Sprache. Das Werden der abendländischen Musik dargestellt an der Vertonung der Messe*. Berlin: Springer, 1954.

———. *Musik und Rhythmus bei den Griechen. Zum Ursprung der abendländischen Musik*. Hamburg: Rowohlt, 1958.

Gerigk, Herbert. "Würfelmusik." *Zeitschrift für Musikwissenschaft* 16 (1934):359–63.

Goldschmidt, Hugo. "Wilhelm Heinse als Musikästhetiker." *Hugo Riemann-Festschrift*. Leipzig: Hesse, 1909. 10–19.

———. *Die Musikästhetik des 18. Jahrhunderts*. Leipzig: Rascher, 1915.

Goldschmidt, Harry. "Über die Einheit der vokalen und instrumentalen Sphäre in der klassischen Musik." *Deutsches Jahrbuch der Musikwissenschaft* 1966:35–49.

Goodman, Nelson. *Languages of Art*. Indianapolis: Hackett, 1976.

Gossmann, Lionel. "Time and History in Rousseau." *Studies on Voltaire and the Eighteenth Century* 30 (1964):311–49.

Gurlitt, Wilibald. "Musik und Rhetorik. Hinweise auf ihre geschichtliche Grundlageneinheit." *Helicon* 5 (1944):67–86.

Guthrie, William Keith Chambers. *Orpheus and Greek Religion. A Study of the Orphic Movement*. 1935. N.Y.: Norton, 1966.

Guyer, Paul. *Kant and the Claims of Taste*. Cambridge: Harvard UP, 1979.

Haase, Rudolf. *Leibniz und die Musik: Ein Beitrag zur Geschichte der harmonikalen Symbolik*. Hommerich: Eckhardt, 1963.

Handschin, Jacques. "Die Musikanschauung des Johannes Scotus (Erigena)." *Deutsche Vierteljahrsschrift für Literaturwissenschaft und Geistesgeschichte* 5 (1927):316–41.

Harvard Dictionary of Music. Ed. Willi Apel. 2d ed. Cambridge: Harvard UP, 1972.

Heartz, Daniel. "Diderot et le Théâtre lyrique: 'le nouveau stile' proposé par *Le Neveu de Rameau*." *Revue de Musicologie* 64 (1978):229–52.

Helm, Eugene. "The 'Hamlet' Fantasy and the Literary Element in C. P. E. Bach's Music." *Musical Quarterly* 58 (1972):277–96.

Heninger, S. K. *Touches of Sweet Harmony: Pythagorean Cosmology and Renaissance Poetics.* San Marino: Huntington Library, 1974.

Hilbert, Werner. *Die Musikästhetik der Frühromantik.* Remscheid: Schmidt, 1912.

Hobson, Marion. *The Object of Art.* Cambridge: Cambridge UP, 1982.

Hollander, John. *The Untuning of the Sky; Ideas of Music in English Poetry 1500–1700.* 1961. N.Y.: Norton, 1970.

Hosler, Bellamy. *Changing Aesthetic Views of Instrumental Music in 18th-Century Germany.* Ann Arbor: UMI Research P, 1981.

Howard, Vernon A. "On Musical Expression." *British Journal of Aesthetics* 11 (1971):268–80.

Huber, Kurt. "Herders Begründung der Musikästhetik." *Archiv für Musikforschung* 1 (1936):103–22.

Huray, Peter le, and James Day, eds. *Music and Aesthetics in the Eighteenth and the Early-Nineteenth Centuries.* Cambridge: Cambridge UP, 1981.

Isherwood, Robert M. *Music in the Service of the King: France in the Seventeenth Century.* Ithaca: Cornell UP, 1973.

Jacobi, Erwin. *Die Entwicklung der Musiktheorie in England nach der Zeit von Jean-Philippe Rameau.* 2 vols. Strasbourg: Heitz, 1957.

Jacoby, Günther. *Herders und Kants Ästhetik.* Leipzig: Dürr, 1907.

Jansen, Albert. *Jean-Jacques Rousseau als Musiker.* Berlin, 1884.

Jensen, H. James. *The Muses' Concord. Literature, Music, and the Visual Arts in the Baroque Age.* Bloomington: Indiana UP, 1976.

Jullien, Adolphe. "La Musique et les philosophes au dix-huitième siècle." *Revue et gazette musicale de Paris* 40 (1873):250–52, 257–59, 265–67, 273–75, 281–83.

Junge, Gustav. "Die Sphären-Harmonie und die Pythagoreisch-Platonische Zahlenlehre." *Classica et Medievalia* 9 (1947):183–94.

Katz, Erich. "Die musikalischen Stilbegriffe des 17. Jahrhunderts." Diss. U of Freiburg, 1925–26.

Keane, Michaela Maria. *The Theoretical Writings of Jean-Philippe Rameau.* Washington: Catholic UP, 1961.

Kiernan, Colm. "Rousseau and Music in the French Enlightenment." *French Studies* 26 (1972):156–65.

Kirkendale, Ursula. "The Source of Bach's 'Musical Offering': The 'Institutio oratoria' of Quintilian." *Journal of the American Musicological Society* 33 (1980):88–141.

Kivy, Peter. *The Corded Shell. Reflections on Musical Expression.* Princeton: Princeton UP, 1980.

Klinkhammer, Carl. "Kants Stellung zur Musik." Diss. U of Bonn, 1926.

Krehbiel, James Woodrow. "Harmonic Principles of Jean-Philippe Rameau and his Contemporaries." Diss. Indiana U, 1964.

Kretzschmar, Hermann. "Allgemeines und Besonderes zur Affektenlehre." *Jahrbuch der Musikbibliothek Peters* 18 (1911):63–77; 19 (1912):65–78.

———. *Geschichte der Oper.* Leipzig: Breitkopf, 1919.

Krieger, Murray. *Theory of Criticism. A Tradition and its System.* Baltimore: Johns Hopkins UP, 1976.

Kristeller, Paul. "Music and Learning in the Early Italian Renaissance." *Journal of Renaissance and Baroque Music* 1 (1946–47):255–74.

———. "The Modern System of the Arts." *Journal of the History of Ideas* 12 (1951):496–527; 13 (1952):17–46.

Kuhn, Thomas. *The Structure of Scientific Revolutions.* 1962. 2d ed. Chicago: Chicago UP, 1970.

Lang, Paul Henry. *Music in Western Civilization.* N.Y.: Norton, 1941.

———. "Diderot as Musician." *Diderot Studies* 10 (1968):95–107.

Laudan, Larry. *Progress and Its Problems. Towards a Theory of Scientific Growth.* Berkeley: U of California P, 1977.

Leahy, M. P. T. "The Vacuity of Musical Expression." *British Journal of Aesthetics* 16 (1976):144–56.

Leichentritt, Hugo. *Music, History, and Ideas.* 1938. Cambridge: Harvard UP, 1970.

Lenneberg, Hans. "Johann Mattheson on Affect and Rhetoric in Music." *Journal of Music Theory* 2 (1958):47–83, 193–236.

Lessem, Alan. "Imitation and Expression: Opposing French and British Views in the 18th Century." *Journal of the American Musicological Society* 27 (1974):325–30.

Levin, Flora R. *The Harmonics of Nicomachus and the Pythagorean Tradition.* State College: American Philological Assoc., 1975.

Lichtenhahn, Ernst. "Zur Idee des goldenen Zeitalters in der Musikanschauung E. T. A. Hoffmanns." *Romantik in Deutschland.* Ed. Richard Brinkmann. Stuttgart: Metzler, 1978. 502–19.

Lipking, Lawrence. *The Ordering of the Arts in Eighteenth-Century England.* Princeton: Princeton UP, 1970.

Lowens, Irving. "St. Evremond, Dryden, and the Theory of Opera." *Criticism* 1 (1959):226–48.

Lowinsky, Edward E. "Music in the Culture of the Renaissance." *Journal of the History of Ideas* 15 (1954):509–53.

———. "Taste, Style, and Ideology in Eighteenth-Century Music." *Aspects of the Eighteenth Century.* Ed. Earl Wasserman. Baltimore: Johns Hopkins UP, 1965. 163–205.

Ludwig, Hellmut. "Marin Mersenne und seine Musiklehre." Diss. U of Halle, 1933.

Mace, Dean T. "Marin Mersenne on Language and Music." *Journal of Music Theory* 14 (1970):2–35.

Malek, James S. *The Arts Compared: An Aspect of Eighteenth-Century British Aesthetics.* Detroit: Wayne State UP, 1974.

Man, Paul de. "The Rhetoric of Blindness: Jacques Derrida's Reading of Rousseau." *Blindness and Insight. Essays in the Rhetoric of Contemporary Criticism.* N.Y.: Oxford UP, 1971. 102–41.

Marks, Paul F. "The Rhetorical Element in Strum und Drang: Christian Gottfried Krause's 'Von der musikalischen Poesie'." *Music Review* 33 (1972):93–107.

———. "Aesthetics of Music in the Philosophy of Sturm und Drang: Gerstenberg, Hamann, and Herder." *Music Review* 35 (1974):247–59.

Marschner, Franz. "Kants Bedeutung für die Musik-Ästhetik der Gegenwart." *Kant-Studien* 6 (1901):19–40, 206–43.

Masson, Paul-Marie. "Les Idées de Rousseau sur la musique." *Société Internationale de Musique* 8 (1912):6.1–17; 7–8.23–32.

———. "Le 'Lettre sur Omphale'." *Revue de Musicologie* 24 (1945):1–19.

Menzer, Paul. *Kants Ästhetik in ihrer Entwicklung*. Berlin: Akademie Verlag, 1952.

Meyer-Baer, Kathi. *Music of the Spheres and the Dance of Death; Studies in Musical Iconology*. Princeton: Princeton UP, 1970.

Miller, Norbert. "E. T. A. Hoffmann und die Musik." *Akzente* 24 (1977):114–35.

Mönch, Walter. "Diderot und Goethe. Gespräche über die Kunst." *Das Gastmahl. Begegnungen abendländischer Dichter und Philosophen*. Hamburg: von Hugo, 1947. 234–330.

Montgomery, Franz. "Early Criticism of Italian Opera in England." *Musical Quarterly* 15 (1929):415–25.

Moos, Paul. *Die Philosophie der Musik von Kant bis Eduard von Hartmann. Ein Jahrhundert deutscher Geistesarbeit*. 1902 [under the title *Moderne Musikästhetik in Deutschland*]. Stuttgart: Deutscher Verlagsanstalt, 1922.

———. "E. T. A. Hoffmann als Musikästhetiker. " 1906–07. *E. T. A. Hoffmann*. Ed. Helmut Prang. Wege der Forschung 486. Darmstadt: Wissenschaftliche Buchgesellschaft, 1981. 7–27.

Mortier, Roland. *Diderot in Deutschland 1750–1850*. 1954. Stuttgart: Metzler, 1967.

Moser, Hans Joachim. "Goethe und die musikalische Akustik." *Festschrift Freiherr von Liliencron*. Leipzig: Breitkopf, 1910. Facs. rpt. Westmead: Gregg, 1970. 145–72.

———. *Goethe und die Musik*. Leipzig: Peters, 1949.

Müller, Hans. "Wilhelm Heinse als Musikschriftsteller." *Vierteljahrsschrift für Musikwissenschaft* 3 (1887):561–605.

Müller-Blattau, Joseph Maria. "Gluck und die deutsche Dichtung." *Jahrbuch der Musikbibliothek Peters* 45 (1938):30–52.

———. *Das Verhältnis von Wort und Ton in der Geschichte der Musik: Grundzüge und Probleme*. Stuttgart: Metzler, 1952.

———. "Größe und Glanz der Barockoper." *Festschrift Ernst Hermann Meyer*. Leipzig: Deutscher Verlag für Musik, 1973. 223–32.

Murat, Michel. "Jean-Jacques Rousseau: Imitation musicale et origine des langues." *Travaux de linguistique et de littérature* 18 (1980):145–68.

Musik in Geschichte und Gegenwart. Ed. Friedrich Blume. 14 vols. Kassel: Bärenreiter, 1949–68.

Neubauer, John. *Symbolismus und symbolische Logik. Die Idee der ars combinatoria in der Entwicklung der modernen Dichtung*. Munich: Fink, 1978.

Neumann, Alfred Robert. "Gottsched versus the Opera." *Monatshefte* 45 (1953): 297–307.

Newcomb, Anthony. "Sound and Feeling." *Critical Inquiry* 10 (1984):614–43.

New Grove Dictionary of Music and Musicians. Ed. Stanley Sadie. 20 vols. London: Macmillan, 1980.

Nivelle, Armand. *Les théories esthétiques en Allemagne de Baumgarten à Kant*. Paris: Belles Lettres, 1955.

Nufer, Wolfgang. *Herders Ideen zur Verbindung von Poesie, Musik und Tanz*. Germanische Studien 74. Berlin: Ebering, 1929. Facs. rpt. Nendeln: Kraus, 1967.

O'Gorman, Donal. *Diderot the Satirist*. Toronto: Toronto UP, 1971.

Oliver, Alfred Richard. *The Encyclopedists as Critics of Music.* N.Y.: Columbia UP, 1947.

Osmont, Robert. "Les théories de Rousseau sur l'harmonie musicale et leurs relations avec son art d'écrivain." *Jean-Jacques Rousseau et son oeuvre. Commemoration et colloque de Paris* (1962.) Paris: Klincksieck, 1964. 329–48.

Palisca, Claude. "Scientific Empiricism in Musical Thought." *Seventeenth-Century Science and the Arts.* Ed. Hedley Howell Rhys. Princeton: Princeton UP, 1961. 91–137.

———. "The Camerata Fiorentina: A Reappraisal." *Studi Musicali* 1 (1972):203–34.

———. "The genesis of Mattheson's style classification." Buelow *New Mattheson Studies.* 409–24.

Pappas, John N. "Rousseau and d'Alembert." *PMLA* 75 (1960):46–60.

———. "Diderot, d'Alembert et l'Encyclopédie." *Diderot Studies* 4 (1963):191–208.

———. "D'Alembert et la querelle des bouffons d'après des documents inédits." *Revue d'histoire littéraire de la France* 65 (1965):479–84.

Paul, Charles B. "Music and Ideology: Rameau, Rousseau, and 1789." *Journal of the History of Ideas* 32 (1971):395–410.

Pirro, André. *Descartes et la musique.* Paris: Fischbacher, 1907. Facs. rpt. Geneva: Minkoff, 1973.

Pischner, Hans. *Die Harmonielehre Jean-Philippe Rameaus.* Leipzig: VEB Breitkopf, 1963.

Popper, Karl. *The Philosophy of Karl Popper.* Ed. Paul Schilpp. The Library of Living Philosophers. 2 vols. La Salle (Ill.): Open Court, 1974.

Porset, Charles. "L'Inquiétante étrangeté de l'Essai sur l'Origine des Langues." *Studies on Voltaire and the Eighteenth Century* 154 (1976):1715–58.

Pousseur, Henri. "L'Apothéose de Rameau. Essai sur la question harmonique." *Musiques nouvelles.* Numéro spécial, *Revue d'Esthétique* 1968. 105–72.

Ratner, Leonard. "Ars Combinatoria. Chance and Choice in Eighteenth-Century Music." *Studies in Eighteenth-Century Music; A Tribute to Karl Geiringer.* Ed. C. Robbins Landon. London: Allen and Unwin, 1970. 343–63.

Récy, René de. "Rameau et les Encyclopédistes." *Revue des Deux Mondes* 76 (1886):138–64.

Reed, Arden. "The Debt of Disinterest. Kant's Critique of Music." *Modern Language Notes* 95 (1980):563–84.

Reichert, Georg. "Literatur und Musik." *Reallexikon der deutschen Literaturgeschichte.* Ed. Paul Merker and Wolfgang Stammler. 2d ed. Berlin: de Gruyter, 1965.

Riemann, Hugo. *Geschichte der Musiktheorie im IX.–XIX. Jahrhundert.* 1898. Berlin: Hesse, 1921. Facs. rpt. Hildesheim: Olms, 1961.

Rogerson, Brewster. "'Ut musica poesis.' The Parallel of Music and Poetry in Eighteenth-Century Criticism." Diss. Princeton U, 1945.

Rosen, Charles. "The Musicological Marvel." Review of *The New Grove Dictionary of Music and Musicians.* Ed. Stanley Sadie. *New York Review of Books,* 28, no. 9, May 28, 1981:26–38.

Rosenkaimer, Eugen. "Johann Adolph Scheibe als Verfasser seines 'Critischen Musicus'." Diss. U of Bonn, 1929.

Ruhnke, Martin. *Joachim Burmeister. Ein Beitrag zur Musiklehre um 1600.* Kassel: Bärenreiter, 1955.

Sacaluga, Servando. "Diderot, Rousseau et la querelle musicale de 1752: nouvelle mise au point." *Diderot Studies* 10 (1968):133–73.

Salmen, Walter, ed. *Beiträge zur Geschichte der Musikanschauung im 19. Jahrhundert.* Regensburg: Bosse, 1965.

Schäfke, Rudolf. "Quantz als Ästhetiker. Eine Einführung in die Musikästhetik des galanten Stils." *Archiv für Musikwissenschaft* 6 (1924):213–42.

———. *Geschichte der Musikästhetik in Umrissen.* Berlin: Hesse, 1934.

Scharlau, Ulf. *Athanasius Kircher (1601–1680) als Musikschriftsteller. Ein Beitrag zur Musikanschauung des Barock.* Marburg: Görich, 1969.

Schenker, Manfred. *Charles Batteux und seine Nachahmungstheorie in Deutschland.* Leipzig: Haessel, 1909.

Scher, Steven Paul. "Comparing Literature and Music: Current Trends and Prospects in Critical Theory and Methodology." *Proceedings of the IXth Congress of the International Comparative Literature Association.* Innsbruck: Gesellschaft zur Pflege der Geisteswissenschaften, 1981. 3:215–21.

———. "Literature and Music." *Interrelations of Literature.* Ed. Jean-Pierre Barricelli and Joseph Gibaldi. N.Y.: MLA, 1982. 225–50.

———, ed. *Literatur und Musik. Ein Handbuch zur Theorie und Praxis eines komparatistischen Grenzgebietes.* Berlin: Schmidt, 1984.

Schering, Arnold. "Christian Krause." *Zeitschrift für Ästhetik und allgemeine Kunstwissenschaft* 2 (1907):548–57.

———. "Die Musikästhetik der deutschen Aufklärung." *Zeitschrift der Internationalen Musikgesellschaft* 8 (1907):263–71, 316–22.

———. "Die Lehre von den musikalischen Figuren." *Kirchenmusikalisches Jahrbuch* 21 (1908):106–14.

———. "Geschichtliches zur 'ars inveniendi' in der Musik." *Jahrbuch der Musikbibliothek Peters* 32 (1925):25–34.

———. "Bach und das Symbol." *Bach-Jahrbuch* 22 (1925):40–63; 25 (1928):119–37.

———. "Kritik des romantischen Musikbegriffs." *Jahrbuch der Musikbibliothek Peters* 44 (1937):9–28.

———. "C. Ph. E. Bach und das redende Prinzip in der Musik." *Jahrbuch der Musikbibliothek Peters* 45 (1938):13–29.

———. *Das Symbol in der Musik. Gesammelte Aufsätze.* Ed. Wilibald Gurlitt. Leipzig: Koehler, 1941.

Schlapp, Otto. *Kants Lehre vom Genie und die Entstehung der Kritik der Urteilskraft.* Göttingen: Vandenhoeck, 1901.

Schlösser, Rudolf. *Rameaus Neffe. Studien und Untersuchungen zur Einführung in Goethes Übersetzung des Diderotschen Dialogs.* Berlin: Duncker, 1900. Facs. rpt. Geneva: Slatkine, 1971.

Schmitz, Arnold. *Die Bildlichkeit der wortgebundenen Musik J. S. Bachs.* Mainz: Schott, 1950.

———. "Die Figurenlehre in den theoretischen Werken Johann Gottfried Walthers." *Archiv für Musikwissenschaft* 9 (1952):79–100.

Schueller, Herbert M. "Literature and Music as Sister Arts: An Aspect of Aesthetic Theory in Eighteenth-Century Britain." *Philological Quarterly* 26 (1947):193–205.

————. "'Imitation' and 'Expression' in British Music Criticism in the 18th Century."
Musical Quarterly 34 (1948):544–66.

————. "The Pleasures of Music: Speculation in British Music Criticism 1750–1800."
Journal of Aesthetics and Art Criticism 8 (1950):155–71.

————. "The Use and Decorum of Music in British Literature 1700–1780." *Journal of
the History of Ideas* 13 (1952):73–93.

————. "Immanuel Kant and the Aesthetics of Music." *Journal of Aesthetics and Art
Criticism* 14 (1955):218–47.

Schweitzer, Albert. *Johann Sebastian Bach.* 1905. Trans. Ernest Newman. 2 vols. London: Black, 1923.

Serauky, Walter. *Die musikalische Nachahmungsästhetik im Zeitraum von 1700 bis 1850.*
Munster: Helios, 1929.

————. "Die Affekten-Metrik des Isaac Vossius in ihrem Einfluss auf Johann Kuhnau und Johann Sebastian Bach." *Festschrift Max Schneider.* Ed. Walther Vetter.
Leipzig: Deutscher Verlag für Musik, 1955. 105–13.

Shirlaw, Matthew. *The Theory of Harmony.* 1917. De Kalb, Ill.: Coar, 1955.

Spitzer, Leo. "The Style of Diderot." *Linguistics and Literary History. Essays in Stylistics.*
Princeton: Princeton UP, 1948. 135–91.

————. *Classical and Christian Ideas of World Harmony. Prolegomena to an Interpretation of the Word 'Stimmung'.* Baltimore: Johns Hopkins UP, 1963.

Starobinski, Jean. *Jean-Jacques Rousseau. La transparence et l'obstacle.* Paris: Gallimard,
1971.

Steblin, R. *A History of Key Characteristics in the 18th and early 19th Centuries.* Ann Arbor: UMI Research P, 1983.

Stege, Fritz. "Die deutsche Musikkritik des 18. Jahrhunderts unter dem Einfluss der
Affektenlehre." *Zeitschrift für Musikwissenschaft* 10 (1927):23–30.

Sternfeld, Frederick William. *Goethe and Music. A List of Parodies and Goethe's Relationship to Music. A List of References.* N.Y.: New York Public Library, 1954.

Stravinsky, Igor. *Stravinsky: An Autobiography.* N.Y.: Simon and Schuster, 1936.

Strunk, Oliver. *Source Readings in Music History. From Classical Antiquity through the
Romantic Era.* N.Y.: Norton, 1950.

Suaudeau, René. *Introduction à l'harmonie de Rameau.* Clermont-Ferrand: Ecole Na-
tionale de Musique, 1960.

Szenczi, Miklós. "The Mimetic Principle in later Eighteenth-Century Criticism."
Studies in Eighteenth-Century Literature. Ed. Miklós Szenczi and László Ferenczi.
Budapest: Akadémiai Könyvkiadó, 1974. 9–54.

Terras, Rita. *Wilhelm Heinses Ästhetik.* Munich: Fink, 1972.

Teuber, Eugen. "Die Kunstphilosophie des Abbé Dubos." *Zeitschrift für Ästhetik und
allgemeine Kunstwissenschaft* 17 (1924):361–410.

Thayer, Alexander Wheelock. *Ludwig van Beethovens Leben.* 1866–79. Trans. Hermann
Deiters. 5 vols. Leipzig: Breitkopf, 1907–17.

Thomas, Jean. "Diderot, les Encyclopédistes et le grand Rameau." *Revue de synthèse*
69 (1951):46–67.

Tiersot, Julien. *J.-J. Rousseau.* Paris: Alcan, 1912.

Todorov, Tzvetan. *Théories du symbole.* Paris: Seuil, 1977.

Tormey, Alan. *The Concept of Expression; A Study in Philosophical Psychology and Aesthetics*. Princeton: Princeton UP, 1971.

Trilling, Lionel. *Sincerity and Authenticity*. Cambridge: Harvard UP, 1972.

Uehling, Theodore Edward. *The Notion of Form in Kant's Critique of Aesthetic Judgment*. The Hague: Mouton, 1971.

Unger, Hans-Heinrich. *Die Beziehung zwischen Musik und Rhetorik im 16.–18. Jahrhundert*. Würzburg: Triltsch, 1941. Facs. rpt. Hildesheim: Olms, 1979.

Vickers, Brian. "Figures of rhetoric / Figures of music?" *Rhetorica* 2 (1984):1–44.

Wachs, Morris. Response to Pappas's article. *Revue d'Histoire littéraire de la France* 66 (1966):546–48.

Walker, D. P. "Musical Humanism in the Sixteenth and Early Seventeenth Centuries." *Music Review* 2 (1941):1–13, 111–21, 220–27, 288–308; 3 (1942):55–71.

———. "Ficino's 'Spiritus' and Music." *Annales Musicologiques* 1 (1953):131–50.

Waniek, Erdmann. "Karl Philipp Moritz' Concept of the Whole in His 'Versuch einer Vereinigung . . .'." *Studies in Eighteenth-Century Culture* 12 (1982):213–32.

Weimar, Klaus. *Versuch über Voraussetzung und Entstehung der Romantik*. Tübingen: Niemeyer, 1968.

Weinberg, Bernard. *A History of Literary Criticism in the Italian Renaissance*. 2 vols. Chicago: U of Chicago P, 1961.

Weisstein, Ulrich. *The Essence of Opera*. N.Y.: Norton, 1969.

Wellek, René. *The Rise of English Literary History*. Chapel Hill: U of North Carolina P, 1941.

———. *A History of Modern Criticism 1750–1950*. 5 vols. to date. New Haven: Yale UP, 1955– .

Werkmeister, Wilhelm. *Der Stilwandel in der deutschen Dichtung und Musik des 18. Jahrhunderts*. Berlin: Junker, 1936.

Werner, R. M. "Gerstenbergs Briefe an Nicolai nebst einer Antwort Nicolais." *Zeitschrift für deutsche Philologie* 23 (1891):43–66.

Wessel, Frederick T. "The Affektenlehre in the Eighteenth Century." Diss. Indiana U, 1955.

Wilson, Arthur. *Diderot*. 2 vols. N.Y.: Oxford UP, 1972.

Winn, James Anderson. *Unsuspected Eloquence. A History of the Relations between Poetry and Music*. New Haven: Yale UP, 1981.

Wiora, Walter. "Herders Ideen zur Geschichte der Musik." *Im Geiste Herders*. Ed. Erich Keyser. Kitzingen: Holzner, 1953. 73–128.

———. "Herders und Heinses Beitrag zum Thema 'Was ist Musik?'." *Die Musikforschung* 13 (1960):385–95.

Wöhlke, Franz. *Lorenz Christoph Mizler: Ein Beitrag zur musikalischen Gelehrtengeschichte des 18. Jahrhunderts*. Würzburg: Triltsch, 1940.

Wokler, Robert. "Rameau, Rousseau and the Essai sur l'Origine des Langues." *Studies on Voltaire and the Eighteenth Century* 117 (1974):177–238.

Wustmann, Rudolf. "Tonartensymbolik zu Bachs Zeit." *Bach-Jahrbuch* 8 (1911): 60–74.

Zenck, Hermann. *Numerus und Affectus*. Ed. Walter Gerstenberg. Kassel: Bärenreiter, 1959.

Ziller, Ernst. *Der Erfurter Organist Johann Heinrich Buttstädt (1666–1727)*. Halle: Waisenhaus, 1935. Facs. rpt. Hildesheim: Olms, 1971.

Zimmermann, Jörg. "Wandlung des philosophischen Musikbegriffs: Über den Gegensatz von mathematisch-harmonikaler und semantisch-ästhetischer Betrachtungsweise." *Musik und Zahl*. Ed. Günter Schnitzler. Bad Godesberg: Verlag für systematische Musikwissenschaft, 1976. 81–135.

Zoltai, Dénes. *Ethos und Affekt. Geschichte der philosophischen Musikästhetik von den Anfängen bis zu Hegel*. Budapest: Akadémiai Könyvkiadó, 1970.

INDEX